Colonialism and the

The post-colonial world has seen a major re-evaluation, political as well as theoretical, of the institutions and ideologies of colonialism. In addition to historical and literary studies, innovative theoretical analyses have opened up new approaches to this subject area. In the light of this new thinking, *Colonialism and the Object* discusses the impact of colonial contact with other cultures on the material culture of both the colonised and the imperial nation.

Drawing together an international group of scholars from a variety of disciplinary and cultural backgrounds, *Colonialism and the Object* demonstrates that the intensive analysis of museum objects and their contexts can provide timely and substantive insights into issues of global importance. The volume includes intensive case studies of objects from India, Pakistan, New Zealand, China and Africa, all of which were collected by or exhibited in the institutions of the British Empire. Other chapters address issues of racial identity across cultural barriers, and the hybrid styles of objects which can emerge when cultures meet.

Colonialism and the Object is essential reading for all those interested in post-colonial theory, museum studies, material culture and design history.

Tim Barringer is a lecturer in History of Art at the University of Birmingham, following earlier positions at Birkbeck College, University of London and the Victoria and Albert Museum, London. **Tom Flynn** is Henry Moore Fellow in the history of sculpture at the University of Sussex. He is currently preparing a book on mixed media sculpture in the nineteenth century.

Museum Meanings

Series editors

Eilean Hooper-Greenhill

Flora Kaplan

The museum has been constructed as symbol in Western society since the Renaissance. This symbol is both complex and multi-layered, acting as a sign for domination and liberation, learning and leisure. As sites for exposition, through their collections, displays and buildings, museums mediate many of society's basic values. But these mediations are subject to contestation, and the museum can also be seen as a site for cultural politics. In post-colonial societies, museums have changed radically, reinventing themselves under pressure from many forces, which include new roles and functions for museums, economic rationalism and moves towards greater democratic access.

Museum Meanings analyses and explores the relationships between museums and their publics. 'Museums' are understood very broadly, to include art galleries, historic sites and historic houses. 'Relationships with publics' is also understood very broadly, including interactions with artefacts, exhibitions and architecture, which may be analysed from a range of theoretical perspectives. These include material culture studies, mass communication and media studies, and learning theories and cultural studies. The analysis of the relationship of the museum to its publics shifts the emphasis from the museum as text, to studies grounded in the relationships of bodies and sites, identities and communities.

Also in this series:

Museum, Media, Message
Edited by Eilean Hooper-Greenhill

Colonialism and the Object

Empire, material culture and the museum

Edited by
Tim Barringer and Tom Flynn

London and New York

First published 1998
by Routledge
11 New Fetter Lane, London EC4P 4EE

Simultaneously published in the USA and Canada
by Routledge
29 West 35th Street, New York, NY 10001

Selection and editorial matter © 1998 Tim Barringer and Tom Flynn

Individual chapters © 1998 individual contributors

Typeset in Sabon by Keystroke, Jacaranda Lodge, Wolverhampton
Printed and bound in Great Britain by Butler & Tanner Ltd, Frome and London

British Library Cataloguing in Publication Data
A catalogue record for this book is available from the British Library

Library of Congress Cataloging in Publication Data
Colonialism and the object / edited by Tim Barringer and Tom Flynn.
p.   cm.
Includes bibliographical references and index.
1. Art, Primitive. 2. Art, Colonial. 3. Art, Colonial–Foreign
influences. 4. Colonies–Relations–Europe. 5. Europe–Relations–
Colonies. I. Barringer, Tim, 1965–   . II. Flynn, Tom.
N5311.C65 1998
704.03–dc21   97–3320
CIP

ISBN 0–415–15775–7 (hbk)
ISBN 0–415–15776–5 (pbk)

Vas Prabhu PEM
April 03

Contents

Figures

Notes on contributors

Tim Barringer is a lecturer in History of Art at the University of Birmingham, following previous positions at the Victoria and Albert Museum and Birkbeck College. He has published widely on Victorian visual culture and is currently editing a book on Frederic Leighton.

Catherine Pagani is Assistant Professor of Asian Art History, University of Alabama. She has published several articles on Chinese material culture in the eighteenth century.

Craig Clunas is Professor of History of Art at the University of Sussex and author of a number of books on Chinese art including *Superfluous Things: Material Culture and Social Status in Early Modern China*.

Deborah Swallow worked at the Cambridge University Museum of Archaeology and Anthropology before moving in 1983 to the Victoria and Albert Museum, where since 1988 she has been Curator of the Indian and South East Asian Department.

Naazish Ata-Ullah is a practising painter and printmaker. She is an Assistant Professor (in charge of printmaking) at the Department of Fine Art, National College of Arts, Lahore, Pakistan. She is currently researching the history of the institution.

Rachel E. C. Layton studied at Mount Holyoke College, Massachussetts and in the Winterthur Program at the University of Delaware. Now based in England, she was formerly Assistant Curator of Decorative Arts, Carnegie Mellon Museum of Art, Pittsburgh.

Karen Kettering is Assistant Professor of History of Art at the University of Dayton. Her doctoral thesis on 'Natalia Danko and the Lomosov Porelain Factory' was completed in 1997.

Nima Poovaya-Smith is Keeper of Ethnic Arts, Cartwright Hall, Bradford City Museums. She has curated a series of exhibitions including *Islamic Calligraphy*, *A Golden Treasury*, *Manuscript Paintings from the Ramayana* and *An Intelligent Rebellion: Women Artists from Pakistan*.

Eilean Hooper-Greenhill is Director of the Department of Museum Studies at the University of Leicester. She is the author of *Museum and Gallery Education* (1991), *Museums and the Shaping of Knowledge* (1992), *Museums and their Visitors* (1994) and several edited volumes.

Ngapine Allen is a lecturer in the Department of Fine Art, University of Canterbury, New Zealand. A practising artist herself, she has published widely on Maori culture.

Jeanne Cannizzo teaches in the Department of Social Anthropology at the University of Edinburgh. She was co-curator of *David Livingstone and the Victorian Encounter with Africa*, 1996, for the National Portrait Gallery.

Nicholas Mirzoeff is Assistant Professor of Art History at the University of Wisconsin-Madison. He is the author of *Silent Poetry: Deafness, Sign and Visual Culture in Modern France* and *Bodyscape*.

Tom Flynn is Henry Moore Fellow in the history of sculpture at the University of Sussex. His book *The Body in Three Dimensions* will be published in 1998 and he is currently preparing a book on mixed media sculpture in the nineteenth century.

Acknowledgements

This book is based on papers given at a session of the Association of Art Historians' Conference in 1995, and we would like to thank all who contributed to the success of that event: primarily, of course, those who presented papers. We would also like to thank Iain Cartwright and Elizabeth McKellar for administering the conference. Much of the organisational work of bringing together speakers from around the world was undertaken from the Research Department of the Victoria and Albert Museum, supported by Charles Saumarez Smith and later Malcolm Baker. Ghislaine Wood and Richenda Binney assisted with the ensuing welter of international faxes and telephone calls. The editorial process was aided by the support of Lynn Nead and Jane Gough at Birkbeck College, and the text could not have been finished without the material assistance of Shearer West and Yvonne Locke at the University of Birmingham. We have been fortunate to benefit from the supportive and creative help of Eilean Hooper-Greenhill and Vicky Peters, Steven Jarman and Nadia Jacobson at Routledge.

Chapter 4 originally appeared as Craig Clunas, 'Oriental Antiquities/Far Eastern Art', *positions* 2:2 (Fall 1994). Copyright 1994, Duke University Press. Reprinted with permission. Chapter 13 is reprinted with permission from Nicholas Mirzoeff, *Bodyscape: Art, Modernity and the Ideal Figure*, 1995.

Introduction

Tim Barringer and Tom Flynn

The 1995 British Association of Art Historians' Conference, hosted by the Victoria and Albert Museum and entitled 'Objects, Histories and Interpretations', focused attention on the understanding and interpretation of objects and on the role of museums of material culture. Many of the chapters in the present book have grown out of papers presented in the conference session, convened by the editors, which examined the influence of colonialism, its ideologies and power relations, on the ways in which objects are understood. The papers stimulated lively debate and it became clear that the session had raised a range of historical and interpretative issues crucial to museum professionals and their publics in the post-colonial era, questions which are of equal import and urgency across the academic fields of museum studies and cultural studies, anthropology and ethnography, and the histories of art, design and material culture. These are: What impact did the imposition of colonial power have on indigenous societies and on cultural production within them? How have objects imported or appropriated from colonies been displayed at the imperial centre? What effects did the importation of objects and materials from the colonies have on artistic production in the imperial nation? What impact do the power relations of colonialism have on the interpretation of objects? What are the possibilities for the display of 'colonial' objects in the present day and how can contemporary museum practice address the inheritance of colonialism?

The location of the conference at the Victoria and Albert Museum in South Kensington – itself a formidable colonial institution, situated only yards from the sites of such imperial spectacles as the Great Exhibition of 1851, the 1886 Indian and Colonial Exhibition, and the former Imperial Institute – could not have been more appropriate, indicating the web of continuities between colonial past and post-colonial present. Many of the conference speakers examined case studies of objects enmeshed in the complex colonial history of South Kensington, such as the Gwalior Gateway, made by Indian craftsmen under the authority of the British Raj and subsequently built into the very fabric of the Victoria and Albert Museum, and the Maori House removed from New Zealand and exhibited at South Kensington and then at the British Empire Exhibition in Wembley in 1924. As Swallow and Allen indicate in their respective analyses, when such objects are removed from their original contexts, and are subjected to appropriation and exhibition, their meanings undergo radical changes.

The essays gathered in *Colonialism and the Object* demonstrate that the intensive analysis of museum objects and their contexts, once considered the province of curators and specialist connoisseurs alone, can provide timely and substantive insights into issues of more general – indeed of global – interest. The intersection between colonialism, museums and objects unites three major disciplinary areas, and three substantial bodies of contemporary theory; post-colonial theory, museum studies and material culture studies/design history. The post-colonial world has seen a major re-evaluation, political as well as theoretical, of the institutions and ideologies of colonialism. In addition to a vast array of purely historical studies, innovative theoretical analyses have opened up new approaches to this subject area. Among the most powerful and influential analyses of colonialism's effects on the culture of the coloniser and the colonised is the work of Edward Said. In *Culture and Imperialism* (1993) Said's avowed intention was to

> connect these different realms [culture and imperialism] to show the involvements of culture with expanding empires, to make observations about art that preserve its unique endowments and at the same time map its affiliations. . . .
>
> (Said 1993: 5)

This book is intended as a contribution to such a project. From *Orientalism* (1978) onwards, Said's critique laid the foundations for an enquiry into colonial culture which has had wide repercussions across the humanities. Said's work, like that of a younger generation of cultural critics, such as Homi K. Bhabha and Gayatri Spivak, has taken language as its subject matter, achieving its most brilliant effects through analyses of the novel. The essays collected in Bhabha's *The Location of Culture* (1994), in which a theory of 'colonial discourse' is deployed to emphasise the ambivalence and hybridity of colonial culture and the paradoxical interdependency of coloniser and colonised, have provided an interpretative framework taken up by many of the contributors to this volume. Flynn applies the concept of fetishism to Belgian colonial cultural practices in the 1890s, while Ata Ullah explores the making and meaning of an object which seems the very epitome of the notion of inter-cultural hybridity. The screen made by the master craftsman Ram Singh under the tutelage of Lockwood Kipling draws deeply on the skills and traditions of Punjabi woodworking, while remaining a European object-type both produced and consumed within a colonial economy. Layton deals with questions of 'race' and identity, detailing the fascinating life history of a silversmith born in the Danish West Indies of 'free coloured' status (having a mother of mixed race and a white father) and who, conforming to essentialising definitions of neither 'white' nor 'black', found himself, as Layton writes 'on a boundary or seam between cultures: European and African (free and slave); Danish West Indian and American; African-American and European'. Himself a direct product of a colonial liaison, Bentzon was ultimately unsuccessful in his attempts to settle securely in either St Croix or in Philadelphia. His hollow-ware silver objects are typical of a Philadelphia-trained silversmith of the period, and they are displayed today in the 'Old World and New' Gallery of the Carnegie Museum of Art in Pittsburgh, Pennsylvania (see Fig. 7.3), indicating a move on the part of museums towards addressing issues of colonialism and acknowledging the contribution of African-American craftspeople. None the less, as his presence in this collection attests, Bentzon's work is, after a century and a half, still refracted through the discursive prism of race and colonial social relations.

Historians of visual culture have responded to developments in post-colonial theory with a range of sophisticated studies of race and representation: the influential work of Linda Nochlin on 'Orientalist' paintings has now been supplemented by a plethora of works questioning the legacy of 'Primitivism' in modern art (e.g. Pollock 1993) and examining representations across visual culture through issues of race (Biddick *et al.* 1996). A number of important studies of ethnographic photography have emerged (Edwards 1992) and Mirzoeff's chapter here contributes to that body of work, revealing the role of photography in constructing 'a cultural geography of colonialism in a specific time and place', in this case the Congo region of West Africa between 1900 and 1915. Kettering and Flynn demonstrate how three-dimensional artefacts can mediate the power relations that underlie the colonial project. As Flynn maintains, the revival of ivory-based mixed-media sculpture in Belgium in the 1890s became part of a broader programme designed to sell the colonial adventure to the Belgian people. The appropriation of ivory – colonial material par excellence – adds layers of meaning beyond the objects' specific iconographies. Kettering notes, in her analyses of ceramic figurines made at the Lomonosov factory in Moscow, how objects which might be considered to be ephemeral, or even 'kitsch', can play an important ideological role in popular culture. As Kettering argues, the very domestication of Uzbek figures through their representation in such an innocuous format could naturalise for the Soviet consumer the centralisation of political control over the Central Asian population. The figures simultaneously represent the Uzbek as exotic – and therefore attractive – and as backward, and subject to liberation through Westernising reforms. While Soviet Central Asia was not, in name, a colony, Kettering demonstrates a colonial imbalance of power in the relationship of centre to periphery.

While representations of all kinds have been subjected to critical scrutiny within the general project of post-colonial enquiry, the broader category of functional, or non-representational three-dimensional objects (whether considered as 'the applied arts', 'the decorative arts', or less restrictively as 'material culture') has largely been ignored in the context of debates about colonialism. There is a certain irony in this since the circulation of goods and the increase of trade was a primary underlying motivation for imperial expansion. The absence of considered accounts of the relationship between colonialism and the object is hardly surprising given the dearth of publications in general devoted to material culture when compared to the seemingly inexhaustible literature on the fine arts of painting and sculpture. The designations 'fine' and 'decorative' arts, which imply a hierarchy of value, prove particularly inappropriate when applied to the products of cultures where such a distinction is meaningless (such as the multiple artistic traditions of India, China and the Islamic world). None the less, as Clunas argues below, the notion of 'art' 'remains a site of conflicting interpretations, fissured along class and gender lines, among others, and the right to define something as "art" is typically seen as an important attribute of those dominant in society at a given moment'. Only when the status of 'art' is conferred on a body of work can it begin to generate a history; as Allen notes 'ten years ago, no one would have accepted that Maori could have an art history'.

A second historiography with which this collection engages is that of museum studies. This field has attained in recent years the status of a separate academic discipline, a discipline marked by its close and fruitful links with actual curatorial practice in museums. Since Peter Vergo's announcement of a 'new museology' (1989), critical studies both of museums in general (most recently Macdonald 1996) and of fine art in particular (Duncan 1995) have proliferated, informed by critical theory and by ideas drawn from such disciplines as anthropology, sociology and archaeology. As Clunas argues in the present volume, the official ideology of museums has, until recently, insisted that they stand outside of time and historical process; museums and their curators have tended to constitute themselves as the recorders of history, rather than as committed participants. The very existence of museum studies as a discipline implies that the museum is now seen as an object of study in itself, subject to the same historical influences as other institutions and representations. Pioneering work in this field with regard to colonialism and issues of race and multi-culturalism can be found in Ivan Karp and Steven Lavine's collection *Exhibiting Cultures* (1991), which is largely concerned with contemporary issues, and Annie Coombes's major historical study *Re-inventing Africa* (1994). Coombes's book is of particular value in examining in detail the construction through exhibitions of an idea of 'Africa' in Britain in the era of frantic European colonial expansion in sub-Saharan Africa. This area of scholarship has been influenced by recent anthropological critiques of ethnographic writing, notably the work of James Clifford, for whom ethnography is 'always caught up in the invention rather than the representation of cultures' (Clifford 1988: 9). The same problem faces the ethnographic museum, or indeed any display purporting to represent a culture or civilisation through objects or artefacts: can representations of culture ever be anything other than partial? What are the limits to the stories objects can tell, or be made to tell?

In this volume, the role of the museum is problematised both historically (Barringer, Swallow) and in the present; senior museum professionals (Clunas, Poovaya-Smith) offer searching analyses of their own practice in relation to colonial ideologies and objects. Many of the contributors have themselves organised galleries and exhibitions, confronting in practice the very issues under theoretical consideration here. Deborah Swallow and Craig Clunas both played pivotal roles in the rethinking of (respectively) the Nehru Gallery of Indian Art and the T. T. Tsui Gallery of Chinese Art at the Victoria and Albert Museum, two major curatorial initiatives which, along with re-displays of the Museum's Japanese and Korean collections, have reformulated one of the great 'imperial archives' of non-Western art for the 1990s. As the authors of major galleries, Clunas, Swallow and their colleagues are of course the direct successors of the original curators of the South Kensington Museum discussed by Barringer. Though on the face of it there might seem to be little common ground between the didactic and triumphalist displays of the nineteenth century and the self-reflexive, technologically and intellectually sophisticated galleries of the 1990s, each undoubtedly and unsurprisingly conforms to the broad ideological expectations of its own day.

Jeanne Cannizzo, whose essay 'Gathering Souls and Objects' discusses missionary collecting in Africa, was curator of the controversial exhibition *Into the Heart of Africa* on the same subject at the Royal Ontario Museum in 1989. In line with James Clifford's ideas, and those of most contributors to this volume, Cannizzo sees the museum as a 'cultural text, one that may be read to understand the underlying cultural or ideological assumptions that have informed its creation, selection and display' (Cannizzo 1991: 151). Yet one influential group of visitors produced a reading of Cannizzo's exhibition dramatically at variance with her own avowed intentions of producing 'a self-reflexive critique of the colonial collecting practices of the museum' (Riegel 1996: 89–90). Cannizzo's ironic critique of the ideas of Canadian missionary collectors in Africa (one of whom, Walter Currie, is discussed in her essay below), stressed the ideological assumptions behind missionary collecting. However the exhibition was the subject of protests from a group calling itself the Coalition for Truth About Africa (Riegel 1996: 90), which claimed to represent Toronto's African-American community, for whom the exhibition failed to distance itself clearly enough from the agenda of its subjects.

Other contributions (Swallow, Barringer, Flynn) assess the historical role of museums, collections, art exhibitions and temporary displays in the promotion and presentation of the colonial project, revealing them as potent mechanisms in the construction and visualisation of power relationships between coloniser and colonised. The relationship between the interpretation of objects in the past and their display in the present is a recurring theme (Mirzoeff, Layton, Allen), while the possibilities for a celebratory, post-colonial museology in a modern, multi-ethnic British city are explored by Poovaya-Smith. Hooper-Greenhill and Allen both present life histories of Maori houses which have been integrated into the culture of the coloniser: one, Mataatua, as a museum piece ('a desirable feature in the Colonial Annexe' at South Kensington in 1882); the other, Hinemihi, ending up as a boat house at Clandon Park, a National Trust property near Guildford, Britain. In 1995, Mataatua was the subject of a restitution claim and, writing as a Maori, Ngapine Allen explains the basis of this claim and the cultural role of the house. Happily, a satisfactory resolution of this issue was achieved shortly before this book went to press, as Allen notes in her postscript. Hooper-Greenhill's account opens with a description of the ceremony of 'blessing of carvings for Hinemihi meeting house in England' and proceeds to plot the specific conditions which marked the passage of the ancestral house from the periphery to the centre of empire, in the process drawing attention to the diverse meanings and associations – the 'disjunctions and dislocations' – generated by Hinemihi on its colonial journey from the southern to northern hemisphere. Underlying the entire process of colonial collecting, which implies a severe imbalance of economic and political power between coloniser and colonised, is the question of legitimacy. These issues, although not the main focus of the present collection, are of prime ethical concern to museum professionals across the world and the subject of lively and often impassioned debate (Knell 1994: 54–6; Simpson *et al.* 1996: 19–23).

While each chapter negotiates theoretical and museological issues, this book is concerned with the impact of colonialism on the production, consumption and interpretation of material objects, and some limiting definition should perhaps be placed on this capacious term. Susan Pearce has offered an initial definition of museum objects as 'selected lumps of the material world to which cultural status has been ascribed' (Pearce 1992: 4), while another term commonly used for material objects is 'artefact'. However, as Pearce notes, 'artefact' in itself often implies an inferior status to the work of art through its connections with 'artisan'. Useful in this regard is a final methodological ingredient: the developing field of material culture studies, also known as design history, which offers broader and more sophisticated contextual readings of a wide range of objects than that allowed by traditional art-historical and museum scholarship. It is in this vein that Flynn and Ata-Ullah address the ambivalences implicit in the production and consumption, display and interpretation of objects whose very existence was premised on the colonial system. The work of Igor Kopytoff and Arjun Appadurai (1986) on the biographies of objects offers models for discussing the 'social life of things', indicating that while social contexts encode objects with changing meanings, a close examination of the object can also provide insights into the societies which produced and consumed them. Clunas notes below that these approaches to single objects may also be applied to collections, and to museums: all the chapters in this volume may be considered as contributions to this broad project. Biographies of objects and their interactions with collections are deeply revealing of the contradictions of colonial culture. None is more poignant than that of the Gwalior gateway discussed by Swallow, a huge stone construction which, for all its magnificence, was only ever appreciated during its brief tenure at South Kensington's Colonial and Indian Exhibition of 1886. Presenting a constant headache to its subsequent custodians, the gateway now lies concealed behind partition walls in a gallery devoted to those monuments of European high art, Raphael's cartoons. It is hard not to see in this post-war history a denial of Britain's colonial past; as Swallow demonstrates, the unravelling of layers of meaning inscribed in and around such an object offer rich insights into colonialism's culture.

This book, then, consists of a collection of case studies, histories of individual objects and collections, firmly rooted in archival and physical analysis of objects and contexts. And while a range of theoretical positions is adopted by the contributors, most begin by focusing on a particular object or collection, subsequently broadening out their arguments to encompass more general historical and theoretical concerns. In this way, an elision can be effected between what are often perceived as opposing strands in the culture of museums: 'object-based' and 'theoretical' approaches. It could be said, indeed, that the contributors to this volume are object-based, but not object-limited, in their analyses.

Our concern has been to incorporate a plurality of voices and perspectives, though we make no claim to complete coverage of the field. The authors are based variously in New Zealand, Pakistan and the USA, as well as Great Britain, and draw their case studies from around the world. We write as museum curators – of ethnographic, Far Eastern, Indian, fine and decorative art collections – and university teachers of anthropology, art history, design history, critical theory, museum studies and studio art. The interdisciplinary nature of this shared project may be discerned from the fact that the contributors to the present volume come from across these disciplines but their essays are informed as much by the continual exchange of ideas between the various communities as by developments in their own subject area.

On 1 July 1997, the Union Jack was lowered for the last time over the British colony of Hong Kong, and power was transferred to the new Hong Kong Special Autonomous Region, regarded by some Hong Kongers as a new colonial regime, this time based in Beijing. Such events serve as a reminder that colonialism continues to affect the daily lives of millions of people across the world, and indicate too that many of the cultural processes and dilemmas discussed in this book continue in a world which describes itself as post-colonial. The complex negotiations surrounding the hand-over of Hong Kong and the sometimes caricatured representations of China and its rulers offered by the British press can be viewed in the context of a long history discussed in this volume (Pagani, Clunas). For Clunas, the fascination of twentieth-century Britain for objects from Imperial China results from a process by which 'nostalgia for one empire became nostalgia for all and souvenirs of empire became fetishes of consolation'. The 'imperial archive' (Richards 1993), losing all pretence of relevance, becomes a mere souvenir, the only surviving token of imperial power. In a further fascinating development, as British colonial influence over the colony of Hong Kong waned, and economic decline restricted government spending on museums, it was members of the economically prosperous Hong Kong business community who sponsored two major redisplays of Chinese objects in national museums in Britain in the early 1990s: the T. T. Tsui Gallery at the Victoria and Albert Museum (1991) and the Joseph Hotung Gallery of Oriental Antiquities at the British Museum (1992).

Recent developments in the colonial history of Hong Kong have also had their effect on objects and collections: news reports at the time of writing suggest that 'works of art worth one billion pounds may have been moved out of Hong Kong as the colony prepares for the handover to Chinese rule' (Glaister 1997). This instance, in which the exchange value of objects in question – 'one billion pounds' – momentarily takes precedence over their significance as 'works of art', serves to remind us of the complex role which objects continue to play in the shifting economic and political geography of the 'post-colonial' world. The present book is intended as a start, rather than the last word, on colonialism and the object. As these early reports from Hong Kong suggest, the social life of things in the post-colonial world looks set to be equally problematic, equally contentious, and equally ripe for analysis.

Part 1
Institution, object, imperialism

2

The South Kensington Museum and the colonial project

Tim Barringer

'Come' said my friend, Professor Omnium, one clear morning, 'let us take an excursion round the world'. . . . 'My dear friend', said I, 'it is among my dreams one day to visit India, China, Japan, California, but at present you might as well ask me to go with you to the moon.' 'You misunderstand', replies Professor Omnium 'I do not propose to leave London. We can never go round the world, except in a small, limited way, if we leave London. . . . Ten thousand people and a dozen governments have been at infinite pains and expense to bring the cream of the East and of the West to your own doors'.

(Conway 1882: 21–3)

The destination of the inter-cultural day trippers in Moncure Conway's book, *Travels in South Kensington*, published in 1882, was the South Kensington Museum, which came into being on the present site in 1857, and survived until 1899 when it was renamed the Victoria and Albert Museum. There was nothing new in Conway's conceit; from the Renaissance cabinet of curiosities onward, the museum had been viewed as a microcosm, an ordered representation of the world in miniature (Shelton 1994). Yet South Kensington's presentation of the world (unlike that of the older British Museum) enshrined a uniquely modern world-view, that of Victorian imperialism. As the collections grew from modest beginnings in the 1850s to include objects from India and South East Asia, China, and Japan, as well as European fine and decorative arts from the Byzantine to the contemporary (though excluding the work of so-called 'savages'), the museum struggled to impose order over a cultural field of bewildering diversity. The representations of the world which it offered were deeply imbedded in the developing culture of Victorian imperialism. Thomas Richards has described the Victorian fixation with the central collection of information, and its ordering and re-ordering, as characteristic of the 'Imperial archive', a fantasy of knowledge made into power (Richards 1993). The acquisition of objects from areas of the world in which Britain had colonial or proto-colonial political and military interests, and the ordering and displaying of them by a museum which was a department of the British state, formed, I suggest, a three-dimensional imperial archive. The procession of objects from peripheries to centre symbolically enacted the idea of London as the heart of empire.

The meaning of an object is inflected, even re-invented by the context in which it is displayed; the removal of objects from a colonial periphery to the imperial centre profoundly alters the ways in which they are understood. Accordingly, rather than addressing the museum's collections in isolation, I shall consider the museum as a cultural formation. Seen in this way, a museum is comprised of objects ordered into taxonomies, whose interpretation is determined by labels, guides and catalogues, by lectures and tours, and (in the case of South Kensington) by buildings encrusted with didactic texts and images. In looking at South Kensington's strategies of display and interpretation as they relate to non-Western objects, I shall distinguish three periods which broadly conform to the wider political and ideological development of British Imperialism. The first, from 1851 to about 1870, was a didactic moment in which the formal quali-ties of Indian objects, especially, were promoted for the purposes of reforming design to improve national economic performance; the second from about 1870 to the mid-1880s, was a moment of academic imperialism, characterised by an increasingly prominent assertion of scholarly and popular interest in, and authority over, non-Western objects and the non-Western world; and finally, from about 1885 to the end of the century, a period of popular imperialist triumphalism, marked by the 1886 Colonial and Indian exhibition, and con-cluded by the erection of Aston Webb's new building for the Victoria and Albert Museum in 1909.

An empire of things: free trade and design reform

The South Kensington project was inaugurated by the Great Exhibition of the Industry of All Nations, held in the Crystal Palace in Hyde Park, in 1851. It was organised, like the future Museum, by Henry Cole under the patronage of Prince Albert. The 1851 exhibition provided a benchmark in changing popu-lar attitudes to Britain's colonial possessions, and its organisers emphasised the commercial importance of more than thirty colonies and dependencies whose manufactures and raw materials were displayed (Greenhalgh 1989: 53–6). The Indian Court, appropriately for the grandest of British territories, covered 30,000 square feet, and its array of exotic objects was highly signifi-cant in popularising Indian design for the British consumer market. Prominent in representations of the Indian Court was a *howdah* with magnificent trappings in gold and silver, given to Queen Victoria by the Nawab of Murshidabad, displayed with some panache on a stuffed elephant found at the last minute in Saffron Walden (Guy and Swallow 1990: 220) (Fig. 2.1). Royal gifts from subordinate colonial rulers and peoples would repeatedly be displayed at the South Kensington Museum, which offered a popular forum for the display of imperial tributes for the next fifty years. Despite their spectacular presentation, the Indian manufactures shown in 1851 were subordinate in quantity and importance to the display of Indian raw materials – coal, oil, precious stones, saltpetre and spices – symptomatic of the direct economic interests under-pinning British involvement with India.

12

Figure 2.1   The Indian Court at the Great Exhibition. Coloured lithograph. From Dickinson, *Views of the Exhibition*, 1851. (Courtesy of the Trustees of the Victoria and Albert Museum.)

The 1851 Exhibition was the direct progenitor of the Museum (Purbrick 1994; Barringer 1996); the £186,000 profit from admission tickets was used to purchase the Museum's site while the core of its collections derives from Great Exhibition purchases, made using £4217 1s 5d of a government grant of £5000 voted for the purpose (Wainwright 1994: 359). About half of this was spent on continental European objects, acquired to assist the competitiveness of British designers; but next in order of magnitude – greater than the amount spent on British objects – was a sum of £1276 10s 0d for items from the East India Company, still effective rulers of India, which had organised the massive Indian court. It was believed by the members of the purchasing committee, Owen Jones, Henry Cole, Richard Redgrave and A. W. N. Pugin, that the formal qualities of Indian design 'illustrate correct principles of ornament, [even if they] are of rude workmanship' (*Catalogue of the Articles* 1852: iv). Prior to the erection of a museum building at South Kensington, some of these objects were temporarily exhibited at Marlborough House, a vacant Royal Palace, where the catalogue included a laudatory article by Owen Jones on Indian design. Jones also reproduced examples from Indian fabrics in the collection in his theoretical work, *The Grammar of Ornament*, in 1856, and in later editions insisted that 'The Indian collection at the South Kensington Museum should be visited and studied by all in any way concerned with the production of woven fabrics' (Jones 1865: II, 79). For Jones and his colleagues, the stylised ornament of Indian textiles contrasted favourably with the jarringly naturalistic ornament of contemporary British designs such as those featured in Henry Cole's infamous Gallery of 'False Principles' of design at Marlborough House (Mitter 1977: 221; Wainwright 1994; Barringer 1996).

The institution which grew up at South Kensington from 1856 was not just a museum. Also on the site were a large art school and the offices of the Department of Science and Art, which controlled government art and design education though a centralised network of art schools with standardised methods of teaching and examination which extended throughout Britain and Ireland. In 1858 John Charles Robinson, the first curator of the museum drew attention to 'the Art-Library, Schools, and general Departmental Machinery, at Kensington, the action of which, be it remembered, is emphatically *Imperial* rather than *Metropolitan*' (Robinson 1858: 404).

Robinson exaggerated, for though South Kensington might hope to have an influence throughout the colonies and dominions, it had no official remit beyond the shores of Britain and Ireland. None the less, teachers trained in South Kensington were employed throughout the British empire, from Sydney and Adelaide to Calcutta, Madras and Bombay, where the School of Art was headed from 1865 to 1875 by Lockwood Kipling, who thereafter moved to the Mayo School of Art in Lahore (Guy and Swallow 1990: 227; Ata-Ullah, Ch. 6). The early administration of the museum strikingly paralleled the methods of colonial authorities. Objects were sent to the provinces in touring exhibitions organised by a circulation department, and tight central control was exerted over local art education with regular inspection by officers from the centre, strategies which underscored the authority of the central institution. The first museum building in Kensington was an unsatisfactory prefabricated iron structure, soon nicknamed the 'Brompton Boilers', designed by Charles Young and Company and reflecting Young's speciality in exporting prefabricated iron buildings to the colonies, for hospitals, barracks and houses (Physick 1982b: 23). Close links were established between the Museum and the military; much of the manual labour was carried out by a division of sappers, drafted to the site, and throughout the century the hierarchy of the institution was dominated by military figures (Denis 1995).

The project of the museum was didactic; central to the intentions of its founders was the idea of promoting good design among both producers and consumers, and more broadly the pursuit of increasing general standards in education, especially among artisans and skilled labourers. The Science and Art Department's *First Report*, drafted by Henry Cole, claimed:

> A museum presents probably the only effectual means of educating the adult, who cannot be expected to go to school like the youth, [yet] the necessity for teaching the grown man is quite as great as that of training the child. By proper arrangements a Museum may be made in the highest degree instructional.
>
> (*First Report* 1853: 30)

The museum aimed to instil a culture of self-education and self-help into the artisan community and to improve the profitability and competitiveness of industry by doing so. It could also open up economic and cultural possibilities of empire to a general public. The interior of the 'Brompton Boilers' in the late 1850s featured an educational collection, including geographical materials, scientific apparatus, and models of foods: a special display of Chinese food was mounted in 1859. Non-Western objects were prominent in the Museum, providing examples of good design for manufacturing, as its pedagogical six-penny guide noted: 'a court is appropriated to specimens of ornamental art manufactures, especially rich in Indian tissues – Chinese and Japanese porcelain and lacquered work, decorative arms, bronzes, objects in marquetrie, dama-scene work, etc.' (*South Kensington Museum Guide* 1857: 3). Although, as contemporary illustrations make clear, the early displays were somewhat chaotic, didactic considerations were uppermost in the organisers' minds: 'It is intended that every specimen should, as soon as possible, be accompanied by a descriptive label, containing the name, date and all other details of the object judged necessary' (*South Kensington Museum Guide* 1857: 3). Henry Cole had written of the museum as 'an impressive schoolroom for everyone' (*First Report* 30), and as a part of this strategy, coloured drawings by Owen Jones, 'illustrative of oriental art generally' were situated near the Chinese and Japanese objects.

The successor to this early installation was far more ambitious. It took a more prominent place in the magnificent glass and cast-iron South Court, designed by a co-opted military man, Captain Francis Fowke, and opened in 1862 (Physick 1982b: 52–6). One of the cloisters to the sides of the grand central arcades was, from 1863, set aside for the display of the Oriental collections – Indian, Chinese, Japanese and Persian objects being subsumed under this rubric (Sheppard 1975: 110). Here the fabric of the building, rather than a mere housing for the objects, took on an interpretative role, impressing upon the visitor not only the splendour of the institution, but also (it was hoped) the specific significance of the objects displayed. The commission for polychrome wall and ceiling decorations (Fig. 2.2) and tile pavements went to Owen Jones, who had installed elaborate decorative schemes evoking historic styles of orna-ment – Greek, Egyptian and Indian – at the Crystal Palace in its new position at Sydenham (Phillips 1857: 141–3). South Kensington's desire for a similarly evocative interior for the Oriental Courts indicates the Museum's use of display techniques balancing education and popular entertainment. The decorations served to enhance the 'otherness' of the objects by creating an 'oriental' ambi-ence and also demonstrated the ways in which Indian, Japanese and Islamic decoration could serve as source materials for contemporary British design. The Oriental courts, in fact, stood as an example of the type of design the museum's founders hoped would catch on in Britain. *The Builder* responded favourably to the Indian court, first to be finished, in 1863:

> The decoration on the ceiling and piers, which is very elaborate, is from the designs of Mr. Owen Jones. . . . The whole is treated on the non-naturalistic, non-imitative, or conventional principle; but, in one

of the ceilings especially, there is a right and perfect bringing of 'realities to mind'.

(Physick 1982a: 117)

Even the windows in the cloister area were quite different from those in the rest of the museum; commissioned specially from the architect J. W. Wild, they were decorated with plaster tracery in the Moorish style (Physick 1982a: 117) indicating the resemblance of the courts to later and more fanciful examples of Victorian architectural orientalism such as Arab Halls by George Aitchison at Leighton House (1877–80) and William Burges at Cardiff Castle (1878–81) (Campbell 1996; Crook 1981). The Oriental Courts, through their very separateness, served the orientalist function, described by Said, of asserting an absolute difference between the Orient and the Occident, while collapsing differences within the category of 'Oriental' (Said 1978). Oriental art was grouped together and set apart from the mainstream, its otherness emphasised

Figure 2.2 Owen Jones, Design for the decoration of the Oriental Courts, South Kensington Museum. (By courtesy of the Trustees of the Victoria and Albert Museum.)

through isolation and exoticisation. Ultimately, however, such spectacular strategies of display drew attention to themselves rather than the objects in the collection, and indeed press coverage of the Oriental Courts concentrates almost exclusively on the building. Visitors frequently complained that the garish decoration reflected in the glass of the cases and obscured the exhibits; an example of the colonial object literally being subordinated to the imperial design (Conway 1882: 43–4).

Power and knowledge: academic orientalism and critique

My second period, that of academic imperialism, coincides with the next major development of the South Kensington buildings in the early 1870s, General Henry Scott's Architectural Courts (Physick 1982b: 156–60). They were intended to house the museum's collection of plaster casts of great monuments of Western art, notably Trajan's column – significantly, one of the greatest monuments of Imperial Rome, often seen as a parallel to the British empire – and Michelangelo's *David* (Baker 1982). The Architectural Courts epitomise the museum as the Victorian sublime: the visitor is overwhelmed by the sheer physical size, the cultural scope and technological prowess of the museum, which functions as a metonym of the state itself.

The erection of the Architectural Courts coincided with a growing popular interest in India which peaked with the ceremonial and publicity generated by Queen Victoria's creation as Empress of India in 1876. At this time, India provided a vital market for the sale of British goods and large numbers of middle- and upper-class Britons found employment in the Indian Army and colonial administration (Cain and Hopkins 1993: 329–36). Around 1870 large numbers of casts of Indian ancient monuments and sculpture began to arrive in South Kensington, largely as a result of the work of Lieutenant Henry H. Cole, son of the museum's Superintendent, who as a Royal Engineer was himself Superintendent of the Archaeological Survey of India's North Western Provinces. It was symbolic of an increasing consciousness of empire in South Kensington, that by the time the vast new courts opened in 1873, a large part of the Eastern court was occupied by over a hundred casts of Indian architecture and sculpture. The space was dominated by what the *Art Journal* described as 'a cube-like erection of uncouth proportions containing a cast of Akhbar Khan's throne'. A 'clever piece of scene-painting' (*Art Journal* 1873: 276) on one end of this structure represented the spectacular site of Fatehpur-Sikri, the red sandstone city built in the 1570s by Jalal ad-Din Muhammad Akbar (1556–1605), one of the key sites of Mughal culture. Once again, a potentially rarefied and academic display was couched in terms of a populist rhetoric.

In a photograph of the court in 1872, with decorative work in hand, can be seen a cast of the Eastern Gateway of the Great Stupa at Sanchi in India, 33 feet high (Fig. 2.3). A new departure is signalled by the copying of an ancient Indian object dating from the late first or early second centuries AD, considered as a work of art rather than an example of ornamentation, craft

Figure 2.3 The Architectural Courts under construction with plaster cast of the Sanchi Gateway. Photograph, *c.*1872. (By courtesy of the Trustees of the Victoria and Albert Museum.)

or manufacturing (Harle 1986: 31–4). The Sanchi site, rediscovered in modern times in 1818 by a British officer, General Taylor, had been partly excavated by various military expeditions and published by James Fergusson in *Tree and Serpent Worship* (1868) (Irwin 1972). But the presence of a physical copy of the gateway far outshone any textual or photographic representations: Moncure Conway enthused, 'the intricacy and fineness of all this work, constituting, as Fergusson has said, the "picture bible of Buddhism", are indescribable' (Conway 1882: 88). The cast was made by the Royal Engineers in 1869, at a cost of £900, in a campaign described by Conway in the rhetoric of the exploration literature of the period:

> the party set out with twenty eight tons of materials, chiefly plaster-of-Paris; these were drawn by bullocks one hundred and eighty miles; and in a year three full-size casts of the magnificent structure were completed without a flaw.
>
> (Conway 1882: 87–8)

An account of the workforce underpinned a colonial hierarchy of expertise and authority, offering a kind of microcosm of the colonial ideal, with an efficient military administration and native labour directing colonial production to the home market:

> The work has been effected in a most satisfactory manner by a trained corps of sappers of the Royal engineers and a body of nine native workmen under the direction of Lieut H. H. Cole. . . . The cast was completed on February 21st, and being packed in suitable sections, arrived at Liverpool early in June [1869] *via* Hoshungabad, Bombay and the Suez Canal.
>
> (*Art Journal* 1870: 65)

Copies of the cast were made at South Kensington and were exhibited in Berlin and Paris. Their political significance was unmistakable: the monument was situated in British India, rediscovered, excavated, photographed and published by officers of the British army; the South Kensington cast was proudly displayed at the imperial centre as a symbol of responsible British custodianship of, and authority over, Indian history and culture. The arrival of the cast was prefaced by a scholarly article in the *Art Journal* (1871: 65–8), and the Sanchi gateways became a recognisable symbol of Indian art, reproduced on the covers of the museum's publications (Birdwood 1881). Through the presence of such elaborate simulacra, the universal survey museum of South Kensington could claim authority over the cultural terrain of Britain's Asiatic empire as well as the history of Western art and design. The cast courts were a three-dimensional equivalent of Richards's imperial archive. From the balcony, the visitor could experience an equivalent of that key trope of imperial travel writing, described by Mary Louise Pratt as 'the monarch-of-all-I-survey' description (Pratt 1992: 201). Conway, predictably, rose to the challenge:

> Vista upon vista! The eye never reaches the farthest end in the past from which humanity has toiled upwards, its steps traced in victories over

chaos, nor does it alight on any historical epoch not related to himself: the artisan, the artist, the scholar, each finds himself gathering out of the dust of ages successive chapters of his own spiritual biography.

(Conway 1882: 25)

The complex history of the Victoria and Albert Museum's Indian collections is given elsewhere (Skelton 1978), but it is important to recognise the centrality of Indian objects to the South Kensington Museum. Henry Hardy Cole published in 1874 a *Catalogue of the Objects of Indian Art Exhibited in the South Kensington Museum*, documenting a considerable collection of objects particularly strong in textiles; Cole's introduction suggested, however, that South Kensington should also assume control of the much larger collections of India Museum, formerly the property of the East India Company and open to the public in crowded conditions at the India Office in Whitehall since 1861. After complex negotiations this was achieved in 1879 and, in 1880, Sir George Birdwood, of the India Office staff, oversaw as Art Referee the arrangement by Caspar Purdon Clarke of the amalgamated Indian collections in new galleries occupying a vacant building separate from the museum on the west side of Exhibition Road. Birdwood evinced a Ruskinian abhorrence of industrialisation foreign to the earlier generations at South Kensington (Mitter 1977: 236ff). For him the beauty of Indian art was the result of its roots in village life: 'In India, everything is hand wrought, and everything, down to the cheapest toy or earthenware vessel, is more or less a work of art' (Birdwood 1880: 131–2).

The galleries adopted a didactic, rather than an aesthetic presentation of the objects: photographs and casts of Indian architecture and 'Sepia drawings of native handicraftsmen' by Lockwood Kipling were displayed alongside original objects. Kipling's picturesque vignettes, which were reproduced in the museum's *Portfolio of Indian Art* (1881), according to Birdwood,

> have been objects of particular interest, during the last ten years, at the Indian Museum. They are from life and being rendered with perfect truthfulness, and skill, they serve to give a remarkable reality to the Museum in which it would be wanting without them, as an exhibition of the industrial arts of India.
>
> (Birdwood 1881: Preface)

These images, while replicating familiar tropes of racial difference, indicate a response to Indian handicraft skills among the Arts and Crafts group redolent of a critique not only of industrialisation but also of the imperial project itself. The anxiety of Birdwood, Kipling and others about the effects of mechanisation and industrialisation at the imperial centre, fuelled by their readings of critics such as Carlyle, Ruskin and Morris, led them to invert the standard account of imperialism's triumphal technological transformation of 'backward' colonised lands:

> We are beginning in Europe to understand what things may be done by machinery, and what must be done by hand work, if art is to be of the slightest consideration in the matter. [To introduce machinery into India

...] would inevitably throw the traditional arts of the country into the
same confusion of principles ... which has for three generations been
the destruction of decorative art and of middle class taste in England ...

(Birdwood 1880: 134–5)

Unlike Owen Jones's adaptation of geometric ornament into mainstream industrial design, the presence of hand-crafted Indian objects in South Kensington now
seemed to expose by comparison the shortcomings of the modern industrial
object.

Imperial spectacle

Despite this note of critique, from the mid-1870s onward, the museum followed
more general cultural trends and evinced an increasingly populist and even ram-
pant imperialism. Henry Cole's successor as Superintendent after his retirement
in 1873, was Philip Cunliffe-Owen who, the *Dictionary of National Biography*
records, 'never professed any special enthusiasm for art' but was a capable
administrator of temporary exhibitions, and these became the main focus of the
museum's attention. Before discussing the greatest of these, the spectacular
Colonial and Indian Exhibition of 1886, it is important to acknowledge that
the museum had never eschewed popular imperial display at any time in its
history.

There are earlier examples of temporary displays relating directly to colonial
military action. One, which brought forth press responses couched in language
of violent triumphalism, included the royal regalia of King Theodore of
Abyssinia, captured during a military campaign in 1867 (Pakenham 1991:
470–1). An essayist in the *Gentleman's Magazine* wrote of contemplating 'at
South Kensington ... this show-case full of victorious trophies, *spolia opima* of
our late enemy, his Majesty King Theodore' and mocked 'a blue robe hung
with what look like extinguishers ... tinsel and royal rubbish'; yet a portrait of
'Theodore's head as he lay defunct and bloody on the hill-top at Magdala' drew
some respect for the 'princely thought of savage kingliness [and] ... air of
unsubdued pride upon his jaws and lips' (Arnold 1868). Twenty years later, it
was still felt to be worth recording in the *Museum Guide* that the 'vestments
and garments' had been 'captured during the Abyssinian campaign under Lord
Napier of Magdala' (*Guide to the South Kensington Museum* 1888: 46). Such
displays made no contribution to the museum's original mission in relation to
design and social reform but rather offered the Victorian public the spectacle of
the remains of a defeated enemy whose perceived status as a racial and cultural
inferior was implicit in the mode of display.

The exhibition of some African objects seized during a bloody campaign
in 1873–4 against the Ashanti leader Kofi Kari-Kari, described by Robinson
and Gallagher as 'a sharp act of supremacy' (1981: 31), proved enormously
popular. Through the reporting of H. M. Stanley, the war with 'King Koffee'
became well known to a wide public. Some of the objects, notably 'King

21

Koffee's Umbrella', remained on permanent display, causing Conway to remark in 1882 'These African trophies are unpleasantly reminiscent of the worst phase of British policy' (Conway 1882: 71). Undoubtedly the South Kensington authorities welcomed the extra publicity gained by such exhibits, even if the museum did pride itself on being 'the ripest fruit of the long Victorian and victorious era of Peace' (Conway 1882: 72).

The exhibition in 1876 of the gifts from the Prince of Wales's tour of India was overtly political in intention, as *The Times* made clear:

> It is understood that HRH desired . . . [that] by the sight of this rare collection of Oriental manufactures . . . the people of this country might have the opportunity of judging for themselves . . . the very great political value of many of the presents as proofs of loyalty of some of the most famous of the historical sovereign families and tribal chiefs in India to the British government.
>
> (*The Times* 22 June 1876)

Ultimately, however, *The Times* correspondent was unimpressed, regretting that

> the collection is overloaded with objects which would be very interesting in a museum but are certainly incongruous among the treasures of a prince. . . . The whole contents of an Indian bazaar have been emptied out of the hold of the Serapis.
>
> (*The Times* 22 June 1876)

Some of these objects were reproduced in the museum's *Portfolio of Indian Art* (Birdwood 1881: Part 12), but in most cases their significance was political rather than aesthetic, and they appeared in the exhibitions as tokens of loyalty to the heir to Queen Victoria, newly created Empress of India, rather than examples of Indian manufactures.

In addition to its traditional function of providing a storehouse of designs and techniques in the decorative arts, it was believed that if the South Kensington Museum had an encyclopaedic collection of Indian goods and manufactures, importers and potential customers could examine specimens in the museum and then apply to purchase similar items from the makers in India. In this case, specific information would be needed about the source of each item. As a museum memorandum noted:

> What importers and art students equally desire to know is the exact place of production of a particular manufacture. It is not enough to say that it is Indian . . . the merchant who desires to import Indian articles of art interest can do nothing unless he knows the exact town of their manufacture.
>
> (Skelton 1978: 301)

The museum came to be understood almost as a giant three-dimensional mail order catalogue for Indian manufactures, and an aggressive policy of Indian acquisitions was undertaken in order to ensure the comprehensiveness of the collection. Caspar Purdon Clarke, later Director, was sent to India to make purchases from a sum of £2000 from the museum's funds, plus an extra £3000 provided by the India Office. He returned from India in 1883 'having collected a vast number of objects, useful and ornamental, great and small,' *The Times* noted, including

> specimens of pottery, metal-work, papier-mâché, lacquerware, inlaid sandal-wood and ivory, embroideries, printed cottons, glass vessels &c. His best acquisitions are built into the great court and are principally of a modern and architectural character . . . [including] a complete wooden house front, lavishly painted and somewhat gaudily coloured.
>
> (*The Times* 21 May 1883)

Such a lavish array of colonial spoils certainly buttressed the museum's claim to encyclopaedic status, but they had of course been appropriated from their original context. Amid the euphoria of Purdon Clark's campaign, *The Times* sounded a note of dissent: 'Pleasant though it may be to have these original relics at South Kensington, is not their removal a veritable vandalism – in short, a defiance of the system of using plaster casts?' (*The Times* 21 May 1883). This illustrates the dilemma of the imperial collector, balancing the desire or need to present colonial objects at the centre and the wish to be seen as a just and benevolent power in the colonies.

In addition to building up the permanent collection, Cunliffe-Owen organised a highly successful series of exhibitions on the large site west of Exhibition Road, culminating in the key event of South Kensington's popular imperialism, the Colonial and Indian Exhibition of 1886, which was attended by 5.5 million people (Mackenzie 1984: 101–2). It opened in a blaze of ceremonial glory, a part of the invented traditions of empire (Fig. 2.4). *The Graphic* carried a large engraving of the Queen, also Empress of India since 1876, depicted ''twixt East and West', processing through an architecture of colonial simulacra, and standing at a fulcrum of race, history and culture. The catalogue featured colour-coded maps of the exhibition and of the world, with British possessions in pink, offering the visitor the chance to process through the empire in miniature, just as Professor Omnium suggested. The exhibition was a massive exercise in publicity for the imperial ideal and a bonanza of national self-aggrandisement:

> No alien, of whatever race he may be – Teuton, Gaul, Tartar or Mongol – can walk through the marvellous collection at South Kensington and look at the innumerable variations of our national Union Jack, without feeling the enormous influence that England has had, and still has, over every part of the globe.
>
> (*The Graphic* 8 May 1886)

The Graphic's commemorative map (*The Graphic*: 24 July 1886) demonstrated the diverse racial types of the empire and a key feature of the Indian court was a display of models of ethnic types made from body casts, simulated figures providing popular entertainment under the guise of ethnology, and offering a grotesque reprise of the high-minded cast collecting from ancient monuments in the 1870s. The press admired the 'lifelike casts of natives – all, be it said,

Figure 2.4 The opening of the Colonial and Indian Exhibition. From *The Graphic*, 8 May 1886.

taken actually from life' which indicated 'the immense variety of . . . race and customs . . . found in our Indian Empire. Not even the most experienced traveller can look upon the stalwart Sikh and the comparatively puny Andaman Islander, without feeling this' (*The Graphic* 8 May 1886).

The exhibition was entered through the spectacular Indian section, access to courts representing specific areas and provinces provided from a central 'Provincial Art Ware Court' stacked with objects of Indian manufacture. Once again, Empire was commodified and reduced to the sum of its material productions. At the heart of the exhibition lay the 'Indian Palace' constructed by Purdon Clarke using diverse elements including windows cast from buildings in the city of Fatehpur-Sikri. Even the loyal *Graphic* was forced to acknowledge the bizarre hybridity of Clarke's 'Palace':

> A Hindu structure is made the entrance to a Mahomedan *serai* and Sikh modern carved woodwork has been adapted in the interior fittings of an ancient Mahomedan palace, and, still more incongruous, old English stained windows have been added to this aggregation of ideas.
>
> (*The Graphic* 15 May 1886)

The Palace's 'Durbar Hall', in which the Prince of Wales held receptions during the exhibition, was perhaps the most elaborate aspect of his design. Superbly carved by the Punjabi craftsmen, Muhamma Maksh and Juma, it remains, like the Gwalior Gateway and the Screen of Ram Singh, a somewhat unhappy hybrid of British demands and Indian workmanship. Expensive, political in conception, contingent and impermanent in execution, and finally useless, the room's melancholy grandeur marks it out as the ultimate example of the official colonial object (Fig. 2.5).[1]

So successful had been South Kensington's imperial jamboree that the Prince of Wales proposed a permanent building on the site to commemorate the Jubilee of Queen Victoria in 1887:

> It appears to me that no more suitable memorial could be suggested than an Institute which should represent the Arts, Manufacture and Commerce of the Queen's Colonial and Indian Empire. Such an institution would . . . illustrate the progress already made during Her Majesty's reign in the Colonial and Indian Dominions, while it would record year by year the development of the Empire in the arts of civilization.
>
> (*The Times*, 20 September 1886)

Figure 2.5 The Durbar Hall. Originally created for the Colonial and Indian Exhibition in 1886, this hall was re-installed in the home of Lord Brassey, on Park Lane in London, before reaching its final resting place in Hastings Museum and Art Gallery. (Photograph: Hastings Museum and Art Gallery.)

Despite these fine words, no one seemed quite sure what an Imperial Institute might be for. The financiers of the City of London, conceiving of it as primarily a commercial centre, argued against South Kensington as the site. However, South Kensington had become so embedded in the symbolic geography of London as a point of intersection between empire and scholarship, between learning and display, education and entertainment, that the new Imperial Institute was erected there, to a grandiose design by T. E. Colcutt (Fig 2.6). The laying of the foundation stone provided the opportunity for one of the greatest of all imperial ceremonies, attended by 10,000 people on 4 July 1887; it was emulated, however, by the opening of the building, in brilliant sunshine on 10 May 1893, which was attended by 25,000. The Institute's functions were listed as being: to display Imperial produce; to illustrate the Empire's economic growth; to collect and disseminate commercial and other information; to hold special exhibitions, promote commercial and industrial education in the colonies and 'to advance systematic colonisation'. As John Mackenzie notes in a witty discussion of the Institute, it failed in each of these respects (Mackenzie 1984: 122–46).

The Institute was physically adjacent to the existing India Museum and the so-called Link gallery ran through the new building, joining the Indian museum with the Chinese, Japanese and Near Eastern collections. Although never

Figure 2.6 The Imperial Institute, South Kensington. Designed by T. E. Colcutt. (Photograph: Victoria and Albert Museum.)

formally a part of the Imperial Institute, these collections formed a spectacular display of non-Western art in a complex closely identified with the imperialist policies of late-Victorian Britain. However, parts of these collections also remained on the main site across Exhibition Road, where, increasingly, they were separated by media and integrated with the Western collections. The tension between rival taxonomies – culture and history versus materials and techniques – persists in the Victoria and Albert Museum's displays to this day, where European and Islamic objects are distributed throughout the material-based departments (Textiles, Metalwork, etc.) but separate departments administer Indian and South East Asian and Far Eastern collections.

The demise of the South Kensington Museum coincided with the Queen's last public appearance on 17 May 1899 when, amid great pomp and circumstance, she laid the foundation stone for Aston Webb's grandiose new building and renamed it 'the Victoria and Albert Museum'. When the new building opened in 1909 its role was confirmed as the most spectacular repository of the material culture of empire, though the redisplay under the patrician eye of Sir Cecil Harcourt Smith toned down the didactic mission, links with populist forms of display and jingoistic tone which had characterised its recent history.

This chapter has emphasised the significance of the interaction between buildings, objects and texts for an understanding of the museum as a cultural formation, and suggested that the South Kensington Museum occupied a central location in the symbolic geographies of the British capital, the nation and the empire. By 1909 the green fields of Brompton, purchased by the free trade reformists of 1851, had been transformed into a matrix of imperial archives, its geography blocked out by institutions whose purview extended across the discursive spaces not only of art, design and material culture, but also technology, natural history and geography. Today, the empire has gone, but the archives still remain, fluctuating as ever between the popular and the scholarly, desperately starved of that funding which the empire was supposed to supply, and awaiting a fundamental reassessment of the role of imperial institutions in the post-colonial period.

Note

1 Adapted after the exhibition to provide a smoking room for Lord Brassey's Park Lane residence, it is now permanently installed in the Hastings Museum and Art Gallery.

3

Chinese material culture and British perceptions of China in the mid-nineteenth century

Catherine Pagani

One result of the British victory in the Opium War (1839–42) was a change in English perceptions of the Chinese. Previously, China was the land of the exotic and unusual, the 'home of wisdom, virtue and good faith' and 'a model for all nations of the earth' (Honour 1961: 22). English opinion of the mid-eighteenth century considered the Chinese to be a happy pig-tailed race dwelling in fanciful pavilions whose institutions were to be admired. One result of the Opium War and its shift in economic power in favour of the British was a decline in the esteem felt for China and the Chinese. In the nineteenth century, the Chinese continued to be stereotyped in the West as a curious people; now, however, they were considered to be a 'lawless race' of 'lazy' and 'stupid' people who were 'filled with the most conceited notions of their own importance and power' (Fortune 1847: 2–3, 5, 8). These attitudes are revealed in writings of the day, particularly in the popular press. However, while the British were feeling a certain disdain for the Chinese people, their attitudes regarding Chinese art were far more positive. Chinese art was praised, and was described as being 'interesting', 'splendid' and 'magnificent'. China thus was seen as both the land of the uncivilised and as a country which produced wonderful and exotic goods.

How could two such different attitudes co-exist? How did they develop? Furthermore, why was Chinese art regarded favourably while the Chinese themselves were not? This chapter will explore these apparently contradictory views and their resolution by examining the reception of Chinese art in 1842, a time when relations between England and China changed dramatically. In this year, the Opium War ended with the signing of the Treaty of Nanking. Regular wartime reports provided the population with a wealth of information on China, and anti-Chinese sentiment in Britain was high. This year also saw the opening of Nathan Dunn's Chinese Collection at St George's Place, London. This successful exhibition, well documented in the press, gave the public a chance to see a wide variety of objects from China as well as read about them in the detailed catalogue. These events were presented simultaneously to a British public eager to know about a country with which they had been at war, and whose goods, including tea, porcelain and silk, they had consumed in great quantities. Examining Chinese art in England within its social and economic context reveals that these attitudes are not so dissimilar. Both show that China was regarded as a marketable commodity just as were her products, sentiments linked to feelings of cultural and economic superiority which came about through victory in the Opium War. Moreover, although China was at the periphery of Britain's colonial enterprise and this conflict was one of trade, British attitudes to the Chinese culture could be characterised as colonial, for the situation after the war was very similar to a colonial one. In order to understand better these phenomena, a discussion of the events surrounding the Opium War is necessary.

Decades-long tensions brought about by the trade imbalance between China and England culminated in the Opium War of 1839 to 1842, the most dramatic conflict between China and the West in the nineteenth century. Britain's formal trade with China had begun in 1600 with the establishment by royal charter of the Honourable East India Company which held the monopoly for trade with China and India. By 1715, trade was regular with tea as the most important commodity.[1] By the end of the eighteenth century, other trade goods passed between England and China, including silk and porcelain, although these goods did not exceed two per cent of the value of the cargo with tea as the most important commodity. The bulk of this trade flowed in favour of the Chinese, largely owing to the taste that the British had acquired for Chinese products. The Chinese, on the other hand, had little use for English goods. By the late-eighteenth century, tensions arose between the two nations over Chinese regulation of the trade: the British wished to have a representative residing in Beijing, increase the level of trade and have more treaty ports open for trade. Compounding the problem was the fact that the Chinese would accept only silver as payment, which accordingly drained from England at an alarming rate. Beginning in 1773, the British chose to redress the trade imbalance with opium grown in regions of India under British control. The East India Company regarded opium as a commodity which could be exchanged for the highly sought after Chinese goods such as tea. The opium habit grew quickly among every level of Chinese society, eventually making opium the single most important trade good passing between Britain and China. Despite Imperial edicts against both the smoking of the drug and its importation, the trade continued to grow.

In 1839, Lin Zexu (1785–1850) was appointed Imperial High Commissioner at Canton by the emperor to deal with the opium situation. He ordered the foreign merchants to surrender all of their opium. The smuggling continued in spite of Lin's orders. After cutting off the food supplies and water to the foreign factories, Lin confiscated 20,000 chests of opium and destroyed them by mixing the contraband with salt water and lime. The English retaliated with force, sending in gunboats to Canton; and on 3 November 1839, Britain declared war. China was ill-prepared to counter Britain's military superiority. The ensuing attack devastated the Chinese, and from that point on, China was in many ways subservient to the West.

The signing of the Treaty of Nanking on 29 August 1842 marked the end of the Opium War. The terms of the agreement forced the Chinese to cede Hong Kong to the British; to open Canton and four other ports for regular trade;[2] and to pay to Britain as indemnity just over 21 million dollars in silver, the currency of trade, most of which was to cover the cost of opium destroyed in pre-war conflicts. According to the British press, the 'vast hordes' of Chinese, thanks to the new freedoms offered by British political and commercial influence, were at last able to 'break through the ignorance and superstition which has for ages enveloped them, . . . come out into the open day, and enjoy the freedom of a more expanded civilization, and enter upon prospects immeasurably grander (*Illustrated London News* 1/31: 469).

This war was followed closely in the British newspapers. The weekly *Illustrated London News* (*ILN*) was one important source of information. The paper first appeared in May 1842 with an initial circulation of 60,000 which rose to 200,000 in less than a decade and a half (Herd 1952: 210). It is of interest for both its written reports on China and its illustrations, many of which were based on sketches made in the field. However, the *ILN* also relied on previously published illustrations, some of them dating from the mid-seventeenth century. An important and well-respected source was Jan Nieuhof's (1618–1672) famous account of the Dutch embassy to China of 1665, translated by John Ogilby and first published in English as *Embassy from the East India Company . . . to the . . . Emperour [sic] of China*, in 1669. For English readers, this work remained the authority on China into the mid-nineteenth century. The newspaper's 'Ground-plan of the Emperor's Palace, Pekin', for example, was adapted from Nieuhof's 'The Groundplot and Forme of Ye Palace or Imperial Court in Peking' (Fig. 3.1), and the 'Imperial Palace, Pekin' was adapted from 'Prospect of Ye Inner Court of the Emperours Palace at Pekin.'[3]

It is not surprising to find that at this time the popular press was not complimentary in its portrayal of the Chinese. The accounts of progress in the war characterised them as untamed savages. One particularly sensationalist item in the *ILN* highlighted their 'revolting cruelty' through the capture and subsequent imprisonment of Mrs Noble, wife of the captain of the armed brig, *Kite*, wrecked in 1840 (Fig. 3.2). According to the report, Mrs Noble was carried about in a wooden cage measuring but two feet eight inches in length, one foot six inches in breadth, and two feet four inches in depth. She could only sit in this box with her head protruding through a hole in the top. The *ILN* reported that Mrs Noble was held for six weeks in this cage when in fact she was caged for approximately thirty-six hours. The newspaper further reported that a replica of this cage was to be sent to the British Museum on the Indiaman *Wellesley* (*ILN* 1/14: 220).

British successes in the war contributed to a sense of cultural and economic superiority over the Chinese. The outcome of the war made for biting satire. A lengthy illustrated poem of 1842 entitled 'The Chinese War' published in *The Comic Album: A Book for Every Table*, contained the following lines:

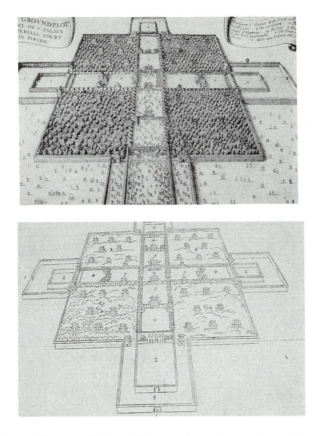

Figure 3.1 Above: 'The groundplot and forme of ye palace or imperial court in Peking'. (From Jan Nieuhof (1669) *Embassy from the East India Company... to the... Emperour [sic] of China*.) Below: 'Ground-plan of the Emperor's Palace, Pekin'. (From *The Illustrated London News*, 14 January 1843.)

Figure 3.2 A Chinese cage. (From *The Illustrated London News*, 13 August 1842.)

With this nation so deluded
Peace is happily concluded:
Let us now no longer teaze
The unfortunate Chinese.
We are ready to befriend them;
Cotton night-gowns we will send them;
For their use we will import
Articles of every sort – . . .
Everything, in fact, to please
And enlighten the Chinese,
England, this time forth supplies them,
Only just to civilize them
(*Comic Album* 1842: n.p.)

The caricature of a Chinese official which accompanied the text was reproduced in the *ILN* of 10 December 1842 (*ILN* 1/30: 509) as a companion to a short piece also found in *The Comic Album* entitled 'The Chinese Ambassador' (Fig. 3.3).

However, there were other factors which shaped British perceptions of China. Important among these was art from China, made for both export and native

Figure 3.3 The Chinese Ambassador. (From 'The Chinese War' in *The Comic Album: A Book for Every Table* (1842), reprinted in *The Illustrated London News*, 10 December 1842.)

Chinese consumption. In particular, export art made for the British market played an important role in reinforcing British notions of the Chinese.[4] In order to ensure the saleability of goods in England, the exporters found it necessary to dictate the shape and decoration of the goods. The results were hackneyed and stereotyped images of China made by the Chinese according to what the British felt was 'Chinese style'. The Chinese produced what the Western market demanded, and in the nineteenth century these images consisted of an exotic and fanciful East showing scenes of Chinese life: of pagodas and mandarins, of colourful flora and fauna; and to a lesser degree, China the land of the opium smoker, an image which was seen for the most part in small-format export paintings. This art thus confirmed what the British already thought about China and the Chinese. The 'Blue Willow' pattern on ceramics is one example of English intervention in the design of export art (Fig. 3.4). The now-famous stylised Chinese landscape in blue on a white ground was designed originally by Thomas Minton in 1780 and shows a Western interpretation of a Chinese design. In the nineteenth century, the Chinese copied this pattern for the export market, thus producing their own version of the British vision of China.

The images found on nineteenth-century Chinese export art, products which were geared to the Western imagination, were taken by many in Victorian England at face value. A newspaper article of March 1843 on trade issues was

Figure 3.4 Chinese export porcelain plate. Underglaze blue painted design, late-eighteenth or early-nineteenth century. (Royal Ontario Museum.)

accompanied by an illustration of two mandarins. The text, in which decorative motifs on ceramics are mentioned, reads in part, 'These Chinese dignitaries are habited in the costume which has long been familiar in England upon "china". Tea cups have not inappropriately acquainted us with Chinese appearances'; and Viscount Joscelyn, in his recent work, remarks 'It is wonderful how correct they are in the main features' (*ILN* 2/45: 174). As there were no competing images for comparison, the population interpreted such motifs as accurate representations of the Chinese.

The consumption of Chinese art, including the manner in which it was displayed and discussed, can also reveal much about attitudes toward China. In general, the opinions on art differed from those concerning the Chinese found in the newspapers. It appears that while the Chinese themselves were not always well regarded, their art was. Concerning some 'Extraordinary Chinese Presents to Her Majesty' in 1844, the *ILN* carried a story which told, among other things, of a large bronze bell and a pair of bronze vases sent to England from China and placed in the library at Buckingham Palace. Noting that, 'Her Majesty is becoming rich in Chinese presents', the paper added, 'we have now the satisfaction of presenting [our readers] with some examples of Chinese Fine Art, deposited in Buckingham Palace, which, in value, far transcend their war-like associates [associations], and which are, in fact, the very finest specimens of Celestial civilization which have yet reached this country.' The artists were praised for showing 'a refinement and elevation of taste greatly in advance of the national style' and the overall craftsmanship was said to be remarkable (*ILN* 4/90: 36).

The years of the Opium War saw stoppage of the China trade; regular shipments of goods were no longer arriving in England. This, combined with the coverage of the war in the press, served to fuel interest in China. As reported in 1842: 'At no period in the history of the world, has the attention of civilised nations been so fully directed towards China . . . as at the present moment' (Langdon 1843: 11). By the end of the war, there was a seemingly insatiable interest in China and Chinese goods. This interest was used to its advantage in the promotion of an exhibition known as The Chinese Collection.

During his twelve years in China, the American merchant Nathan Dunn (1782–1844) amassed a large collection of Chinese goods before his retirement from the trade in 1830. His business, Nathan Dunn and Company, was one of few at Canton which refused to traffic in opium on moral grounds (Carpenter 1976: 93). Dunn first exhibited the collection in Philadelphia in December 1838 on the ground floor of the newly-opened Philadelphia Museum. In 1842, at the urging of 'many of the most influential, scientific, and learned persons of the British metropolis and kingdom' (Langdon 1843: 15), the collection travelled to London. One of the enthusiastic visitors to the Philadelphia exhibition was the English author and traveller James Silk Buckingham (1786–1855) who published impressions of his 1840 visit in *The Eastern and Western States of America*. In this work he wrote of visiting the collection often with 'increased pleasure at every successive visit' to such an extent that he felt 'a longing desire to have [the Museum] transferred to London, where it would gratify ten times the number of persons that it can do here, and where the visitors, I think, feel more pleasure, from the more sensitive and ardent temperament of Europeans generally, compared with the coldness and indifference of the Americans' (Buckingham n.d.: II, 42–43).

In London, under the direction of the curator and co-proprietor William B. Langdon, the exhibition was kept up for several years.[5] Langdon enlarged Dunn's catalogue of the collection, *Ten Thousand Chinese Things* (with the Chinese characters *wan tangrenwu* included) of which approximately 50,000 copies sold in Philadelphia; the collection's popularity in England ensured the sale of more than 300,000 copies of the catalogue's London editions. Sometime after Dunn's death in 1844, the collection toured England before being returned to the United States. It was shown at P. T. Barnum's New York museum, and eventually was sold at auction in 1851, its size reduced to about half of the original (Christie and Manson 1851).

With the opening of the Chinese collection in London, the Orient was presented to the public both as an exotic and different culture, and as one worthy of serious academic study. This 'exhibition of extraordinary beauty and interest' was housed in an impressive structure resembling a Chinese residence, so designed to 'make the collection and its building worthy of attracting members from all classes' (Langdon 1843: 15). It was described as being 'resplendent with gold and bright colours, its roof and veranda turned up at the corners, painted green, and supported on columns of red with dragon-shaped brackets – a novel and striking object, and not inelegant' (*Spectator* 730: 616). Visitors entered into a large hall, approximately 225 by 50 feet, and were confronted by a variety of artefacts, among them three colossal gilt Buddhist sculptures (Fig. 3.5).

However, the stated purpose of this collection of 1,341 artefacts was to educate. 'Objects', according to the catalogue, are valuable for they are 'visible and tangible, and, therefore, cannot be easily misunderstood'. Dunn began by collecting 'a few rare specimens for his own gratification' until he had assembled the 'Chinese World in Miniature' (Langdon 1843: 13), and was assisted in his efforts by several of the Hong merchants at Canton including Howqua (Wu Bingzhen) and Tingqua (Guan Lianchang). Presented here was 'at one view an epitome of Chinese life and character, arts and manufacture, scenery and natural productions' (Langdon 1843: 14). Furthermore, these objects, as representations of Chinese culture, were also seen to reflect the moral character of the Chinese. Upon viewing this exhibition, the public would be able to

> analyse the mental and moral qualities of the Chinese, and gather some knowledge of their idols, their temples, their pagodas, their bridges, their arts, their sciences, their manufactures, their fancies, their parlours, their drawing rooms. . . . Here we have, not one object, but thousands; not a single discovery, but an empire with all its variety of light and shade, its experience, [and] its mind.
>
> (Langdon 1843: 13–14)

Figure 3.5 The Chinese Exhibition at Hyde Park. (From *The Illustrated London News*, 6 August 1842.)

Langdon made an effort to provide accurate information and relate only facts in his catalogue. He wrote: 'All fiction and romance have been carefully avoided; and what is stated, has in no instance been committed to these pages, unless on competent authority' (Langdon 1843: 14). The catalogue carried information by such noted authors on China as Sir John Davis (1795–1890), Dr Robert Morrison (1782–1834), Karl Gutzlaff (1803–51) and the eighteenth-century Jesuit missionary Jean-Joseph-Marie Amiot (1718–93). The result was, for its time, an informative and fairly balanced discussion of Chinese culture.

In an atmosphere of hostility toward the Chinese fuelled by the unflattering opinions found in the press, Dunn's collection not only survived but thrived. Competing images of a nation peopled by unenlightened savages with whom Britain was recently at war and one which produced objects worthy of admiration offered sharp contrasts for the public in the early 1840s. The Chinese Collection formed the tangible point of intersection between these attitudes, and Dunn's success may be attributed to his careful and skilful presentation of them. While apparently contradictory, these views in fact complemented one another: both reveal an underlying attitude to China in mid-nineteenth century England as a highly marketable commodity.

Dunn saw in the artefacts he assembled and put on display a means of educating the public on the Orient, and in so doing, connected these objects to the nation which produced them. For Dunn, this collection of goods was representative of Chinese culture, which he then marketed through his exhibition to an interested public. Thus, China itself became a commodity through its goods. Commodity and culture became inextricably linked: Dunn *read* Chinese culture *from* these commodities, and in his presentation of them, he *made* Chinese culture *into* a commodity.

Dunn's collection of China's material culture appealed to those who were interested in the exotic and the sensational through such elements as its brightly-painted Chinese-style building and its melodramatic displays on opium smoking, as well as those who sought a more academic and serious study of Chinese culture through a wide range of objects and extensive catalogue descriptions. Dunn wanted to show what he claimed was the 'real' China, and while this assortment of objects including paintings, porcelains, and manikins dressed as Chinese, was certainly not reflective of Chinese culture as a whole, it was the largest and most comprehensive collection of Chinese goods yet exhibited in London (Altick 1978: 292). Here, Chinese objects stood for Chinese culture as a whole, and as the catalogue exclaimed, the public could experience all of China in its variety, including the moral and mental character of the people themselves (Langdon 1843: 13–14).

Alongside his educational aims for the exhibition, Dunn also intended to reap personal financial benefit from China, which would enable him to mix with London society. Accordingly, he was energetic in marketing the collection, using methods which appealed to the Victorian fascination with the melodramatic, and capitalised on the omnipresent interest in China at the time. Indeed, Dunn could not have found a better time to bring his collection of Chinese objects to London. His exhibition benefited from the reports of the Opium War through which China held a central place in the minds of the British public as never before. As one newspaper reported:

> At any time, such a museum as this, giving an insight into the habits
> and arts of life of a people of whom we know so little, would be
> interesting; but at the present juncture it is most especially so. A few
> hours spent in studying the contents of this collection, with the aid
> of the descriptive catalogue, which is full of information, much of it
> original, will possess the visitor with an idea of the Chinese almost as
> complete and vivid as could be formed by a voyage to China.
>
> (*Spectator* 730:616)

Furthermore, trade with China had stopped during the war years, reducing the availability of Chinese goods. The exhibition presented the timely opportunity to assess this foreign culture through an examination of a wide array of its products. It also gave the public a chance to display its national pride by patronising an exhibition of objects from a country defeated.

In Philadelphia, the exhibition had enjoyed great success, bringing in a reported 100,000 visitors in three years at an admission price of twenty-five cents (Lee 1984: 16). London offered Dunn an opportunity to reach an even larger population. While the potential profits were great, Dunn declared that making money was not the prime motive in exhibiting his collection. Nathan Dunn was one of Philadelphia's wealthiest citizens and, from all accounts, did not need to rely on ticket sales to exhibit his collection in London; he stated publicly that he charged an admission of 2s 6d only to cover basic costs. His price, however, was criticised in the press for being unreasonably high, with other motives suggested for it.

In June 1842, shortly after the Chinese Collection opened in London, a lengthy article appeared in the *Spectator* praising this exhibition of 'products of Chinese ingenuity'. The article also requested that Dunn lower the admission price to one shilling 'for the benefit of the thousands whom the payment of half-a-crown would prevent from visiting it' (*Spectator* 730: 616). Dunn defended his admission price the following week in a letter to the editor. He wrote that it was recommended to him as 'the very lowest charge which the most experienced persons among [the distinguished nobility of England] . . . considered . . . prudent that I should adopt'. The editor of the newspaper countered that Dunn was not only going against the customary one-shilling fee, but that apparently he was concerned with appealing only to the wealthy. By setting a high entrance fee, he was excluding that segment of the population for whom 'the sight of [the exhibition] would give greater gratification and instruction than the fashionables who make it a morning lounge' (*Spectator* 731: 635). Dunn did not immediately reduce the price; but finally he did so in 1843.[6]

The sensational aspects of the collection, highlighted by Dunn's early marketing strategies, became more pronounced in the late 1840s. The original catalogue of 1843 had contained a lengthy section on opium smoking where the 'baneful effects of this deleterious drug', such as the debilitation of the limbs, and a 'discharge of rheum [which] tekes place from the eyes and nose', were detailed (Langdon 1843: 78). By 1851, sensationalism had become the focus in the advertisements for the collection. At this time, attention was no longer placed on the interesting assemblage of artefacts, but rather on several native Chinese who had been placed on display, and in particular to the 'golden water-lily' bound feet ('only Two Inches and a Half in Length!!') of the 'Celestial Belle' Pwan-Ye-Koo.[7]

Thus even China's much-admired arts were not enough to secure her place as an enlightened nation in the eyes of the British for long. In fact, ultimately these arts were the undoing of what little prestige the Chinese enjoyed in the eyes of the British. Over the next two decades, reliance on Chinese goods dropped as overall interest in Chinese art decreased. With this came less favourable reports on China. In 1846, the Scottish botanist Robert Fortune (1813–1880), sent to China as Botanical Collector to the Royal Horticultural Society, wrote that China was no longer an 'enchanted fairy-land'. He continued to say that although the Chinese had 'long since discovered the art of making beautiful porcelain, lacquer-ware, and silks, which have for centuries been so admired in Europe', facts which would speak well for them, instead show how little she has progressed over the centuries, and 'do the very reverse' from 'telling in their favour as an active and intelligent people' (Fortune 1847: 2–5).

Notions of progress had become of central importance. This was especially true in 1851, the year of the Great Exhibition at the Crystal Palace, itself a 'Temple to Progress', where the manufactured commodities of various nations were displayed. Here, China was represented by a rather disorganised assortment of goods including textiles, lacquerware, bronzes, 'curious jars', a printing press, carved ivory balls, and several Japanese objects (*Official Catalogue* 1851: 214–16). These were not China's finest manufactures sent by their proud producers, but appeared rather as a group of odd knick-knacks borrowed from the homes of those who had travelled to the East. These goods were hardly representative of what China had to offer, and differed very little from the objects exhibited by Dunn years before. The objects from 'small-eyed China' included 'fragile porcelain', 'ivory fans, so curiously carved, and . . . mother-of-pearl ornaments, so laboriously and exquisitely graven' (Tallis 1851: I, 5). Comments reflect a passing interest in the intricacy of the workmanship, but recorded nothing novel or remarkable to capture the public's attention. Furthermore, although Chinese skill was praised, it was also asserted that the Chinese were 'capable of wasting any amount of time upon any triviality' (Tallis 1851: I, 113). Chinese art offered nothing new, and the Chinese as a whole were now seen as doing the same old thing. They were perceived as being uninspired, 'so unwilling to learn, and jealous of change' (Tallis 1851: I, 63–4). Worst of all, they did not 'break through the ignorance which for ages had enveloped them' to take advantage of the new opportunities given, as the papers had said, by 'the new freedoms offered by British political and commercial influence'. These 'vast hordes' of Chinese failed to live up to British expectations of artistic evolution, and did not 'enter upon prospects immeasurably grander', as predicted in the *ILN* of 1842. The excitement concerning the Chinese and their products generated at war's end had again changed. The British were bored: the euphoria of the post-war boom was over.

This chapter has explored the complex relationship between British perceptions of Chinese material culture and of the Chinese themselves. Chinese objects (some of them produced specifically for the Western market) could be understood in multiple ways; as refined or barbarous, as quaintly timeless or as testimony to a lacklustre civilisation impervious to Victorian ideas of progress. Such paradoxical readings of material culture are closely linked to the circulation of goods in a market, and Nathan Dunn, for one, was aware of the money and status which could be made by exploiting the vogue for things Chinese, whether promoted as being mysteriously beautiful, or symbolic of vile habits and customs. In either case, a comfortable sense of military, and above all social and political, superiority, marked British attitudes to China. None the less, despite the military defeats of the Opium War, mainland China never became a part of the British Empire, though Hong Kong, of course, did. When the British left Hong Kong on 1 July 1997, a chapter in the history of colonialism closed, though (as British press reporting of the event testified) attitudes to a now powerful China are still stereotyped, complex and contradictory. Meanwhile, the taste for Chinese art objects continues unabated.

Notes

1 Export art had come into England largely as a result of the private trade carried on by the captains, chief negotiators and crews of the Company's ships who were allowed to trade for individual profit.

2 These ports were Amoy (Xiamen), Shanghai, Ningpo (Ningbo), and Foochow (Fuzhou).

3 Jan Nieuhof was part of the Dutch embassy to Peking under Peter de Goyer and Jacob de Keyzer in 1656. He first published his account in 1665 as *L'Ambassade de la Compagnie Orientale des Provinces Unies vers l'Empereur de la Chine ou Grand Cam de Tartarie* . . . (Leyden: Jacob de Meurs). This work saw later translations into Dutch, English, German and Latin. The illustrations contained therein were based on those he made in his diary, which has been published by Blussé and Falkenburg (1987). For information on this Dutch embassy, see Wills (1984).

4 A valuable discussion of the various types of Chinese export art may be found in Clunas (ed.) (1987).

5 For a history of the Chinese Collection, see Saxbee (1990).

6 The admission price of 2s 6d may be found in various advertisements for the exhibition. See, for example, *ILN*, vol. 1 no. 12, 30 July 1842, p. 191. Later, after Dunn's death in 1844, the price was dropped to 1s, and continued at this price into 1851 when the exhibition was moved to Albert Gate, Hyde Park.

7 The collection was now under new proprietorship. Advertisements concerning the display of Pwan-Ye-Koo and four other Chinese, including two children, began appearing in the *ILN* on 10 May 1851 (vol. 18, no. 483, p. 380) under the heading 'Extraordinary Arrival From China'. A second advertisement followed on 24 May (vol. 18, no. 487, p. 444), and interestingly was placed just above one for the display of a royal Chinese junk.

China in Britain
The imperial collections[1]
Craig Clunas

When I was fourteen I went to London with my father. We were on the way to Cambridge, where I was to investigate the possibility of studying Chinese. I visited the Victoria and Albert Museum for the first time, and there in a large room titled 'Far Eastern Art' I was enthralled to see a great carved lacquer seat, labelled 'Throne of the Emperor Ch'ien-lung' (Fig. 4.1). While the uniformed warder looked away (or pretended to), I knelt down and put my forehead to the black linoleum in homage.

These are not the tales curators tell. Their role in maintaining objects (in both senses of the word) demands that they suppress such embarrassing personal engagements and secret fetishisms, which threaten to reopen the space between the viewer and the artefact. The throne was there, and the Emperor of China sat on it. Now it is here, and you the visitor view it. Do not ask how it got here, or where it was from 1770 to now; that does not matter. You are here to engage with 'China', not with 'Britain', so do not ask what the presence of the throne of the emperor of China might tell you about 'Britain', and its narratives about 'China' over the two centuries since the thing was made. Admission of this bit of adolescent theatricality may undermine my professional identification as a member of the staff of that same museum, entrusted by the British state with the power to place that same 'throne', write about it and display it. However, failure to admit to it, to accept the object's presence in South Kensington as being an untroubling and natural occurrence, which need not touch anyone's fantasy life today, can only in the end reproduce a stifling identity of self-regard. What follows is a step towards the compilation of the inventory which Gramsci saw as necessary, if a consciousness of myself and my colleagues as a product of the historical process to date is to be produced. The dates, deeds and institutional affiliations of past scholars which I write down here are presented not simply as 'what happened', but rather as an essential part of any critical elaboration of present practice in the production of 'Chinese Art' in Britain, in a context where the displays of the major public museums are the principal visible constructions from which a discourse of 'Chinese culture' can be derived.

Figure 4.1 Throne. Carved lacquer on a wood core, *c.*1775–80. Taken from the Nan Yuan hunting park in 1901. (Victoria and Albert Museum.)

Possessions/identities

C. B. Macpherson's work (1962) on the political theory of possessive individualism in eighteenth-century England has made familiar the notion that possessions are seen as constitutive of identity within the dominant discourses of political and moral economy in Britain. More recently, the work of Susan Stewart (1993) and James Clifford (1988) has extended this notion to the position that possessing is also central to the generation and sustaining of the identities of collectivities. This is particularly so in the case of the imagined community of the nation state. The National Museum acts as a key site of promotion of the existence and validity of the state formation. It does so with particular force in that the discursive practices at the heart of the museum lay claim to scientific objectivity, to a transcendental mimesis of what is 'out there'. It thus can act with particular force to validate the claims to sovereignty and independence by proving through displays of archaeology and ethnography the inevitability of the existence of the actually contingent conditions which give it its very existence.

The 'British Museum' could never be restricted to British things, for to do so would set a limit to the reach of British power, as well as to the gaze of the all-comprehending and autonomous subject. The British colonial presence in China differed from that in India in duration and intensity, but many of the same practices in the field of culture can be observed, practices constitutive of a 'British' identity differentiated not only from the other of Asia but from more immediate colonial rivals such as France and latterly the United States. In what follows I want to look at some changes in the presentation of material from China in the British Museum and the Victoria and Albert Museum in London, two institutions directly patronised and supported by the British state, conscious that the framing of Chinese objects in these institutions conditions their viewing as expressive of discourses of national and imperial identity. The interplay of private and public possession, between individual collectors and public museums which they patronised and supported, and which ultimately came to possess the objects they had amassed, is of particular importance in forming the collections of material out of which representations of 'China' and 'Chinese art' were manufactured in Britain. I write with intentional ambiguity about Britain's possession of the 'throne' of China, to which I bowed as a teenager.

The institutional framing of 'Chinese art' in Britain

It is impossible to discuss the creation of the broader category 'Chinese art' in Europe and America over the past hundred years without first accepting the existence of a discourse (and a gendered discourse) of China which has its primary locus in the context of domestic consumption, since it is against, or by contrast with, what is done in the home that so much of what happens in the institutional context of museums and of the academy is defined. This is particularly striking in the case of objects of luxury consumption for the Chinese domestic market redirected by the museum, and put under the category 'decorative arts': chairs, items of clothing, ceramic wine jars, personal religious images, to take a few random examples. Chinese elite categorisations of art, as expressed in texts as well as in the practices of the art and craft markets excluded much of the Chinese material subsequently displayed in the museum context in Britain.

Indeed 'art' is not a category in the sense of a pre-existent container filled with different contents as history progresses. Rather it is a way of categorising, a manner of making knowledge which has been applied to a wider and wider set of manifestations of material culture, paralleling the constant expansion of an 'art market' applied to a wider and wider range of commodities. It remains a site of conflicting interpretations, fissured on class and gender lines, among others, and the right to define something as 'art' is typically seen as an important attribute of those dominant in society at a given moment. Crucial to this way of categorising in European museum and academic practice is the strategy whereby notions of function must largely be removed from the objects of the exercise. In order to be an object of 'decorative art' a cup must no longer be drunk from, and questions of how it would be drunk from have to be occluded. Thrones must no longer be bowed down to. Objects transferred from the domain of 'ethnography' to that of 'art' typically find diachronic links privileged at the expense of connections with others which have failed to make the transition (Clifford 1988: 224–5).

But narrative art history is only one interpretative framework into which the things made in China have been construed in Europe and America. Despite its role as the dominant paradigm in the United States today, it is arguable whether it has ever actually taken root in Britain at all. Another framework of representation has historically flourished here, one with an equal power of generating discourse, though this time originating in the study of the natural world: the framework of taxonomy. This in the later nineteenth century, and most particularly in Britain, exercised a powerful hegemony over the ordering of man-made products as well as over those of nature (Stafford 1990: 67–89). It is the programme of a universal taxonomy of 'the industrial arts' which formed the explicit project of the South Kensington Museum, known after 1899 as the Victoria and Albert Museum. In 1863 (immediately after the Second Opium War against China) the Lords of the Committee of the Council on Education had stated 'that the aim of the Museum is to make the historical and geographical series of all decorative art complete, and fully to illustrate human taste and ingenuity' (Earle 1986: 866).

The aim of completeness was qualified by the exclusion from the South Kensington collections of the material culture of those peoples, dubbed 'primitive', who had neither art nor history. They were consigned to the historic present of ethnography collections, represented in 1863 primarily by the British Museum but later in the century by collections such as those of the Horniman Museum in London and the Pitt Rivers Museum in Oxford (Coombes 1988: 57–68).

It is very hard to research the history of a museum. The point of a museum is that it has no history, but represents the objects it contains transparently, in an unmediated form. It is even harder to create a history of the display of Chinese material in British museums, since very little descriptive or pictorial information exists as to what was shown where when, what juxtapositions (almost the most powerful creators of meaning in display) were made, which objects were privileged by particularly prominent positioning, and what was said about them on labels. This is more than an accident, or a piece of forgetfulness on the part of my predecessors. The museum cannot allow itself to document its own frequently changing display arrangements, since then it will have a history, and if it becomes a historical object in its own right then it can investigated, challenged, opposed or contradicted (Lumley 1988; Vergo 1989).

There have in fact been many changes in the contexts and categories into which Chinese artefacts have been inserted in Britain. Only some of these contexts have involved a deployment of the notion of 'Chinese art', but all have operated with the notion of an integral 'Chinese culture', for which certain types of luxury artefact, mediated through the international art market and categorised by British individual and institutional collectors, was a satisfactory synecdoche.

Chinese objects came to the British Museum in the founding bequest of Sir Hans Sloane in 1753, and appear at first to have been included under the rubric of 'Ethnography'. That this was felt to be in some sense inadequate by the mid-nineteenth century is shown by the complaint in David Masson's *The British Museum, Historical and Descriptive* (1850) that works of China and Japan were crammed into 'five paltry cases' among a 'collection of articles illustrative of the manners and customs of nations lying at a distance from our own, as well as of rude ancient races' (Miller 1973: 222). Masson argued that there should be distinct rooms for the antiquities of China, India and Japan, which should be separated from those of more primitive peoples.

There was clear privileging of Chinese and Japanese pictorial works throughout the nineteenth century, though this owed more to Western notions of the hierarchy of the arts than it did to any recognition of their equal prominence in any scheme of things to be found in China. The fact that they were a 'higher' art form is shown by their inclusion in the collections of the Department of Prints and Drawings (formed out of the Department of Antiquities as far back as 1836), where they were collected and curated on a par with European material.

This is a significant point. At a time when Chinese ceramics were still, at least administratively, the same thing as canoes and weapons, a Hiroshige print was the same as a Rembrandt print. A picture could not, by definition, be simply an 'antiquity', a piece of historical evidence, but was of necessity part of the realm of (fine) art. A Chinese picture could be bad art, failed art, but it could not cease to be art at this point. Note, however, that there was no question of including Chinese painting with Western painting in the National Gallery, and it remained alongside items (prints) which occupied a subsidiary, if still honoured, ranking in the Western canon.

London's other major institutional collection, the South Kensington Museum, has also included Chinese material since its inception in the Museum attached to the central design school of the Department of Practical Art in the decades immediately prior to the Great Exhibition of 1851 (Burton 1985: 373–87). The initial aim of the collection was stringently didactic, aimed at improving the quality of British manufactured goods in a situation of intense commercial rivalry, above all with the French. Consequently the South Kensington Museum aimed to concentrate on 'Ornamental Art', which meant excluding pictures and sculpture (though this programme was modified shortly after its inception, and a considerable quantity of Chinese pictures acquired).

In the historicist climate of the time China was a perfectly acceptable source of design solutions, though one held in lower esteem by many. In *The Grammar of Ornament*, first published in 1856, the designer and theorist Owen Jones (someone closely associated with the whole South Kensington project) could write that Chinese art was totally familiar, through the medium of imported goods, and could condemn it thus: 'The Chinese are totally unimaginative, and all their works are accordingly wanting in the highest grace of art – the ideal' (Gombrich 1979: 56). The complaint is really one about 'the Chinese mind', to which an assemblage of designed objects will provide an infallible key. Nevertheless large quantities of objects in a variety of media were accumulated at South Kensington, in an institution which became increasingly confused as the nineteenth century wore on as to whether it was there to educate British craftsmen by exposing them to a broad range of often contemporary practice, or there to assemble a great historical corpus of material in which connoisseurly criteria of quality would be the deciding factor.

Ceramics as the flowering of Chinese art

In the inter-war years and after the Department of Ceramics was broadly responsible for the sustenance and construction of 'Chinese Art' within the Victoria and Albert Museum. With what were, both numerically and in terms of prominence in display, the most important Chinese collections, and with internationally renowned scholars such as William Bowyer Honey (1891–1956) and Bernard Rackham (1877–1964) on its staff, the Department exercised an unofficial hegemony, as guardian of the master narrative in which 'Chinese ceramics' and 'Chinese art' were collapsed into each other.

However, during the inter-war period, the British Museum's sub-department of Oriental Prints and Drawings (established in 1913) employed the young Arthur Waley (1889–1968), nowadays better remembered as a translator of Chinese and Japanese literature.[2] Waley had been employed by Laurence Binyon (1899–1943), author in 1908 of *The Painting of the Far East*.[3] Both Waley and Binyon enjoyed wide literary reputations which gave them an authority not essentially derived from their museum offices. Although his championing of painting might make him seem a more faithful transmitter of 'traditional' Chinese connoisseurly criteria, Binyon's views are those of the classic orientalist position as defined by Said, where 'the East' cannot represent itself, but must be revealed to itself by the Western expert, who has penetrated its essential and unchanging characteristics. They are summed up in a series of lectures delivered at Harvard in 1933–4, and dedicated to his great American contemporary Langdon Warner, Director of the Freer Gallery (Binyon 1936: 16). These construct 'Chinese art' as a reflection of essential and largely historically invariant characteristics of 'the Chinese race', and are full of typically reductive aphorisms – 'The Chinese have kept their eyes fresh', 'This race has always had a turn to the fabulous . . . It [Chinese art] has its roots deep in the earth.' Binyon certainly shared the view described above that it was the early achievements of Chinese culture that were the touchstone of quality, and that these were in some sense unknown to the Chinese themselves; 'for it is only in the present century that the real achievements of Chinese art have been revealed' (Binyon 1936:7). He also provided a theoretical underpinning for the prominent role given to ceramics in museum collections, in his typically florid panegyric in Bergsonian vein to a Tang dynasty ceramic jar.

No less than a great picture or statue, this vase typifies what art is and art does: how it has its being in the world of the senses yet communicates through the senses so much more than we can express in words. You cannot tell the body from the spirit, the thing expressed from its expression. The complete work is filled with a mysterious life like a human personality.

(Binyon 1936: 21)

The anonymity of potters saved the connoisseur from even having to consider any named, individuated Chinese maker as a conscious social or political actor. No actual person had made the pot, it had been made by 'the race'.

Chinese art and imperial decline

The years after the First World War saw a major shift in the valuation of Chinese art in Britain, with a collapse in the status of the types of Qing (1644–1911) porcelain which had been the focus of interest for an early generation of collectors (like Stephen Bushell[4] and those advised by him), and a new engagement with the art of early China. It has been traditional to view this in rather mechanistic terms, as the simple reaction to the increased opportunity to see early Chinese things concomitant with the progress of excavation, legal and illegal, in China. Clearly there was a connection between railway building and the flood of tomb ceramics on to the market. But it is also the case that changed attitudes made for a greater receptivity to early Chinese artefacts. (After all, plenty of bronzes were available above ground in the Qing period, but there is no evidence that they moved Whistler or Oscar Wilde in the same way as Kangxi blue-and-white ceramics). Rachel Gotlieb's description of a tired Europe refreshing itself from the vital springs of more primitive cultures is clearly part of the larger picture of appropriation of the other seen in the art of the Cubists and Surrealists (Gotlieb 1988: 163–7). In the particular case of China, the otherness is seen as distance in time, not space. Chinese culture has a glorious past, a decayed and exhausted present and no future.

Running parallel to this development, expressed above all in critical writing like that of Roger Fry, was a deepening fetishisation by the Victoria and Albert Museum of objects manufactured at what was deemed to be both the apogee and the end of 'traditional China', the eighteenth century. The reign of the Qianlong emperor (1736–95) was held to mark the last era of artistic excellence before the catastrophic nineteenth-century 'decline' (the causes of which, if they are discussed at all in artistic literature, are usually put down to something like 'exhaustion' on the part of the 'tradition'). The role of imperialism in China's 'decline' is not commented on. The Qing empire disappeared in 1911, closely followed by the emperors of Russia, Germany and Austria. By 1920 only the emperors of Abyssinia, Japan and the King-Emperor George V kept their thrones. The latter ruled over territories which were expanded after the First World War, reaching a physical extent from which they were so swiftly to shrink. It is in the light of this that we must examine the fascination with the

Chinese imperial court which was to permeate writing about, collecting and displaying Chinese artefacts in an institution like the Victoria and Albert Museum. The signs of rulership (crowns, thrones and other regalia) had been prominent in the Indian courts of the Great Exhibition of 1851, the event from which the Victoria and Albert Museum rhetorically derived (and continues to derive) legitimacy (Breckenridge 1989: 203–4). The fascination with the imperial provenance of the loot from the 1862 sacking of the Summer Palace was reflected in the museum's collecting in the decades after the event, but the supply of objects of high enough status and sufficient aesthetic quality was seen as necessarily limited before the ending of Qing rule.

In 1922 the museum was given what has remained one of its most famous and most reproduced treasures. It is a late-eighteenth century throne-chair, looted from an imperial hunting park to the south of Peking in the 1901 multi-national invasion of China, and sold on the London art market by Mikail Girs, a White Russian *émigré* who had been Tsarist ambassador there at that time. It cost £2,250, and earned the donor of those funds the thanks of Queen Mary, who was known to have 'expressed a hope that, by some means, it might find a place' in the museum which bore her husband's grandparents' names. The throne has remained on display ever since, labelled until recently, 'The [note the definite article] throne of the Emperor Ch'ien-lung'.[5]

The screen with which it once formed a pair remains unpublished in the Museum of Ethnography in Vienna, but then possession of the screen of China is not the same thing as possession of the throne of China. (It would of course be recognised that Qing political discourse made no room for a 'throne of China', no ruler's seat which is symbolically equated with right of rule. The object's meaning is entirely a product of its context of display.) In Susan Stewart's terms, the throne is more of a souvenir than an item in a collection:

> we need and desire souvenirs of events that are reportable, events whose materiality has escaped us, events that thereby exist only through the invention of narrative. Through narrative the souvenir substitutes a context of perpetual consumption for its context of origin. It represents not the lived experience of its maker but the 'secondhand' experience of its possessor/owner. Like the collection it always displays the romance of contraband, for its scandal is its removal from its 'natural' location. Yet it is only by means of its material relation to that location that it acquires its value.
>
> (Stewart 1993: 135)

As the British Empire became more and more remote, souvenirs of the emperor such as the 'throne of China' played a greater and greater role in the national imaginary, as nostalgia for one empire slid across into nostalgia for all, and souvenirs of empire became fetishes of consolation. British colonial power in China was less effective in 1922 than it had been two decades earlier, at the point of the looting of the 'throne', and was to decline significantly over the next two decades leading to its collapse under Japanese assault. The throne thus comes to signify not the empire from which it was taken, but the equally vanished empire which took it.

Chinese art in the academy

Percival David (1892–1964), while also building up a major private collection of Chinese ceramics, provided in 1930 the funds for an experimental lecture-ship in Chinese Art and Archaeology, to be tenable at the School of Oriental and African Studies (SOAS), London University (Hansford 1956: 3). This lectureship, the first formal teaching to be made available in Britain in the field, was first given to Walter Perceval Yetts (1878–1957), who had no academic background in Chinese art history. In 1932 the post was made into a Chair attached to the Courtauld Institute of Art, and funded by the Universities China Committee in London, a grant-giving body funded by the monies extorted from the Chinese government by Britain as part of the 'Boxer indemnity' after 1901.

Yetts was succeeded as a teacher of Chinese Art and Archaeology at London University by S. Howard Hansford (1899–1973), who initially also had no formal background in art history or academic sinology, having worked rather until his mid-thirties with the family firm of Wright and Hansford, China and Japan Merchants. Hansford's SOAS lectureship was made up to a Chair in 1956, and he held the post till 1966, when he was succeeded by William Watson. In Hansford's inaugural lecture he took the opportunity to review the study of the subject in Britain, but first of all to stress the long history of 'archaeoloatry – the worship of antiquity' in China. In a further statement, very much in the manner of the orientalist concentration on 'essences' he argues that 'all Chinese' are conscious of the antiquity and unity of their civilisation, and adds: 'The Chinese, like the British, are quite sure that they are the salt of the earth, and do not feel the need of proving it by tedious argument' (Handsford 1956:4).

His definition of the field is one which begins with bronzes, then Buddhist sculpture, then 'glyptics' i.e. the jade carving which was his own special field. For the study of these subjects London, with its three major museum collections, its private collections, and above all its thriving art market, 'offers conditions as near ideal as possible', and in particular better than those of China. He accepts that the torch of scholarship in this field has passed to Americans and Germans, while the major collections are all in Japan or the USA. He never mentions China, and we are left with the clear impression that Oriental Art is too important a subject to be left to Orientals.

The end of empire and the art of empire

Hansford's 1956 inaugural lecture was delivered in a context in which the study of Chinese art in Britain seemed to him indeed to be flourishing. What was happening in London at this period was the emergence of a more distinctive profile for 'Chinese art'. Distinguished now from 'ethnography' at the British Museum (in 1946) and recognised at the Victoria and Albert Museum as a distinct phenomenon by the creation of the 'Primary Gallery' (1952), above all enshrined in the prestigious Percival David Foundation of Chinese Art (1952), as well as supported by a flourishing art market and the collectors grouped around an expanded Oriental Ceramic Society, the subject seemed to enjoy a new degree of discursive coherence, but one still centred on museums rather than on academic teaching. The Percival David Foundation remains at the time of writing the only teaching institution in Chinese art, and from 1966 to the present its Head has been a scholar whose career began in a museum (William Watson, 1966–83; Roderick Whitfield, 1983–).

This discursive coherence nevertheless operated in a political climate of massively reduced British colonial power in Asia. After the end of the Malaysian 'emergency' (fought as Britain's contribution to the global containment of communism in Asia) such power was now focused almost solely on China, through the retention of Hong Kong. Yet throughout this period, and down to the present, colonialism was displaced into culture. Hong Kong remained invisible to the public culture represented in museums like the Victoria & Albert Museum and the British Museum, and 'China' remained, the two colliding only in the last decade with the reinstallation of the galleries at both the Victoria and Albert and British Museums using funds donated by individuals from the Hong Kong business community.[6] As government restrictions on museums' budgets mirror national economic decline, and as the private sector of corporate and personal sponsorship becomes the major support for once-imperial institutions, the question of who gets to represent what to who comes to the fore. To a sector of the museum's visitors, the loot of empire is what they expect to see, a literal 'empire of things'. In this world of insecure meanings and private fetishisms, the continued presence of major displays of Chinese art in the national museums, paid for with money from Hong Kong, come to seem in their entirety like souvenirs of that empire which is fast vanishing into the imaginary consolations of the costume drama.

Notes

1 This article is a shortened version of a piece first published as 'Oriental Antiquities/Far Eastern Art' in *positions*, 2: 2 1994. It appears here as published in Benewick, R. and Donald, S., eds, *Belief in China: Art and Politics, Deities and Mortality*, The Green Centre for Non-Western Art and Culture, Royal Pavilion Art Gallery and Museums, Brighton (1996).

2 Waley worked for the British museum from 1913 to 1930 and produced a catalogue of the Dunhuang paintings in 1931, which is still reckoned of some value today. Waley represented the exceptional figure of the self-taught genius and remarked quite correctly in 1923 that it was simply impossible to learn in London the kind of Chinese needed to equip one for a study of Chinese painting (though the idea of going to China to learn it was equally rejected) (Barrett 1989: 47).

3 Laurence Binyon was very much the *fin-de-siècle* aesthete in his views, a man for whom his work on *The Painting of the Far East* was but one strand in a career equally devoted to Western art, poetry, and historical drama.

4 Prior to 1939, only one attempt had been made at South Kensington to address the entire field of 'Chinese art', and to improve the scholarly treatment of the Chinese collections in line with the European holdings, but this had been done right at the beginning of the century by recourse to knowledge held by a private collector, in this case Stephen

Wooton Bushell (d.1908). The South Kensington Museum commissioned his *Chinese Art* (originally of 1904, but with numerous reprints), using the museum's pieces as illustrations almost exclusively.

5   *Nominal File: J P Swift*, Victoria and Albert Museum Registry.

6   The T. T. Tsui Gallery of Chinese Art opened at the Victoria and Albert Museum in 1991, and the Joseph Hotung Gallery of Oriental Antiquities opened at the British Museum in 1992.

5

Colonial architecture, international exhibitions and official patronage of the Indian artisan

The case of a gateway from Gwalior in the Victoria and Albert Museum

Deborah Swallow

That the bulk of the Victoria and Albert Museum's Indian collections at the time of writing lie in storage – or in 'reserve collections' to use the correct museological terminology – is well known to those interested in the arts of the subcontinent. Less well known is the fact that the very largest item in the collection is actually in one of the museum's galleries. But the object in question has been hidden from view since the Second World War. Concealed from public gaze behind constructed partitioning on the southern wall of the Raphael Gallery stands an Indian sandstone gateway. Seen last when it was temporarily revealed, documented and given first-aid conservation during reconstruction work in the Gallery in 1993, this gateway has been known since its creation in 1883 as the 'Gwalior Gateway'. It stands as a symbol of the ambivalence that surrounded British attitudes to Indian art and craft in the nineteenth century, and that left the collection in the post-Second World War period with hardly a seat in the curious game of musical chairs that has characterised the history of display in the Victoria and Albert Museum. The story of the Gwalior Gateway offers an interesting perspective on the local and larger-scale politics of representation throughout this period.

In the latter part of the nineteenth century Britain had no doubts about the advantages of her Indian empire. Lancashire's mills were transforming India into a large market for her manufactures, capital was flowing into the sub-continent, the routes to her shores had improved, and India continued to be the base from which British traders successfully exploited markets further east. India was the key to a specific sort of colonial system, playing a subtle role as the chief support in an extensive eastern trading system. A major function of the British state in India was to protect and promote this infrastructural role.

This meant collecting and guaranteeing the sources of enough revenue to run the administration, to do the minimum necessary to oil the wheels to maintain an army that had the military muscle to protect Britain's wider economic interests. To raise funds the British had to fall back on revenue, the standby of all previous rulers of India, and to be successful the settlements had to be modelled along lines approved by influential sectors of society. As time went on even those involved in the administration of India in London realised that the secret of successful government was to keep taxation low, cultivate policies of salutary neglect, stick scrupulously to strict neutrality in regional matters, keep administration cheap and the British element in it small. As the decades passed and more finance was needed, new ways of winning collaboration were sought, while imperial strategy also entailed a policy of non-interference in a good third of India, the princely states.

Accorded a secure place within Britain's empire, the princes, carefully ranked and ordered, and watched over by political agents posted at their courts, exercised power by courtesy of their British overlords, in a relationship of mutual dependence. Neither benevolent paternalists, nor blatant oppressors, the British, it can be argued, ruled India only in a formal sense, creating the illusion of power by means of drama and pageant, colouring their optimistic pronouncements with a wash of fiction. As the century wore on and communications improved, the British found many occasions for the display of the romanticised pageantry that had become an important part of the imperial self-image, and the princes played a key part in this drama. Whether at court in London, at Osborne House or at durbars in India, the princes had to appear in traditional Indian royal dress and frequently outdid the most extravagant expectations. Yet their states were also expected to be exemplars of the changes that the British hoped to introduce into India. Torn between these conflicting demands, the princes sustained their roles as traditional Hindu or Muslim rulers, maintained the trappings of feudal court life and made religious endowments, but also adopted the external habits of a Westernised life-style. They modernised their states and set up the institutions of new India – schools, colleges, hospitals, courts, charitable and learned societies.

Encouraged by the British, and as part of their own internal battle for symbolic precedence, they also built new palaces. Sir Lepel Griffin, agent to the Governor General of Central India, writing in *The Pioneer* newspaper in 1887, expressed one official view. For those princes

> whose minds have been enlightened by English training, the old, and it may be, picturesque designs of native palaces are odious. They cannot breathe in the confined rooms and narrow passages which were good enough for their fathers. They demand large well-ventilated rooms, light and air, wide staircases and imposing halls. Such conveniences find no place in the conventional designs of native architecture.
>
> (quoted Metcalf 1989: 110)

Although the princes continued to patronise traditional artisans and artists, their tastes inevitably became eclectic, their styles extravagant, and they fell prey to the battles of conflicting opinion on an appropriate form of architecture for India then being waged in the Subcontinent (see Davies 1985; Metcalf 1989; Tillotson 1989; London 1984).

In the early period of their stay in India, the British transplanted overseas the predominant neoclassical model of the time, adopting different variants as tastes changed. By the early nineteenth century, as the East India Company expanded the territory under its control, these neoclassical buildings had taken on an enhanced meaning. The construction in 1803 of Government House in Calcutta, modelled on Robert Adam's Kedleston Hall in Derbyshire (1759–70), reflected the Whig conviction that the country mansion, more effectively than any other structure, expressed the power and authority of government (Metcalf 1989: 12).

The subsequent decades saw the British slowly gaining in knowledge of the indigenous architecture of the subcontinent, but throughout the period British perception of India's historic architecture was dominated by a theory of decline and by the use of religious and communal categories as a mode of explanation. Partha Mitter's excellent study of European reactions to Indian Art (Mitter 1977), traces the history of European failure to understand the architecture, sculpture and complex iconography of the Hindu tradition. The discovery of the early history of Indian Buddhism reinforced these prejudices and allowed the Victorians to argue that the so-called Buddhist period – between the second century BC and the first century AD – when the great *stupas* at Sanchi, Bharhut and Amaravati were constructed and the Greek and western Asiatic influenced arts of the Gandharan region were at their height, represented the Indian classical age. All that came after represented a decline and later medieval Hindu architecture, particularly that of southern India, reflected the decadent end of a tradition. By contrast, the architecture of India's Islamic rulers, who dominated northern India in the centuries after AD 1200 was reassuring, familiar and aesthetically satisfying, even though the term 'Saracenic' which was used to describe it in the nineteenth century, was a reminder of the historical confrontation between Islam and the West. The appeal of this architecture clearly owed as much to its political symbolism as to its aesthetic beauty.

> The constructive truthfulness of the Muslim styles was appropriate to a nation of soldiers equipped for conquest while the exquisite style of decoration of the Hindu marked out a society with an infinite number of artists who could fit their craft to the requirements of their foreign masters.
>
> (Metcalf 1989: 38–9)

The British sometimes found it difficult to fit the buildings they were trying to describe in to standard categories, as many buildings in effect reflected a marriage of elements from different traditions. The architecture of their own Indian capital in Calcutta continued to reflect a monumental civic classicism, and Bombay, India's great trading city, at the height of its commercial expansion, acquired some of the finest Gothic revival buildings in the world. But towards the end of the century they increasingly turned to the combination of

Figure 5.1 The High Court in Madras (completed 1892). One of the most splendid Indo-Saracenic buildings in the city. Architect Henry Irwin; building contractor T. Namberumal Chetty. (Victoria and Albert Museum.)

Muslim and Hindu forms that became known as the Indo-Saracenic style (Fig. 5.1). This they saw as representing the two traditions while firmly subordinating the Hindu, as they themselves tried to encapsulate India's past within their own building – in an architectural equivalent to the feudal pageantry of their imperial durbars.[1]

The princes in turn also now had a wider range of choices than before, and the palaces that were built from the 1870s onwards reflect this variety. A number of the Maharajas mimicked the Palladian style that had been the traditional choice of their European rulers. The Jai Vilas Palace in Gwalior, erected by Jayaji Rao Scindia and made ready in time for the visit of the Prince of Wales in 1876, was designed by Sir Michael Filose, an Italian with several generations' service in the Indian army. This immense construction, standing beneath the sheer rock fortress that commands the road to central India, and incorporating Doric, Tuscan and Corinthian elements in an extensive façade of paired columns and Palladian windows, was judged 'not bad' by the British, but did not entirely meet their approval. The Lakshmi Vilas Palace, built as the town residence of the Gaekwar Sayajirao III of Baroda and designed by one of the leading architects of the Indo-Saracenic style, Major Charles Mant, was completed by another of the

55

great architects of the movement, Robert Fellowes Chisholm, after Mant had committed suicide fearing that the whole immense edifice would collapse.

Some of the princes managed a more comfortable balance than others. The rulers of Amber, having moved down from its fortress at Amber in the eighteenth century to create a new city, Jaipur, with its city palace on the plains below, felt no need to erect a new palace at this period, unlike some of the more parvenu princes whom the British had effectively elevated to their present status. Maharaja Ram Singh II employed a highly accomplished practitioner of the Indo-Saracenic style – an army engineer, Colonel Swinton Jacob – to improve Jaipur's roads and irrigation works, and subsequently allowed him to develop a range of public buildings outside the eighteenth century city, including the splendid Albert Hall and Museum.

The questions raised in the discussion about an appropriate architecture are not unrelated to the wider debate about the aesthetic and economic value of Indian arts and crafts more generally. This discussion, initiated at the time of the Great Exhibition, grew more heated over the following decades and was central to the development of the new art institutions of Britain and India. As Barringer has shown (Chapter I above, and see also Greenhalgh 1989), India had a major presence in the exhibitions from 1851 onwards – at Paris in 1855, London in 1862, in Paris again in 1867 and 1878, and of course in London again at the Indian and Colonial Exhibition of 1886. In the intervening decades the inner contradictions of official art education policy had also been exported to India (Mitter 1994: 29–62), where privately-founded schools of art soon fell into the hands of officialdom.

By 1864 the Departments of Public Instruction, set up in the three Presidencies in 1855, had control of the three main art schools. Those involved in art teaching were caught in a web of tangled aims. The rift between literate artists reared in academies and the growing army of 'confused' craftsmen became more and more evident in both Britain and India. Yet we should spare a charitable thought for those directly involved in the decision making, in the management of the institutions that were in theory supposed to be directing progress. The changes taking place as a result of industrialisation and the emerging globalisation of the world economy must have been as confusing and difficult as those facing us in the new information age, and it is hardly surprising that both their actions and the verbal and written discussion that took place appear to be riddled with contradictions.

Despite the metropolitan praise of the flat ornament typical of Indian and Islamic art, formulated most convincingly by Owen Jones, the schools in India were instructed to introduce the drawing techniques associated with Western naturalism. Robert Chisholm, the head of the Madras school of art in the 1870s, whom we have already met as the architect of Baroda's Lakshmi Vilas Palace and the creator of a range of Indo-Saracenic buildings in Madras, condemned the school's original policy of support for artisans, and reminded an investigating committee of the imperial policy of spreading Western art as part of its larger moral purpose (Mitter 1994: 38). Calcutta during the 1860s and 1870s was transformed into an academy which valued the high arts and relegated the useful arts to a subordinate position (Guha-Thakurta 1992: 46–9). In Bombay a more complex chemistry prevailed. George Wilkins Terry, in Bombay from the 1850s to the 1870s, was arguing by 1851 that the knowledge of figure drawing was the basis of higher art, whether decorative or fine, as it brought Indian designers face to face with nature. Their own tendency, he argued, was to repeat traditional composition. In 1865 Terry had been joined by Lockwood Kipling, father of the more famous Rudyard, and John Griffiths, who were to be responsible respectively for decorative sculpture and painting. Both had a keen interest in Indian art and Griffiths devoted many years to the creation of copies of the frescoes of Ajanta. But it was only after Kipling moved to Lahore to run the Mayo School of Art in 1880 that he was able overtly to champion Indian crafts, taking a leading role in the development of a key organ of contemporary opinion – *The Journal of Indian Art* (later known as *The Journal of Indian Art and Industry*).

But what exactly has this to do with the concealed gateway in the Victoria and Albert Museum's Raphael Gallery? The prologue over, we return to South Kensington and the story can now begin.

In the late 1870s, Indian art was a subject of some interest to at least a small group of people in London. Yet the Government of India was itself ambivalent about the collections that had been added to the East India Company Museum holdings in the period since 1858 and, in a move not unfamiliar to us today, wanted to devolve their care and pass the costs to others (Desmond 1982: 129–89). Fortunately for India, the adoption of the larger part of the collection suited the expansionist policies of the South Kensington Museum. In the course of the transfer, there was an interesting realignment of individuals involved with the collection. John Forbes Watson, the Economic Reporter of the Products of India, best known to Indian curators as the man who cut up large parts of a superb collection of Indian textiles in order to create sample books for distribution to textile manufacturing centres (Swallow, forthcoming), was effectively ousted in favour of George Birdwood, a champion of the Indian craftsman, a former member of the Indian Medical Service who had himself been the first curator and effectively founder of the Victoria and Albert Museum in Bombay. Birdwood had voiced his views on the state of the arts of India in the introduction to the Indian Section of the 1878 Paris exhibition.

> Indian collections are now also unfortunately becoming at every succeeding exhibition, more and more overcrowded with mongrel articles, the result of the influences on Indian art of English society, missionary schools, schools of art, and international exhibitions, and above all, of the irresistible energy of the mechanical productiveness of Manchester and Birmingham, and Paris and Vienna.
>
> (Birdwood 1878: 49–50)

His comments on the display of the gifts made by the Indian princes to the Prince of Wales during his 1875–6 visit to India are couched in even stronger language. But it was Caspar Purdon Clarke, a trained architect who had been Superintendent of the Indian Section of the Paris exhibition who was given the commission to fill the deficiencies in the collection 'both as representative of the art manufactures of India and also as authenticated examples of the work of certain localities'. Birdwood, initially to accompany Clarke, was later 'unable' to go and merely advised from the sidelines.

The papers relating to Clarke's commission give a flavour of the progress that he subsequently made through the subcontinent. Given the concern for protocol during this period, it is not surprising to find that he asked for official diplomatic status (that of a second secretary was considered appropriate), and a uniform to match, as well as letters of introduction to the Viceroy, the Governor General, the Governors and all senior local authorities. He made a stately progress through India, gaining the collaboration of the local authorities, whether British or native. In Gwalior, it was the hero of our story – a Major J. B. Keith, the Curator of the Monuments of Central India – who gave him most help. Clarke was extremely impressed by the range of the architecture and of the carving skills that were evident in the housing in the city, and when informed by Keith that there were craftsmen who could produce perfect copies, commissioned a copy of the tomb of Khan Dowra Khan (Khandola Khan). Major Keith, whose work for the Archaeological Survey of India had given him a considerable understanding of the architecture and monuments of the region, was a man in the mould of Kipling and Birdwood, and had clearly been looking for ways of helping the many local artisans whose livelihood was in danger of disappearing. He was critical of the sterility of the minor architecture of official India, like R. C. Temple, who wrote disparagingly of the influence of the Public Works Department (Temple 1886) and Kipling, who argued: 'There are hundreds of such buildings in India, where cut up into longer or shorter lengths they serve for law courts, schools, municipal halls, dak bungalows, post offices and the other needs of our high civilisation' (Kipling 1884: 2). He too had a healthy disrespect for the official training system's stress on literacy and paper skills. And Keith would have observed the way official architecture was affecting local taste like both Kipling and F. S. Growse. Growse was another champion of traditional Indian architecture whose work in Bulandshahr attracted warm praise from Kipling in an article in *The Journal of Indian Art*, but lost him his job: 'If the mercantile classes of native society are distinguished by their conservative adherence to ancestral usage, the landed gentry, who are on visiting terms with European officials, cherish equally strong aspirations in the opposite direction' (Growse, n.d., quoted in Kipling 1884: 3). Year by year 'good men of the mistry (mason) class grew rare', 'They are scarcely to be found at all in the neighbourhood of our official centres, and when they are employed they are regarded as "hands" merely by overseers who, in artistic sense are their inferior' (Kipling 1884: 2). It is no surprise that Keith, encouraged by Clarke's arrival, hoped that he might be able to use the visit to good purpose.

Clarke, who has left no diary of his travels, and no detailed account of his commissions before they were shipped, only recorded his recollections of the project to construct a gateway over fifteen years later:

So far as I can remember, the stone gateway was especially made for the SK Museum and was the outcome of my visit to Gwalior in 1881. When stopping at the Fort I was shown by Major Keith, the Assistant in Central India to the Curator of Ancient Monuments, some very beautiful stonework in old Gwalior and, upon being informed by him that he had men who could execute work of equal merit, I left a commission with him to copy a section of one of the tombs – that of Khan Dowra Khan. Major Keith put the work in hand and shortly after my return to England the work arrived. Not long afterwards I received a letter from Major Keith informing me that the Maharajah Scindia had upon his recommendation requested him to prepare a magnificent gateway for presentation to the SK Museum.[2]

Barringer (Chapter 1 above) mentions *The Times*'s criticism of Clarke's rapacity in India. In Gwalior at least, as in a large number of other places, he had to be content to acquire contemporary copies of architecture. Here, Keith would never have allowed him to seize any architectural remains. Keith's own record of the instigation of the second part of the Gwalior project published in a notice in *The Journal of Indian Art* not only reveals his own moral stance but also indicates his purposes:

Be it recorded with regret that the Anglo-Indian philistine has been a greater enemy to Indian art than either Mahomedan or Mahratta. When the writer visited Central India ten years ago, an offical in Bundlekhand kept a European to wrench off sculptured heads from the temple porches and sanctums. Within the writer's own experience he may declare that he had the greatest difficulty in preventing the Jain caves of Urwahi valley and the picturesque reservoirs in the Gwalior fort with their porticoes and pillared balconies from becoming a quarry. The greed of a Mahomedan contractor in the Public Works for dressed stone and to spare himself expence was simply insatiable. Rich medieval pillars were ground down into road material, whilst temple friezes and bas reliefs were converted into targets for rifle practice. To remedy this the writer tried to found a Museum for archaeological fragments as well as a place of registry [sic] for decayed workmen. And lastly, by way of invoking popular sympathy for his work, he proposed for the Calcutta exhibition, a piece of representative stone carving. His proposition eventuated in the Gwalior Gateway, which forms the subject of illustration for this notice. It is not the copy of a conventionalised entrance, as hinted, but an eclectic piece of work which the writer elaborated with some care. His object was to assist some 2,000 starving artisans, and he thought that this would be best compassed by illustrating the carving of many periods.

(Keith 1886: 111)

According to the record in the registered papers in the museum, the Maharaja Scindia of Gwalior wrote to the India Office from Simla on 8 October offering the gateway to the South Kensington Museum – apparently on the instigation of Major Keith – some eight weeks before the opening of the Calcutta

International Exhibition. We know that the carving took a period of four months to complete, the journey to Calcutta would have taken several days by rail, and though the letter could have been the formalisation of an earlier verbal understanding, it seems possible that the idea of sending the gateway to South Kensington occurred after the initial conception of the project. The museum, however, graciously accepted the royal gift.

The 1883–4 Calcutta International Exhibition itself seems to have been a rather rushed affair. Although there had been earlier exhibitions of Indian art in Madras, and the Maharaja of Jaipur had himself held an exhibition under the auspices of his local college of art, the Calcutta exhibition was India's first international show. The idea had been suggested by a Mr Jules Joubert, a gentleman of French extraction, naturalised in New South Wales, who had organised the New Zealand International Exhibition. The official report noted that a few of the courts were not ready at the time of the opening, but claimed that 'there is reason to believe that the opening ceremony found the Exhibition more finished than has been the case with any great exhibition of late years' (Calcutta 1885: 5). Certainly we know that the construction work on the Gwalior Gateway had not been completed by the opening, but within a few days it stood in all its glory at the entrance to the Indian courts (Fig. 5.2).

The gateway was dismantled at the close of the exhibition, packed and shipped and reached London in July 1884. Over the following months there was acrimonious correspondence between the museum and Major Keith over payment for his commission on the copy of the tomb, which had also been received. And it is easy to imagine the unrecorded thoughts of those in the museum as the 200 'packages' of stone were unwrapped and the scale of the gateway was realised. The museum, we must recall, was in a period of relative decline (Physick 1982b: 213). The building was ugly, asymmetrical, and incomplete. For some years the construction programme had been frozen, and though there was a chink of light when Lord Carlingford became President of Council in late 1884, the museum was in fact to stagger on for another six years before the Government sanctioned the competition for the completion of the frontage of the building, and it was some years more before the work would finally commence (Physick 1982b: 213). So it is not surprising to find that the gateway was stowed away. A possible loan to the forthcoming Indian and Colonial Exhibition was sanctioned and the hope expressed that it would find a place in the new building for the Oriental collection.

The Colonial and Indian Exhibition of 1886 saw the gateway in its full glory, visible for the first and the last time in an appropriate setting. Here we can start to understand what sort of an object it was meant to be. During the eighteenth and early nineteenth centuries, many of the Rapjut rulers of western and central India expanded their fortress palaces. In Jaipur, as we have seen, a complete new city was built, its palace structure, within the city, based on a series of courtyards and gardens. The passage between palace and city was marked by a prominent gateway – large enough to allow the comfortable passage of caparisoned elephants – a critical royal symbol in a period when, with the decline of centralised Mughal authority, the smaller princedoms all expanded

Figure 5.2 The Gwalior Gateway as displayed in the Calcutta International Exhibition of 1883–4. (Victoria and Albert Museum.)

their own rituals of power. Frequently referred to as *Hathi Pol* (elephant gate), these gateways are found in many of the Rajput palaces as they spill down the sides of the hill on which an earlier fortress is built (Fig. 5.3). Elephant motifs on the gateways, as in the Gwalior Gateway, or painted on the adjacent walls, reinforce the function of the structure. The architectural style of these gateways, like that of the palaces of which they were a part, was frequently just the sort of eclectic mixture of forms that the British, with their communal theories of style, struggled to classify yet found fascinating. Today we have no difficulty in identifying them as distinctive to their period.

It is therefore interesting to look again at Keith's own comments on Indian architecture in his 1886 note. Not surprisingly, he follows the dominant perceptions of the day, and quotes the contemporary authority James Fergusson (Fergusson 1876), tracing the development of Indian architecture from the earliest period to a culmination in the Jain shrines at Mount Abu (eleventh to fifteenth centuries). Yet, like Fergusson, he reasserts that the Buddhist site at Sanchi (third century BC to sixth–seventh centuries AD) is the high point of sculptural carving and all that follows a decline. Then, in keeping with the

Figure 5.3 The Tripoluja Gateway to the City Palace, Jaipur. (By courtesy of the Trustees of the Victoria and Albert Museum.)

tendency to praise the arts of the Muslim rulers of India, he picks out for praise the superb stone carving of floral motifs of the early Mughal period. It is to this standard, he argues, that he is trying to return:

> In his grammar of ornament, Jones declares that it is an anachronism to reproduce the forms of the past into the art of the present. But the forms at Gwalior are not dead, but merely in abeyance and will revive with patronage.
>
> (Keith 1886: 111)

The placing of the gateway in the Indian and Colonial Exhibition must have given Keith great pleasure. There, it fulfilled a ceremonial function as the entrance to the area that represented the Indian 'palace', and inside that area, which was decorated with carved wooden screens and architectural pieces from different parts of India (commissioned and assembled by Lockwood Kipling and his associates) Indian craftsmen demonstrated their skills (see Figs 5.4 and 5.5).

Figure 5.4 The Gwalior Gateway as displayed in the Colonial and Indian Exhibition of 1886. (*Journal of Indian Art* vol.1, 1886, by courtesy of the Trustees of the Victoria and Albert Museum.)

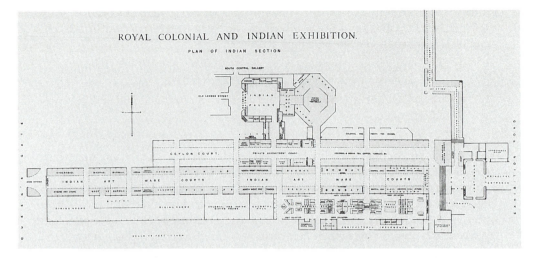

Figure 5.5 Plan of the Indian section, Colonial and Indian Exhibition, 1886. (Victoria and Albert Museum.)

The fate of the gateway since 1886 has been a curious one. Returned to the museum, it was stowed away in sheds to the side of the building and there it remained, despite persistent correspondence from Major Keith and various of the great and the good whom he succeeded in stirring into action. In 1891 Major General Festing, who two years later was to become the Director of the Science Museum, suggested that the gateway be erected on a triangular piece of ground between the Museum and Thurloe Square, the present site of the Ismaili Centre. In 1896, Keith, now retired and back in England, and presumably aware of the planning for the new building, stirred up some press criticism in a little-known journal in Calcutta, entitled *The Truth*. The article criticised the Department of Science and Art, claiming that the citizenry of Calcutta had wanted the Gwalior Gateway to be left in Calcutta and that the refusal to show it constituted an insult to the Maharaja of Scindia in particular and to the princes in general. Sir John Donnelly, Secretary for the Department of Science and Art, besides questioning the authenticity of the cutting, advised against writing to the editor, saying that the gateway was 'a beastly thing' and suggesting that the Imperial Institute might like to have 'this white elephant'. In 1897 Keith protested again. Clarke, now Director of the museum, and managing a generally troubled institution, produced the minute which provides his version of the history of the gateway, and the Vice President of the Council recommended that 'if possible' it should form an entrance to one of the courts in the new building. A site at the southern end of Room 47 was also suggested. A few months later Keith wrote again. The letter was ignored, the Vice President advising that no notice be taken and Donnelly remarking that 'the fact is the poor man is off his head'. But Keith was not to be so lightly dismissed. On 6 May 1899, only a few days before the announcement that Queen Victoria would lay the foundation stone of the new building, the Duke of Abercorn, at Keith's instance, again enquired about the gateway.

And here, to our frustration, the record ends. The next entry, dated 1933, is a simple summary of the earlier correspondence. Yet at some stage in the tortuous discussions that took place as the Aston Webb building that now forms the main frontage of the museum was developed, it must have finally been decided to mount the Gwalior Gateway in the Western Court. Even here the building was not big enough, and the wide spreading eaves and the structure above it, with its paired elephants, were not included. (These remained in the museum's bomb-proof store in the Crypt until the late 1980s when they were transferred to an outside store.) But there are further ironies in this long tale. Clarke resigned as Director in 1905 and left the museum to become Director of the Metropolitan Museum in New York. In 1908 as the new building reached completion, the discussion about the proper management of the museum and the reorganisation of its collections reached a head. The collections were to be reorganised by material, but the galleries were to be organised on both cultural and material lines. The main Oriental display, including both Indian and Far Eastern material, was to be brought back from the galleries to the west of Exhibition Road where they had been situated since the acquisition of Indian material from the India Office. An Oriental gateway was already sited in the western galleries, which could thus become an Oriental gallery.

The museum was not expecting the outcry from the Indian lobby that broke out when its restructuring plans were made known. At the end of a heated campaign led by Lord Curzon the Indian Museum retained its separate identity and remained on its site behind the Imperial Institute. The Near and Far Eastern collections were reincorporated into the Museum's materials departments, and the Gwalior Gateway presided over a mixed display of objects from these cultures until the Second World War (Fig. 5.6). Ironically, when the then Director, Leigh Ashton, reinstated the museum after the War, the Indian collections were replaced in their old premises. By 1955, when they were evacuated from their former galleries and moved to the main site in Cromwell Road, the Gwalior Gateway had been hidden behind partitioning to ensure that the newly installed Raphael Cartoons could be seen in all their splendour.

When recently the gateway was exposed to view as part of the building works for the refurbished Raphael Gallery,[3] the question of the gateway's future was gently raised again. No one involved with the project, unsurprisingly, would even contemplate the idea of the gateway being exposed. And sadly, at the end of the twentieth century, the costs of dismantling the gateway, finding storage for it, and making it potentially available for another site were too prohibitive to be considered.

Today, the debate about the effects of the colonial economy and industrialisation on non-industrial communities continues. In India it is not a historical debate. Artisanal communities still exist in the subcontinent, alongside industrial manufacturing units, nuclear power stations, international stock exchanges, satellite dishes, new information systems and all the other trappings of modernity. Considered against what are still the prevalent canons of Western taste, we may choose to dismiss the Gwalior Gateway as they did in 1933:

Figure 5.6 The Gwalior Gateway as displayed in the Western Galleries in the Aston Webb range of the Victoria and Albert Museum. (By courtesy of the Trustees of the Victoria and Albert Museum.)

The Gwalior gateway is not a copy of any existing gate, but is in the style of the late Mogul architecture with Hindu elements blended in and to that extent is a hybrid. Scindia ordered it, Keith designed it, and Gwalior stone-masons carved it in the local stone, for ultimate presentation to the South Kensington Museum. It was carved in or about 1883, shown at an exhibition at Calcutta in 1883–4, and was eventually delivered to this museum early in August, 1884. Lent by the Museum to the Colonial and Indian International Exhibition of 1886. Stored from 1886–1900?

(Victoria and Albert Museum Nominal File, *Gwalior Gateway*)

I would prefer the record to end otherwise.[4] Major Keith was determined that his gateway be seen. He fought relentlessly to achieve his end, and he almost won. The scale of the object was against him. Given these practical problems he missed the critical moment. But at least the object survives. In 1955, when the Indian collections were evicted from the twenty galleries they occupied to make way for the expansion of Imperial College, many other large items in the collection, both originals, copies and casts, were summarily disposed of. Western attitudes to Indian art remain equivocal, as do attitudes to the decorative arts more generally. Major Keith made an impassioned plea for respect for his stonemasons: 'Indian stone carving requires, like the other arts, the assistance of European enterprise and capital; but this once given, the artisan ought to be allowed to think and work as a Hindu and not as a European' (Keith 1886: 112). Yet ironically those working in the studios of the great Renaissance masters, who still moved easily between what later became the 'fine' and 'applied' arts, might not have found the attitudes or the skills of the Indian craftsman so alien or unworthy of praise:

> In concluding this short notice, the writer wishes to instance the resource of Indian workmen almost on a par with that patience which induces them to work through the long summer's day for a trifling remuneration. In preparing the foundation for the Gateway at the Calcutta exhibition, one Mistri, Musai Ram, found that he had forgotten his spirit level. Equal to the occasion he constructed a small conduit, into this he threw the contents of his lota, on the surface he floated a leaf, and then with straw, proceeded to take measurements, the result being a perfect level on which rested 75 tons of carved masonry.
>
> (Keith 1886: 112)

Notes

1 The debate about an appropriate imperial architecture mirrors contemporary debate in London. In Calcutta, the Indian capital until 1920, monumental civic classicism remained the order of the day, with only one major secular Gothic building – the High Court, based on Gilbert Scott's Hamburg Rathaus. Bombay, with its face firmly directed towards the west, continued until the turn of the century to build in neo-Gothic and Renaissance styles.

2 Caspar Purdon Clarke to Sir John Donnelly, 30 June 1897, Victoria and Albert Museum Nominal file, *Gwalior Gateway*.

3 Housing the cartoons by Raphael (1483–1520) for the tapestries commissioned by Pope Leo X to hang in the Sistine Chapel, on loan from the Royal Collection.

4 At the time of writing the long-term possibility of the former Oriental galleries reverting to their initial purpose is again being mooted.

6

Stylistic hybridity and colonial art and design education
A wooden carved screen by Ram Singh

Naazish Ata-Ullah

The architecture of the British Raj dominates the cityscape of Lahore. As the city prepares for the Golden Jubilee celebrations in 1997 marking fifty years of independence from British rule, the impressive Lahore High Court, General Post Office and the Lahore Museum (each one a memorial of the British Raj) still remain buildings of prime civic importance. In architectural style and administrative function they form a strong contrast with the earlier monuments of the Mughal and Sikh rulers who preceded the British. The Raj buildings present a varied example of nineteenth-century colonial architecture: a curious mix of European classical styles and traditional Indian architecture (Metcalf 1989; Tillotson 1989). Such hybridity characterises objects produced under colonial influence and direction. This chapter explores in detail the making and meaning of one such object: a wooden carved screen which is attributed to the master-craftsman Ram Singh, currently in the collection of the National College of Arts, Lahore (formerly the Mayo School of Arts).[1]

The fertile province of the Punjab came directly under British rule in 1849 with the fall of Lahore. Shortly afterwards the British established control over the whole of India as they rapidly completed the annexation of the north-western region which not only bordered Afghanistan but was also the geographical limit of their Indian Empire. Meanwhile state structures, such as an administrative network and an efficient communications system, were rapidly developed in the Punjab. Additionally, a system of schools and colleges which had earlier been implemented in other regions was likewise established to advance colonial educational policy. Lahore, a historic city and the regional capital, retained its status as one of the major centres of academic and cultural activity in India.

For purposes of good governance an on-going concern of the British state was to understand the political, economic, religious, judicial and cultural aspects, as far as possible, of the vast and diverse country it was ruling. Hence meticulous studies were carried out in all these areas by dedicated scholars and administrators. Almost all existing important histories and other documents were translated into English and extensive surveys such as the *Archaeological Survey of India*, Birdwood's compilation of *The Arts of India* and Fergusson's study of

Indian architecture (to name a few) were commissioned (Cunningham 1875; Fergusson 1876; Birdwood 1880). These detailed studies have formed the basis for information, research and analysis until very recently when modern historians began reconsidering the works of the past executed under colonial direction.

In 1864 B. H. Baden-Powell organised an exhibition of industrial arts of the region in Lahore in a purpose-built exhibition building which later became the famous Tollington Market. The exhibits were compiled by him in a publication known as *The Handbook of the Manufactures and Arts of the Punjab* (1872). The outcome of this exhibition was important both for craftsmen and for policy makers: not only did it provide a complete survey of regional crafts, but it also introduced the concept of directing production for commercial purposes, internally in the Indian market, as well as for overseas trade. The exhibition also made apparent the need for an institution where crafts could be taught and practised.

In 1875, the Mayo School of Arts was founded in Lahore as a fitting memorial to Lord Mayo who was assassinated while on a visit to the Andaman Islands. Funded by subscriptions to the Mayo Memorial Fund in the Punjab, the building (completed in 1883) was designed by the first Principal of the School, John Lockwood Kipling, assisted by his student and master-craftsman Ram Singh, and constructed by Lahore's Executive Engineer, Ganga Ram, in the characteristic architectural style of the period (Latif 1994: 274). The School became an important centre for the teaching and practice of local crafts; and it was in this centre that craftsmen from the region congregated.

By focusing on the activity of the School, this chapter will attempt to show how several objects, such as the wooden carved screen attributed to Ram Singh, were made by adapting the skill of local craftsmen to suit European taste. It will also be proposed that in this way not only was a transformation effected in traditional practice but that soon after its inception, the products of the School, especially wooden and metal functional objects, began to be widely copied because they were regarded to be of a high standard particularly in demand by the rising educated middle classes in India. Thus the influence of the Mayo School of Arts spearheaded a burgeoning activity in the workshops of Lahore and in the region.

The justification for setting up an art school in the Punjab was not merely an economic one: it formed part of a more comprehensive policy for the industrial arts of the country at large. In 1853 Sir Charles Trevelyan had stated the overall motive for establishing schools of art in India on the model of the 'institution at Marlborough House. . . . Art is taught there systematically . . . [as] it is our duty to give our Indian fellow students every possible aid in cultivating those branches of art that still remain to them' (Edwardes 1961: 256). Furthermore he proposed a system that would 'set the natives on a process of European improvement [so that] the national activity [would be] fully and harmlessly employed in acquiring and diffusing European knowledge and naturalising European constitutions' (Tarapor 1980). Three major schools of art had already been set up in Madras (1853), Calcutta (1854) and Bombay (1857). Finally, the

Mayo School of Industrial Arts ('Industrial' was later dropped) was founded primarily as a school of craft. S. M. Latif, the nineteenth-century historian, records that it was established for the 'purpose of instruction in design especially for the development of the indigenous arts of the Punjab' (Latif 1994). With the establishing of the Mayo School, the Director of Public Instruction in the Punjab declared its philosophy:

> our school of art is to be emphatically an industrial one. We do not wish to imitate the ceramic vases of Madras or the foliated capitals of Bombay, but to draw our experience rather from the royal workshops of the Mughals, from the best native specimens of Art and Industry in Modern India, and from the cyclopean forges of the Railway.
>
> (Director, Public Instruction, Punjab 1876)

Once guidelines for the School had been clearly stipulated, an appropriately qualified administrator was selected. John Lockwood Kipling (1837–1911), a sculptor and father of Rudyard, fulfilled the necessary requirements as his experience in India (of ten years' duration at the time) was based on the teaching of architectural decoration at the Sir J. J. School of Art in Bombay. His training in England included working 'on the sculptured and painted decorations of the New Courts and Residences' at the South Kensington Museum (Kipling n.d:n.p.; Physick 1982b: 120). On these grounds he was appointed Principal of the Mayo School of Arts and Curator of the Lahore Museum in 1875, whereupon he set about inducting students and organising the School's courses and curricula.

Most of the pupils who joined the Mayo School of Arts were 'the sons of artisans . . . whilst others [belonged] to the *munshi* or *naukari pesha* [working] class. . . . As might be expected, the sons of artisans shew considerable aptitude and great interest in their work' reported the Director of Public Instruction (Director, Public Instruction, Punjab, 1876). This was not unusual as the Punjab had a highly evolved craft tradition, particularly in woodwork, and of the 88 students in 1875, there were 49 Muslims, 24 Hindus, 12 Sikhs and 3 Christians. In contrast to the Mayo School, in the Calcutta School students were drawn from the middle classes. Partha Mitter attributes this phenomenon to the government's failure in recruiting 'enough artisan children because of their poverty and illiteracy' (Mitter 1992: 29). He also quotes Cecil Burn's report on the Bombay Art School from 1908–9 which states that 'from their commencement the schools of art failed to attract sons of working craftsmen' (Mitter 1982; Mitter 1992: 294–5). Evidence from the records of the Mayo School, however, indicates that the complexion of its students reinforced the government's objective to develop the school as a centre of excellence in the crafts.

Traditionally the arts and crafts were learned in India through an ancient system of apprenticeship whereby artist-craftsmen were members of guilds or *biradaris* which were part of the larger caste system on which the society was structured. The caste system was so deeply embedded in the society that even in Kipling's time he encountered social prejudices among his students. He observed in his reports that there was 'prejudice in favour of the comparative respectability and gentility of mere draughtsmanship . . . with compasses . . . over practical work'. He suggested to one of his students who was engaged in some architectural details that, in order properly to understand the changes of form from a square to an octagon and then to a circle, 'he should get a cube of wood and having cut it to these forms he should draw them in perspective and elevation'. The response came 'with some hauteur – But that is carpenter's work' (Director, Public Instruction, Punjab 1877: 75–8).

The organisation of the Mayo School along the lines of a 'craft school' was a conscious effort by Kipling to draw upon surviving traditions and skills, and to emphasise technical rather than theoretical instruction. Inspired by William Morris's efforts towards the revival of craftsmen's guilds in England and by Birdwood's concerns about the deterioration of crafts in India, Kipling organised workshops at the school for metalwork, carpentry, jewellery, modelling, carpet designing, decoration, wood engraving, photography and lithography. He worked along with his students in the workshops, directing and assisting them by example. The teaching was project-orientated and even in its earliest days the school established links with the local market. Kipling became editor of the *Journal of Indian Art and Industry* which was first published in England in 1886, the year of the Indian and Colonial Exhibition. Several of its contributions were articles on Indian arts and crafts, richly illustrated by students and instructors from the Mayo School of Arts. Kipling personally contributed many well-researched articles, including one on 'Punjab Wood-Carving' which is relevant to this study as it details the processes used by craftsmen in the production of woodwork (in architecture and in objects of utility) in the various areas of the Punjab region (Kipling 1886). The objective of publishing this journal was primarily to promote commercial prospects for Indian products; and it was also envisaged that if Indian craftsmanship could be adapted to European items of utility, the prospects for trade would greatly increase.

Kipling's task as a teacher was both complex and challenging since, even at the Sir J. J. School of Art in Bombay, his personal views on teaching methodology differed from the existing curricula. In Bombay he had observed that students had been forced into practices which were totally alien to their visual experience and culture. For example, drawing was taught by using British Art School methodology and the Sir J. J. School was full of 'antique casts, watercolor sketches, drawing-copies, Gothic mouldings' and plaster casts sent out from South Kensington which were slavishly copied by the students (Tarapor 1980). He was critical of this method and in one of his reports voiced his disapproval by declaring that 'those of my students who have come to me . . . direct from the native town, without having received any instruction in the School of Art, are decidedly the best' (Director, Public Instruction, Punjab 1882). His alternative teaching methods at the Mayo School of Arts, including drawing, can best be explained through a study of his reports. Recognising the basic importance of drawing as an essential skill for learning in the arts, he chose to make his students draw from Asian objects in the Lahore Museum's collection which were undoubtedly of greater relevance to them than plaster casts from the antique. In his report of 1876 he described the various stages through which a student develops a design. In this way he explained his teaching methodology and his methods of direction. He wrote that like all other students, one Muhammad Din, was put through

> a course of outline from the flat and elementary geometry . . . and [he] made drawings of Kashmiri ewers in the Museum and he [was] exercised in original design. . . . He was first required to draw carefully a battle-axe, which is in the Museum, then to make a sketch from nature of some leaves, and lastly to use these leaves as the basis of a new design for a casket.
>
> (Director, Public Instruction, Punjab 1876)

He also believed in and wrote that the indigenous styles of art were capable of indefinite development and that the first aspect to study was the actual work of the country 'which alone can give a rational point of departure for variety of design and improvement of technique' (Director, Public Instruction, Punjab 1876). This revealing description forms the basis for the analysis of the wooden screen attributed to Ram Singh.

A. K. Coomaraswamy, art historian, philosopher, critic and an esteemed pioneer of the nationalist movement in Indian art, believed that the function of the art schools should have been to 'build up the idea of Indian art as an integral part of the national culture, and to relate the work of Indian craftsmen to the life and thought of the Indian people' (Coomaraswamy 1908: 53). He did not accept that any Englishman was capable of doing this as it was impossible for a foreigner to comprehend the complexities, the soul and the spirit of Indians. Having stated this view, how can we assess Kipling's role? There is no doubt that Kipling held views typical of his times and was effectively a member of the colonial establishment and an executor of its policies. However, we cannot deny his contribution to history and his impact on the Mayo School of Arts in its formative years. In his defence, it may be stated that Kipling tried his best to understand his domain: the people, the arts and crafts and the entire region. His personal collection of drawings, prints and watercolours and his own drawings witness his involvement with his surroundings.[2] It is quite evident that he admired and respected both art and artisan and his contribution as the Principal of the Mayo School and Curator of the Lahore Museum was to uphold one of its founding objectives: that the school and the museum should complement each other. He was also responsible for introducing the work of the school to other parts of India and abroad and by doing so he established a high reputation for the institution which he not only founded but administered for eighteen years.

It is not possible to date accurately the wooden screen as neither Kipling nor Percy Brown (Principal of the Mayo School 1897–1909) refer to it in their reports (Fig. 6.1). It is probable that the screen was made at the School between 1893 and 1909 after Kipling's retirement and during W. S. H. Andrew's tenure as Principal. B. C. Sanyal, the Indian painter, recalls it being at the School when he joined the faculty in 1929.[3] It has always been kept in the Principal's room amongst other items of special value such as two terracotta sculptures by

Figure 6.1 Wooden screen by Ram Singh, late nineteenth century. (Collection of the National College of Arts, Lahore.)

Kipling, an oil painting of Kipling by Sher Muhammed (his student), and a *chinidan* or display bracket also by Ram Singh. On the basis of its style and the excellence of workmanship displayed in it, the screen can be attributed to the hand of Ram Singh who, among his many talents, was a highly skilled craftsman in wood.

The screen, carved in teak, measures about 150 cm (60 in) in height and is made of four hinged panels each of which is 46 cm (18 in) wide. The panels are further subdivided into three rectangular parts and each is crowned by a smaller curved section. All the motifs on the screen are traditional floral or bird forms carved in low relief (Figs 6.2–6.4). Surrounding the motifs is very fine *pingra*, the lattice work for which the Punjab was famous. The carving of the screen resembles that of another item of furniture, the *chinidan* or wooden carved display bracket which is also kept in the Principal's room (Fig. 6.5). The screen is derived from and resembles traditional wooden windows, of which there still are many surviving examples in the architecture of the walled city of Lahore. The divisions of the screen's panels are in geometrical straight lines, similar to traditional lattice windows. Kipling offered a detailed description and several valuable observations on the use of traditional techniques in his article on 'Punjab Wood-Carving' (Kipling 1886). For example, he observed that the use of 'geometric tracery is a constant element in Muhammedan design ... and

Figure 6.2 Detail of Fig. 6.1.

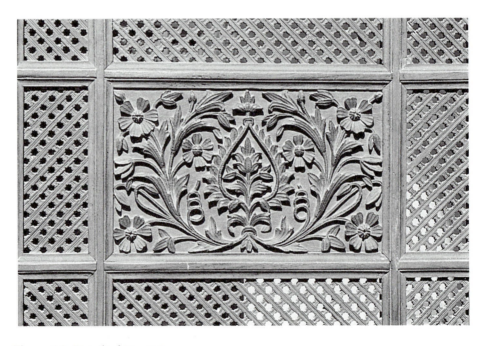

Figure 6.3 Detail of Fig. 6.1.

Figure 6.4 Detail of Fig. 6.1.

Figure 6.5 Carved wooden chinidan by Ram Singh. (Collection of the National College of Arts, Lahore.)

[consequently] the Punjab *pingra* [work] is similar to the lattice-work seen in Cairo'. As Kipling noted, the strongly Islamic character of *pingra*-work is, therefore, the most distinctive feature of the technique. In his description of the thirteen varieties of *pingra* techniques, one closely resembles the screen (Fig. 6.6). This is the '*chhe-barah*, [which is] composed of figures of six and twelve'. In the article, detailed illustrations of each technique are drawn by Ram Singh whose name appears on the plate (Kipling 1886: plate 5). Kipling noted that although each type had a different name (*chhe-barah, ath barah, akbari*, etc.), these were general and not 'scientific' terms and, therefore, could not be used to place a precise order for one or another kind of tracery in the market. Thus, Ram Singh's slight variation on the *chhe-barah* design, in the screen attributed to him, supports Kipling's statement (see Fig. 6.6). In the joinery of *pingra*-work each piece was 'neatly dowelled into its neighbour . . . [but] glue [was] seldom used' wrote Kipling, who also mentioned that the use of the technique was practised at the Mayo School, '[but only] for sideboards, cabinets, brackets, etc.'. He did not, however, mention the use of this technique for making a screen (Kipling 1886: 3).

There is no mention of an article of furniture like the screen in any survey of Indian crafts in the nineteenth century such as in Birdwood's *The Arts of India* (1880) or in Baden-Powell's *The Industrial Arts of The Punjab* (1872). The catalogues of the Calcutta Exhibition (1883), the Paris Universal Exhibition (1878) and the Glasgow Exhibition (1888), to name a few, do not mention a wooden carved screen. However, several carved screens, similar to the one by

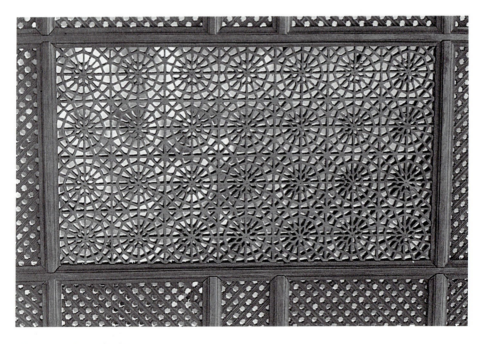

Figure 6.6 Detail of Figure 6.1.

Ram Singh, were exhibited in the Indian Art Exhibition at Delhi in 1904 (Watts and Brown 1979: 102–9; 159–60). This indicates that prior to the Delhi Exhibition, the concept of a movable screen was alien to Indian craftsmen and it was, probably, introduced by the British very late in the nineteenth century or very early in the twentieth century. It also presents the likelihood that there was no widespread use of such screens in India as articles of furniture. They were, however, popular both in Europe and in the Middle East in the nineteenth century. Originating from China these screens came to Western markets through trade. It is possible that the movable and foldable versions, which were adaptations of traditional Chinese screens, were produced for commercial purposes. They may have been imported to India in small numbers for the ruling nawabs. However, they were imported to India in greater quantity for the use of British officials who required many other items of furniture, such as office tables, chairs, cabinets and bedsteads, none of which were indigenous to Indian furniture. It is evident that soon after these articles came to India they began to be copied by Indian craftsmen.

Chinese screens were adapted variously by different cultures. For example, carved wooden screens are found in many 'orientalist' paintings of the Middle East, adding to the exotic atmosphere of imagined interiors, becoming metaphors for the orient in a similar way to oriental carpets or metal lanterns. Other articles of carved woodwork, such as geometrical patterned wooden ceilings and the foldable cross-like stands (*rehel*) for reading the Holy Quran, are also illustrated in 'orientalist' paintings, by artists such as J. F. Lewis. These wooden stands are enlarged versions of a *rehel* which is commonly used in India for the same purpose; and very similar carved wooden ceilings are also found in Indian architecture. As mentioned earlier, Kipling was also aware of the similarity of woodwork techniques between India and Cairo. A closer analysis, however, presents other interesting observations.

In Indian culture, there is a concept of creating a physical barrier or screen between people. The reasons for doing so are multiple: usually the screen segregates the sexes; sometimes it may distinguish between persons of higher and lower social status. A screen, traditionally a fabric curtain for which the Urdu word is *purdah*, would serve this purpose. Often the curtain or *purdah* was made of sheer or perforated material for better viewing (it could then be referred to by the term *jali*, meaning a net or a screen). It could also be made of heavily embroidered velvet to ensure insulation. Carpets could also be used for the same purpose in cold weather, while light, split-bamboo, *chicks* or blinds replaced them in the summer. There is also evidence of the use of the same concept in architecture where perforated screens in stone and wood replace windows not only as ventilation devices but also to provide privacy. Immovable perforated screens in stone or marble, approximately 45 cm (18 in) high, usually part of the architecture, were used both as barriers and to demarcate the area surrounding platforms (or even thrones) where a king or person of noble rank would sit for audience. A smaller sized screen (about 15 to 30 cm (6 to 12 in) in size) could also surround a traditional wooden item of furniture known as a *takht posh* which was used to sit on.

How, then, were these portable screens used? Their portability naturally made them more versatile and they could be shifted from one location to another according to need. They were often used as room dividers instead of curtains as they provided both segregation and privacy. The wooden carved versions were usually commissioned and bought by government officials or by the wealthy elite. Less expensive versions, constructed as simple wooden hinged frames with cloth panels, became more widely accessible.[4]

Ram Singh's screen is currently placed, at an angle, in the Principal's office at the National College of Arts (Kipling's original room), between the entrance door and the Principal's desk creating a temporary barrier between the person entering the room and the official behind the desk. As an article of furniture it offers an excellent example of cultural transformation and hybridity.

By far the most illustrious student of the Mayo School of Arts, in its earliest years, was Bhai Ram Singh (d.1915). Originally a native of Amritsar, a city well known for its woodwork, he belonged to a family of carpenters who were Sikhs (Gupta 1947: 175). In 1874 he joined one of the industrial schools for carpentry set up by the British to train the sons of craftsmen. This school was incorporated into the Mayo School in 1875. Ram Singh's talent was immediately recognised by Kipling who wrote in an *Annual Report* that he was 'amongst the most promising students [and that he] gives promise of being a very capable draughtsman and designer in his own craft' (Kipling 1877) (Fig. 6.7). By 1878, the school was participating in public works in the city and elsewhere in India and Ram Singh was involved in all these projects.

The principles of Kipling's teaching methods were successfully learned and practised by Ram Singh. In his report Kipling mentioned the process by which

Figure 6.7 J. Lockwood Kipling, *Portrait of Ram Singh*. (By permission of the University of Sussex.)

Ram Singh designed and carved a writing desk. Apart from understanding the form of a writing desk (not a traditional item), Ram Singh used for its ornamentation details from wood carvings that he had personally collected in Amritsar. The description indicates that, true to the innovative spirit of Kipling, indigenous craft motifs were being incorporated in creating new designs as early as 1876, shortly after the founding of the school. Ram Singh put into practice the policy of first making and subsequently popularising an article of furniture, otherwise alien to India, by use of traditional, indigenous craftsmanship. This creative hybrid of indigenous and European traditions is a complex and fascinating result of the interaction of colonialism and the object.

Indian crafts were patronised in many ways in the latter part of the nineteenth century when projects were commissioned by royalty for their homes. The first major project in Britain to be executed at the Mayo School was for the Billiard Room at Bagshot Park, the residence of Queen Victoria's son the Duke of Connaught. Kipling and Ram Singh designed its woodwork and between 1885 and 1887, assisted by their students and other craftsmen, they proceeded to carve 241 panels of typical Punjab wood-carving. These were all in *deodar* wood: 'no two panels were the same. They also carved the fireplaces and surrounds, skirtings, ceilings, cornices and display brackets for the corridor' (Director, Public Instruction, Punjab 1887–8). Thus traditional techniques and motifs were transformed and used in a new and different context, this time at the imperial centre.

By 1888, Ram Singh was working on the Mayo School's projects both as a designer and craftsman. The range of designing, supervising and craft activities in the school was very diverse – from book illustrations, interior decoration, woodwork, furniture and mouldings to design of buildings. In 1885, he submitted an 'original architectural design' for the Municipal Hall in Lahore, which was eventually not used. However, he shared a prize with Colonel Jacobs of Jeypore, in the same year, for the Chief's College Competition (Aitchison College, Lahore) as a result of which the ground plan for the college was Colonel Jacob's design and the elevation Ram Singh's.

The pinnacle of Ram Singh's career came with a commission from Queen Victoria to make an 'Indian' Banquet Room for her palace in the Isle of Wight. He was sent to England in 1891, for two years, to supervise the project at Osborne House. Raymond Head writes that 'like the Billiard Room at Bagshot Park, it is one of the best examples of the "Indian style" in Victorian England' (Head 1985: 146). It was here that the Queen commissioned Rudolf Swoboda to paint his portrait (Royal Collection, Osborne House) and – Ram Singh wrote to Kipling – 'on my leaving she gave me Her portrait and a gold pencil case on Christmas Day'. An interesting feature at Osborne, from the perspective of this study, is the sculptured peacock above the mantelpiece. It is similar to the peacock carved on Ram Singh's Lahore screen, providing yet another reason to attribute the screen to him (see Fig. 6.4).

Apart from his involvement in design, Ram Singh was an inspiring and respected teacher. He taught advanced carpentry, wood-carving, architectural drawing, design, model-making and free-hand drawing. In the Principal's Report of 1898–9, which he was obliged to write as the Principal was on leave, he mentions the success of the process of carving from plaster models which he had introduced in the school's curriculum on his return from England. It is obvious that an artist of such diverse talents would have imbibed a great deal from his visit abroad and that he would have disseminated his ideas to his colleagues and his students on his return.

On Kipling's retirement in 1893, Ram Singh was appointed acting Vice-Principal; this position became permanent in 1896–7 and as a mark of public acknowledgement he was decorated with the title of Sardar Bahadur. He continued to work in different media and on a variety of projects such as the marble fountain in the courtyard at the Mayo School of Arts; the statue in front of Assembly Hall, Lahore; the Museum gateway, Lahore; and he is also said to have designed some buildings of the Old Campus, Punjab University. Ram Singh is also mentioned in connection with the Indian Art Exhibition at Delhi (1904), where he assisted Percy Brown, the Assistant Director. An entry in the exhibition catalogue describing a 'Panjab Room and Balcony' indicates the success of the new hybrid forms.

> By far the most instructive exhibit of this division may be said to be the small room specially furnished by the Mayo School of Art, Lahore, to exemplify the adaptablility of the Punjab style to modern house-furnishing.

At the exhibition the first prize with gold medal was awarded to the Mayo School of Art for wood-carving shown on the balcony of the Punjab Room and a second prize with silver medal was also awarded to the Mayo School for a sideboard.

Ram Singh was briefly Principal of the Mayo School after Percy Brown's transfer to Calcutta in 1909. He held this post until 1913 after which he retired (fig. 6.8). He is said to have died shortly afterwards in 1915 in Amritsar. He was of the first generation of traditional craftsmen who worked under Western direction. While retaining his traditional bearings, he is emblematic of the transformation of indigenous culture under the colonial state.

By the time of the Delhi Exhibition in 1904, institutions like the Mayo School had a well established reputation both in India and abroad. The products of the school, including articles of furniture, were bought by government officials, the elite of the city and the region, and also by the growing middle classes. The annual exhibitions of industrial art held in Lahore were frequented by craftsmen from all over the Punjab. These events evoked interest in the design of new objects which were on display. However, the large demand for the 'new' and the gradual development of a 'Westernised' taste resulted in a proliferation of articles in the bazaar, many of which were poor-quality copies. The inadequacy of these mass-market copies was often a result of little understanding of the principles of design involved in making them.

Although the Principal of the Mayo School of Arts was required to inspect

Figure 6.8 Ram Singh (centre), photographed in about 1913 on his retirement. (Archives of the National College of Arts, Lahore.)

many Industrial Schools across the region, in practice he could not always successfully direct the teaching methodology in each one. In this regard colonial art education policy was not properly implemented in the Punjab other than at the Mayo School of Arts itself. The Mayo School was in many ways the most authentic and influential institution in the region. As a colonial institution, it effected a transformation in traditional practice. Broader economic and cultural considerations, also indissolubly linked with colonialism, forced traditional craftsmen into adapting their work to suit new markets and a taste for new objects.

Notes

1   The Mayo School of Arts was upgraded in 1958 to become the National College of Arts. This is the leading institution in Pakistan for the teaching of art, design and architecture.
2   Some of his personal drawings and writings are part of the Kipling Papers at the University of Sussex. His collection of bazaar prints and paintings, including his own drawings of various craftsmen at work, are in the Indian Section in the Victoria and Albert Museum.
3   Interview with B. C. Sanyal which was conducted by me in Delhi, India, in December 1994.
4   *Hayat Furnisher's Catalogue*, Lahore, 1911. Hayat Furnishers was founded by a Kashmiri woodwork craftsman after the fall of the Sikhs to the British in 1849. The printed catalogue contains a range of furniture which was made in their workshop. The business was vast and very successful. It had strong links with the Mayo School of Arts and employed many of its graduates. A number of carved wooden screens are advertised in this catalogue.

7

Race, authenticity and colonialism

A 'mustice' silversmith in Philadelphia and St Croix, 1783–1850

Rachel E. C. Layton

> The inauthentic Negro is not only estranged from whites – he is also estranged from his own group and from himself. Since his companions are a mirror in which he sees himself as ugly, he must reject them; and since his own self is mainly a tension between an accusation and a denial, he can hardly find it, much less live in it. . . . He is adrift without a role in a world predicated on roles.
>
> (Broyard 1950:63)[1]

This mid-twentieth century passage by an American author of mixed racial ancestry demonstrates the problematic ambiguities of race and identity. In his essay 'Portrait of the Inauthentic Negro', Anatole Broyard – who for most of his adult life concealed his black genealogy and passed for white – describes the 'strategies' that those who find themselves in the no-man's-land between one clearly defined racial community and another often adopt to 'evade' the uncertainty of their situation. These he characterises as 'avenues of flight' (Broyard 1950: 57).[2] The author secretly practised these self-same tactics in his own life. The subject of this chapter, Peter Bentzon, who was also of mixed racial identity, seems also to have adopted such tactics – that is passing as white and attempting to erase his blackness. Bentzon's 'avenues of flight', as will be seen below, included frequent movements between the colonial society in the Danish West Indies where he was a free coloured silversmith, to the American city of Philadelphia where it seems that he was passing as white. The silver objects made by Peter Bentzon, however, demonstrate nothing of his hybrid background. His silversmithing trade was firmly rooted in an Anglo-American tradition. In what way, then, can colonial objects like Bentzon's inform our understanding of the component parts of a mixed racial identity, and, likewise, how does the racial background of a nineteenth-century craftsman affect the way that we look at the objects he produced?

Peter Bentzon, a hitherto unknown craftsman from the Danish West Indies, is the first silversmith of African descent to be identified by his own mark – in

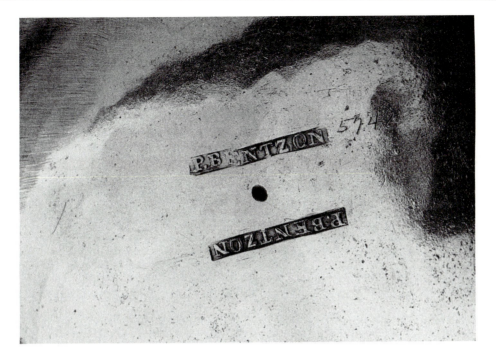

Figure 7.1 Bentzon's two identical marks on the bottom of the teapot shown in Figure 7.2.

fact, through this research a total of four marks may now be added to the body of scholarly information on American silver (Fig. 7.1). Although we are aware that there were at least four other silversmiths of African descent working in America in the first half of the nineteenth century alone, none has yet been associated with a known mark, which, like an artist's signature on a painting, is a fundamental aid to the identification of an individual's body of work. On first encountering Bentzon, collectors, students and enthusiasts of African-American decorative arts might be tempted to pigeonhole him as an African-American craftsperson because he is known to have worked in America. However, on a closer consideration of Bentzon's life and racial descent the picture becomes somewhat more complicated.

Born into freedom in the Danish West Indian Island of St Thomas in about 1783, to a mulatto mother and a white father, Bentzon was called a 'mustice'. His father may have been the Norwegian lawyer, Jacob Bentzon, who from the late 1770s until his return to Norway in 1803, lived in St Thomas and was for a number of years a royal judge advocate.[3] Like other terms used in the West Indies to describe the percentage of an individual's African ancestry, mustice or mustee identified Peter Bentzon as the offspring of a European and a mulatto. Defining and enumerating African ancestry was deemed necessary because by the nineteenth century there had emerged in the Danish West Indies an intermediate group of non-European free persons of mixed racial ancestry called free coloured. These 'freedmen' as they were also called were neither slaves nor wholly free; together with free blacks they formed a class whose civil liberties were severely circumscribed, and whose political rights were nonexistent (Hall 1992; Cohen and Green 1972). All freedmen were required to wear a cockade, a rosette on their hat or scarf made of red and white ribbon or leather (Lawaetz 1979: 3), designed to distinguish them from specious claimants to free status. Civil rights remained inaccessible to the free coloured population until 1834. As in other New World slave societies, sexual exploitation and liaisons between Europeans, Africans and people of partial African descent were not uncommon in the West Indies. By 1797 the ratio of free people of African descent to Europeans had become one to two (Lawaetz 1979: 5).

In 1818 Governor General Adrian Bentzon – no relation to Peter – reported to the Danish government that there was growing tension between slaves and freedmen in St Croix and suggested that light-complexioned freedmen received greater favour because they were similar to Europeans in appearance. Because of the perception in the Danish West Indies that the free coloured population's connection to and familiarity with slaves might lead to unrest, the further separated a freedman could be from his African ancestry and from the slave community the less suspicion he aroused. A later governor, Peter von Scholten, remembered today for his benevolence toward the slaves, in 1830 defined the parameters of contemporary local prejudice in a report sent to Frederick VI of Denmark:

> Where free persons of colour of both sexes assimilate in colour to the whites, and they otherwise by a cultivated mind and good conduct render themselves deserving to stand according to their rank and station in life, on an equal footing with the white inhabitants, all the difference which the colour now causes ought to cease.
>
> (Hall, N. 1989: 209)

The preoccupation with physical appearance and the concern to correlate skin complexion with legal status shaped the experiences of the free coloured in St Croix and the other Danish West Indian islands.

The racial diversity of the population of St Croix, like that of other colonial islands in the West Indies, was a function of a slave-supported, imperialist industry which was more often than not connected to the production of sugar cane. The Danish government purchased St Croix from the French crown in the early eighteenth century along with the islands of St Thomas and St John. Some fifty English families from Tortola and other English islands lived in St Croix with about four hundred slaves (Lawaetz 1979: 1). Some of the families cultivated small plots but their main occupation was the cutting and selling of timber for a local island trade. The Danish government subsequently succeeded in attracting experienced colonists from other West Indian islands, and the resulting expansion of sugar cultivation there necessitated a larger labour force. The first colonists had brought slaves with them, but as the demand for labour increased, Africans were imported directly from the Danish settlements in Guinea, West Africa in what is now Ghana. This vast labour source of African slaves underpinned the sugar economy of the Danish West Indies. In 1815 the slave population outnumbered the European, with over 24,000 Africans to less than 2,000 Europeans. Located about forty miles south-east of St Thomas, the island of St Croix is a mere seventy-four square miles with two main towns: Christiansted and Fredericksted. Built on land sloping down to the sea, Christiansted was the main port of the island and the centre of trade and politics in the Danish West Indies. Except for the two British occupations in the early nineteenth century, Denmark continued to own the island until 1917 when it disposed of St Croix, St Thomas and St John to the United States (Lawaetz 1977, 1979).

In 1803 a law became effective which banned the slave trade, specifically the importation of African slaves into the Danish West Indies (Lawaetz 1979: 5). This aside, those already in slavery in the Danish West Indies continued their lives within a strict social hierarchy. As in the slave societies of plantation America, there had emerged an intermediate group of non-European free persons, situated between the Europeans and enslaved Africans. The existence of such a category of 'free' persons upset the neatly symmetrical schema in which European – and white – was virtually a synonym for free, and African – and black – for servitude. The social contradiction entailed in the existence of this group was compounded by the appearance of free persons of mixed racial ancestry, who owed their existence to the sexual exploitation of enslaved women by European men (Hall, N. 1992: 139).

The free coloured population was perceived as a danger to the state. It was known as 'the plague of the colonies', supposedly capable of the worst and the most dangerous forms of social deviance (Hall, N. 1992: 174). Until 1815, whites were separated by law from the free coloureds, most of whom were required to live in the Free Gut, the freedmen's ghetto. In 1747 the government designated the 'Guts' as the special quarters of town where freedmen were required to live. But by the early nineteenth century freedmen generally lived and worked in what had formerly been white areas; conversely whites occasionally lived in the Guts, sometimes as tenants of freedmen.[4] Freedmen themselves were stratified on the basis of wealth, occupation, skin complexion and the method by which they had achieved freedom. Because so many free people in St Croix were of partial African descent the authorities attempted to codify racial purity on the basis of ancestry because by then many European families could trace African descent.

All free coloured men were required to serve in the 'Free Negro Militia' with a free coloured captain. The militia was used both for patrolling the towns and for quelling slave uprisings. Three hundred free coloured men – most of whom served in the militia – lobbied for their citizenship in 1816 with a petition brought to King Frederick VI in Copenhagen. They insisted that instead of a certificate of freedom, which had to be carried at all times, they be granted Burgher Briefs which gave a man licence to practise a trade in Christiansted. The petitioners also disputed the law that all freedmen were required to wear the identifying cockade. Their petition was refused and civil rights remained inaccessible to the free coloured population until 1834 (Lawaetz 1979: 5–8).

The silversmith Peter Bentzon was part of the community of free coloured by birth and situation, although his occupation and education in the elite trade of silversmithing, his international travel, and no doubt his light skin complexion placed him in the upper class of that group. The unique circumstances which shaped Bentzon's future must have been the result of connections and financial support provided by an outside source, such as his European father or the European relations of his mulatto mother. As noted above, Bentzon was a 'mustice' born in about 1783 to a free mulatto mother and a white father. At the age of eight he was sent from the West Indies to Philadelphia for his education. He was probably at school prior to serving his apprenticeship to a currently unidentified silversmith in Philadelphia from 1799 to 1806. For the next four decades Bentzon lived and worked in Philadelphia and St. Croix, travelling frequently between the two places. His movements to and from Philadelphia and the West Indies can be tracked from records in the Danish National Archives in Copenhagen and the National Archives in America.[5]

After completing his apprenticeship in 1806 at the age of twenty-three, Bentzon returned to Christiansted, St Croix to start up his business as a silversmith. Upon arrival, port officials recorded Bentzon's plans to stay with John Daly, the only free coloured plantation owner and one of three attorneys in St Croix. Daly may have managed the funds which enabled Bentzon to obtain his education and apprenticeship, and which subsidised his peripatetic silver-smithing career. Bentzon practiced his trade in St Croix for ten years and during this period he made several trips to St Thomas. One visit to the neighbouring island in 1816 was with his wife Rachel (de la Motta) Bentzon, who was also identified as a mustice – they had married in about 1813 when she was approximately fourteen. In 1816, Bentzon also began a series of journeys back and forth to Philadelphia to organise the relocation of his business and family to America.

Until their departure, Bentzon and his growing family and the three slaves who worked for them lived in Christiansted at 53A Company Street, one of the main thoroughfares of the port town. The two-storey, four-room building which was probably both Bentzon's shop and residence, survives today in the historic district of Christiansted. Although Bentzon was a freedman of African descent, his property was outside the 'Free Gut'. Bentzon offered 53A Company Street for sale in the *St Croix Gazette* in August and September of 1815, and by the time of his departure from St Croix the property had been sold and listed in the tax register as 'F.N. [fri-neger/frinegerinde] Peter Bentzon's, now Rigallon's house where he and his family live.'

In 1816, the year of Peter Bentzon's departure to Philadelphia, the Danes repossessed the islands of St Croix, St Thomas and St John from the British who had occupied them during the Napoleonic Wars in 1801 and again from 1807 to 1816. During the British occupations, there was fairer and more equal treat-ment of the free coloured population (Hall, N. 1992: 167). Not surprisingly, Peter Bentzon chose to relocate to Philadelphia in 1816 upon the return of the Danes. In 1817, Bentzon makes his first appearance in the Philadelphia directories though he continued to travel to and from the West Indies. The family lived in a racially diverse commercial district north-east of Market Street where Bentzon rented property from Robert Dawson, with whom he may have had Cruzan connections. On one return trip from St Croix to Philadelphia, he carried, 'A quantity of Old plate, American manufactured, for repairs' as well as an old looking glass, a box of sweetmeats and one dozen coconuts.[6] Bentzon probably called his silver 'American manufactured' to avoid taxes on silver made outside of the United States. When Bentzon visited St. Croix a year later, he described himself as a 'practising goldsmith and jeweller.'[7]

After more than a decade in Philadelphia, during which period he moved four times within the commercial district, Peter Bentzon returned to St Croix. In November 1829, Bentzon arrived in Christiansted stating that he 'wanted to stay on St. Croix.'[8] He continued to trade and to move goods across the ocean but ran into trouble in 1831 when he was accused of illegally trading silver spoons. Having recently returned to the West Indies, Peter Bentzon pleaded ignorance of the tariff regulations. By 1832, Bentzon had returned to Company Street, near his first dwelling and place of business. Exactly why Bentzon returned to St Croix after more than ten years in Philadelphia, where he had learned his trade and had established his initial business contacts, is unclear. His movements may reflect an unstable business climate or racial politics.

A growing unrest amongst the slave population, and the tension between slaves, free coloureds and Europeans in St Croix which reached its violent climax in the 1848 slave revolt, most likely prompted Bentzon's second relocation of family and business to Philadelphia. He may have also left the island because of his involvement in a lengthy court case in which a young female slave named Rosa stole and pawned some of her mistress's jewellery to Bentzon. Incidentally, Rosa's owner was Madame Cappel, the mulatto mother of Anna Heegaard, the free coloured mistress of Governor General von Scholten. Unknowingly, Bentzon accepted Madame Cappel's jewellery and was therefore implicated in the crime. Bentzon was charged with receiving stolen goods and the case progressed in turn from the police in Christiansted, St Croix, to the West Indian upper court, to the High Court of Copenhagen. The transaction between Bentzon and the slave girl gave the authorities immediate cause for suspicion. Bentzon acknowledged the Chief Constable's previous admonitions 'not to indulge in buying or receiving such things from suspicious persons', but when he remarked that so many young people were pawning their gold that it was impossible to decide who was legitimate, the Constable reminded him that all the unfree were suspicious (Garde 1993: 68–74). Although the court found Bentzon not guilty of a crime, ignominiously his free coloured status was made public and he was required to pay an allowance for court fees. With this incident resolved, although hardly satisfactorily, Bentzon left St Croix for the last time.

Once back in Philadelphia, he and his family joined his daughter and newlywed husband, and they lived together in the Spring Garden ward. Almira Louise Bentzon and Albert Crantz Stabell, of St Croix, were married in 1848 in the

Catholic Cathedral of Saints Peter and Paul by Bishop F. P. Kendrick. Witnesses at the wedding were a Cruzan couple, possibly free coloured, which indicated that Peter Bentzon and his family may have been part of a Cruzan, if not African-American community in Philadelphia. The marriage ceremony by a bishop is also intriguing, perhaps pointing to the family's status in the church.

Peter Bentzon pronounced himself Danish Lutheran and Anglican at different times, perhaps a pragmatic reflection of the successive presence of the Danish and the British in St Croix, although his wife Rachel was Catholic. The Bentzons had six daughters and one son. The five eldest children were Catholic and the youngest two Lutheran. The sixty-seven-year-old Peter Bentzon, his wife, six daughters, one son and their son-in-law were listed in the 1850 Philadelphia census. After that date there is no trace of the family in historical records in either Philadelphia or St Croix.

Of the nine known objects marked by Peter Bentzon, only two are hollow-ware containers, the rest flatware.[9] Their existence reflects the narrow scope of Bentzon's silversmithing business which was probably limited to smallwork and repairs rather than a consistent stream of commissions for tea and coffee services. Bentzon most likely made the diminutive silver teapot when he first started working in Philadelphia (Fig. 7.2). The object reflects his Philadelphia

Figure 7.2 Teapot by Peter Bentzon. Philadelphia, *c.* 1817. Marked 'P. BENTZON' twice on the bottom (see Figure 7.1) and inscribed 'Rebecca Dawson' on the edge of the base. The cipher 'MC' on the side is a later addition. Silver and wood: height 7 in, length 12 in. (Private collection: photograph by Wayne Gibson.)

88

training, as opposed to his exposure in the West Indies to imported Danish and English silver. The teapot's shape, and especially the incised oval plate on the end of the spout, are characteristic of Philadelphia silver. The heaviness of the teapot is unusual for the second decade of the nineteenth century when many silversmiths used rolling mills to make lightweight sheet silver. The characteristics and quality of Bentzon's teapot indicate that it was made by a silversmith whose business was not well organised for prolific hollow-ware production. The engraved 'Rebecca Dawson' on the foot probably refers to a relative of Robert Dawson, from whom Bentzon rented his house and workshop in Philadelphia. The cipher engraved on the side of the teapot was a later addition for a different owner. The teapot is the only known object which Bentzon made in America. Based on the scarcity of silver marked by Bentzon and because of the change in his occupational title from goldsmith to jeweller in 1817, just one year after his arrival in Philadelphia, he probably concentrated on 'smallwork' (jewellery and repairs) rather than the production of hollow-ware. Bentzon was probably ill-equipped to compete with the changing face of silversmithing in Philadelphia as industrialisation encroached on the workshop.

The second hollow-ware object is the 1841 footed cup presented to Reverend Benjamin Lucock by the superintendent and teachers of St John's Episcopal Church Sunday School in St Croix (Fig. 7.3). St John's was a racially mixed congregation of Europeans and free coloured people. English by birth, Lucock went to the West Indian island of Montserrat in 1822, received an honorary degree from Columbia University in New York City, and in 1832 moved to Fredericksted, St Croix, to run the Episcopal parish. Lucock received the cup before returning to England, weakened after a carriage accident. As a gift to their minister, the superintendent and teachers of the Sunday School chose to patronise a silversmith in St Croix rather than purchase an imported object from England or Denmark (Fig. 7.4). The choice of Bentzon for the commission of the cup may have been because he was a member of the congregation, for apart from Peter Bentzon there were at least two other silversmiths in St Croix. In any event, the patronage of a free coloured individual was not uncommon; in the diverse community of St Croix, there were many free coloured people who offered services and goods that were readily purchased by Europeans. Whites and free coloureds alike, for example, patronised the successful restaurateur Apollo Miller who was born a slave and became free by self purchase (Hall, N. 1989).

Peter Bentzon was a member of a free coloured community in St Croix although his occupation and education as a silversmith, his international travel, and probably his light skin complexion, placed him in the upper class of that group. Even though he was moderately successful in St Croix, owning property and able to travel frequently, his free coloured position prevented him from achieving equality with the resident Europeans. In Philadelphia, where he ran a small silver, jewellery and repair business, his African ancestry does not appear to have been a political or social impediment, making his experience as an African American in Philadelphia very separate from his life in St Croix.

Figure 7.3 Footed cup made by Peter Bentzon for presentation to Benjamin Lucock (1792–1846), St Croix; 1841. Marked 'P. BENTZON' three times on the inside rim of the base (see Figure 7.4) and 'PB' four times under the foot. Inscribed 'Presented/ To/REV. B. LUCOCK/By The/Superintendent and Teachers/of/St. John's Church Sunday School/Christiansted St. Croix/As a token of their/Esteem & Respect April th 1841 (*sic*)'. Silver: height 6¾ in, width 5½ in. (Philadelphia Museum of Art, purchased with the Thomas Skelton Harrison Fund and partial gift of Wynyard Wilkinson, photograph by R. C. Cooper, Ltd.)

Peter Bentzon's is only one story in an uninvestigated group of African American silversmiths. Henry Bray and Anthony Sowerwalt were both listed as silversmiths and 'Persons of Colour' in the 1813 and 1818 Philadelphia directories, and Joseph Head, 'Black Man Silversmith', had business trans-actions with the better-known early nineteenth-century silversmith Samuel Williamson.[10] And as cited by James Porter in *Modern Negro Art*, John Frances was a runaway silversmith of colour employed by John Letelier in Philadelphia (Porter 1992: 16). To date, little is known about the careers of Bray, Sowerwalt, Head or Frances, and no objects bearing their marks are known. In a business that we currently perceive as European American, there was a diverse African American or African European presence.[11]

The preoccupation with physical appearance and the concern to correlate skin

Figure 7.4 One of Bentzon's three identical marks on the inside rim of the base of the footed cup.

complexion with legal status shaped the experiences of the free coloured in St Croix and the other Danish West Indian islands. The surviving documentary evidence shows Bentzon consistently responding and reacting in ways most convenient for the prevailing moment – transporting goods into America under the auspices that they were 'American manufactured', or relaying to the Philadelphia census-taker that he and his family were all US citizens, or that he had taken out citizenship papers when really they were his charter of freedom as a free coloured Cruzan, or his fluctuating religious affiliations which were dependent on the coloniser at hand. When asked about his Burgher Briefs, Bentzon claimed that his had been 'lost by fire in America'. The court researched Bentzon's claim only to find that there was no proof that he had ever applied for citizenship papers. But these reactions and adaptations may be because Bentzon was an individual residing on a boundary or seam between cultures: European and African (free and slave); Danish West Indian and American; African American and European. Furthermore, such snippets and scraps of paper and information were all conspiring to reduce Bentzon to an identity that other people had invented. Bentzon responded with distance and denial, and half-denials and cunning half-truths. Over the years he became a virtuoso of ambiguity and equivocation.

Even though Bentzon experienced economic mobility in St Croix, his free coloured position prevented him from achieving an equality of status. In

Philadelphia, however, he and his family, as mentioned earlier, may have passed for white. In 1850, the instructions to the census marshals, under the heading 'Colour', read: 'in all cases where the person appears white leave the space blank; in all cases where the person appears black, insert the letter B; if mulatto, insert M. It is very desirable that these particulars be carefully regarded'. Although the instructions are vague, they indicate that skin shading, not ancestry, was the census marshal's sole determinant of 'race'.

In St Croix, Bentzon and his family were regarded as 'coloured' because of their publicly known African ancestry, but in America they were not considered to be of African descent because their skin complexion suggested otherwise. Although Bentzon was of African descent and worked in America, he neither experienced Philadelphia as an African American nor produced work there that remotely suggested an African affinity. Instead, Bentzon appears to have taken advantage of his multiple social identities, picking and choosing as he moved through different places and communities at different times.

Just as the racial hybridity of individuals such as Peter Bentzon complicates the sociologist's attempt to pigeonhole by community, so too the objects produced by those without clear allegiance to one social grouping or another must

Figure 7.5 Teapot by Peter Bentzon (see Figure 7.2), as exhibited in 'Old World and New', part of the Sarah Mellon Scaife permanent collection galleries at the Carnegie Museum of Art, Pittsburgh, Pennsylvania. (Photograph by Richard Stoner, courtesy of the Carnegie Museum of Art.)

necessarily challenge traditional cultural classification systems conventionally used by the museum curator. How then do museums present and interpret objects born of colonialism – implicitly the product of a forced marriage of cultures? The National Museum in Copenhagen, Denmark displays in its West Indian gallery an American sideboard with silver drawer pulls by Bentzon, so emphasising the importance of Denmark's colonial history in the Caribbean. In contrast, at the Philadelphia Museum of Art the footed cup by Bentzon is presented within the specific context of that city's silversmithing tradition. A third object, a silver tablespoon marked by Bentzon, has taken on a different cultural value by virtue of its acquisition by the Center for African-American Decorative Arts. The 1994 reinstallation of the permanent collection in the Sarah Mellon Scaife galleries at the Carnegie Museum of Art in Pittsburgh, Pennsylvania (Fig. 7.5) afforded an opportunity to look anew at the relationship between objects without the constraint of commonly employed museum classifications such as nationality, school or medium. American, European and non-Western decorative arts, paintings and sculpture were here combined to produce thematic rather than national, typological or chronological groupings. Bentzon's *c.*1817 teapot is exhibited at the entrance to these galleries in a section entitled 'Old World and New' which examines the transference of style from the former to the latter in early Anglo-American culture. In the case of the teapot, evidence of any techniques or stylistic traits imported from continental Africa, however, are non-existent. Residual African characteristics in early African-American decorative arts were attractive to groundbreaking historians such as James Porter and Alain Locke because they confirmed suspicions of an alternative transference of style. In Bentzon's case, any evidence of his African ancestry was erased by his colonial experience, which in turn was the cause of his hybrid identity. In the absence of telling visual information which reveals the colonial origin of an object such as Bentzon's teapot, the museum visitor can acquire a full understanding of its cultural significance only by means of its association with and juxtaposition to other carefully selected exhibits and with the benefit of enlightened, cross-related labelling.

Notes

1 As cited in Gates 1996: 68.
2 Broyard took the expression 'avenues of flight' and some of the concepts in his own essay from Jean-Paul Sartre's 1948 'Portrait of the Inauthentic Jew' (*Commentary* 1950).
3 Genealogical material on Bentzon and his family was derived from the following: H. F. Garde, 'Peter Bentzon – en vestindisk guldsmed', *Personalhistorisk Tidsskrift*, 1 (1993): 68–77; Hugo Ryberg, comp., and Mrs. Rigmor de Vicq, ed., 'A List of Names of Inhabitants of the Danish West Indies from 1650–*c.*1825', (photocopy, Danish National Archives, 1945); *Philadelphia Public Ledger*, October 10, 1848; Philadelphia Archdiocesan Historical Research Center, St Augustine's microfilmed baptismal register, November 6, 1828; Philadelphia Archdiocesan Historical Research Center, Cathedral of SS Peter and Paul, marriage register, 1847–1868, October 11, 1848; Philadelphia Census, 1850.
4 I am indebted to Elizabeth Rezende of St Croix for sharing with me her research on the Guts.

5 Rigsarkivet (Danish National Archives), Vestindiske lokalarkiver, Christiansted byfoged 1734–1900, Politimester, Protokoller over ankomne og bortrejste personer, 1817; incoming passenger lists, National Archives, Mid-Atlantic Region, Philadelphia, Pennsylvania, USA.

6 Entry for 1 October 1816, Incoming Passenger Lists for Philadelphia (National Archives, Mid-Atlantic Region).

7 Vestindiske lokalarkiver, Christiansted byfoged 1734–1900, Politimester, Protokoller over ankomne og bortrejste personer, 1817, p. 36.

8 Ibid., 1829, p. 138.

9 Objects bearing Bentzon's mark are as follows: teapot (private collection, currently on loan to the Carnegie Museum of Art), presentation cup (Philadelphia Museum of Art), tablespoon (The Center for African American Decorative Arts), tablespoon (St Croix Historical Society), four silver drawer pulls on an American sideboard (Nationalmuseet, Copenhagen). Additionally, two pastry, or 'klejner', tools, a fish slice, and a gold buckle are in private collections in Denmark.

10 The Henry Francis duPont Winterthur Museum and Library, Downes Collection of Manuscripts and Printed Ephemera, Samuel Williamson account books, daybook, 105.

11 Other sources which note the African American presence in the early American silver trade are Driskell (1976); Lewis, S. (1976); Locke (1940); Porter (1992).

8

Domesticating Uzbeks
Central Asians in Soviet decorative art of the twenties and thirties

Karen Kettering

During the 1920s and 1930s, Soviet Russian decorative arts produced for audiences in Moscow and Leningrad were replete with images of Central Asians, typically Uzbeks.[1] Because the multi-ethnic Soviet Union was made up of hundreds of nationalities and language groups, the consistent selection of Uzbeks is puzzling. What did the generalised image of a Central Asian often resembling an Uzbek express which that of a Iakut, Bashkir or Ukrainian could not? It is my argument that the numerous objects featuring Central Asian figures performed a specific function for Soviet *Russian* viewers that can be recovered only by attending to two important conditions surrounding their production: the Russians' inability to bring this region completely under their political control and the objects' intended function as decoration for the Soviet Russian home. For both Soviet Russian producers and viewers with an investment in the success of Soviet power, orientalist discourse was a convenient means by which intransigent forces defying the Soviet state and its programmes could be 'domesticated' into charming or coy figures. As any number of basic textbooks on Russian civilisation have noted, many Russians continued to conceive of Russia as neither a European nor an Asiatic nation, but a mixture of the two and, moreover, to consider themselves as technologically backward, or 'Asiatic', in relation to their European neighbours both before and after the October Revolution. Indeed, in the early Soviet period, the noun *aziatshchina*, a negative term denoting an 'Asian' way of life, was used to describe the worst parts of Russian daily life (Blank 1994: 40). These decorative works tended to reinforce *Russian* identity as civilised bearers of culture and did so at the expense of an internationalist *Soviet* identity in which all citizens, whatever their nationality, were considered equals.

While Orientalist painting had been produced in Russia during the nineteenth and twentieth centuries, the number of such works was small compared to the unprecedented quantity of images of Central Asians that began to appear after Soviet troops had brought the former Russian Imperial colony of Turkestan, which had briefly managed to establish its independence, under Soviet control. In 1924, the Soviet government declared that insurgent forces had been defeated and divided the former colony into the republics of Uzbekistan, Tajikistan,

Kirghizstan and Turkmenistan. Although the level of open armed conflict had declined after 1924, resistance had moved underground and took the form of guerilla warfare and assassinations of Soviet officials. For Russians during the 1920s, it was simplest to explain the Soviet forces' inability to attain a decisive political or military victory in the region by making reference to traditional accounts of the character of its inhabitants. These accounts portrayed the residents of Central Asia as savage: brutal, cruel and obstinately clinging to a backward social and cultural structure that was feudal at best.

In examining the development of the representation of Central Asians in Soviet decorative art, I shall focus on works made at the Lomonosov Porcelain Factory in Leningrad for several reasons. First, in the most general sense the decorative arts are particularly well-suited to historical moments in which both artists, and a wide number of viewers, seek to 'domesticate' a threatening culture. This process of 'domestication' entails rendering a menacing culture or nation unthreatening by producing appealing, charming or sentimental images of the group. After a given nation or minority culture has been effectively defeated or marginalised, it has been quite common for decorative artists to present members of that culture as essentially content with their subordinate status. One need only think of the thousands of inexpensive ceramic 'Mammy and Uncle Mose' salt and pepper shakers that circulated throughout the United States during the early twentieth century or the more costly Rookwood vases and silver Tiffany candlesticks adorned with images of Native Americans made after most had been relegated to reservations (Owen 1995). Likewise, the production in the 1920s and 1930s of figures of 'exotics' familiar from the history of European and Russian decorative arts provided a site for the inscription of Soviet concerns about Central Asia. Examples of this tradition were available to factory artists: the Russian Museum's Department of Everyday Life (*bytovoi otdel*), for example, contained several late eighteenth-century Russian porcelain mugs in the shapes of the heads of a male and female Turk (Farmakovskii 1923: 16–17). At the time of their making, the meaning of such figures would have been inflected by the knowledge of Russia's wars with the Ottoman Empire, while in the early twentieth century they were drained of their original power and had now simply become interesting curiosities on the museum's shelves. Porcelain factory artists appropriated such well-worn stylistic and thematic conventions in order to render benign the purportedly violent and savage Muslim residents of Central Asia who resisted Soviet power.

Second, after the October Revolution, the Lomonosov Porcelain Factory pursued the decoration of the domestic sphere as its primary duty. Both critics and cultural policy makers of the period praised the factory's production almost exclusively for its acceptability, indeed desirability, as domestic decoration (Kettering 1997). They felt that the factory artists produced wares decorated with 'ideological motifs' commemorating and propagandising Soviet government programmes which were both attractive and tasteful in style. That a factory only recently the private property of the Imperial family was now producing works adorned with portraits of Lenin and Red Army men or women workers was a matter of considerable political value. Furthermore, it was believed that works such as those produced by the Lomonosov factory might subtly win over their owners to various government agitational, educational and cultural programmes. The power Soviet critics accorded to the object within the domestic sphere at this time cannot be underestimated. Numerous writers suggested that something as innocuous as a scrolled or gilded handle on a tea cup could have a negative impact on the party's political struggle by lulling the user into bourgeois desires for luxurious consumer goods (Kettering 1996). In the period prior to the outbreak of the Second World War, such influential figures as Mikhail Kalinin (Chairman of the Presidium of the Supreme Soviet), Anatoly Lunacharsky (Commissar of Education) and Grigorii Ordzhonikidze (Commissar of Heavy Industry) each intervened on different occasions to secure financial subsidies to keep the factory open and working, although the high production costs of artistic objects meant that the factory rarely made a profit on these goods. As the magazine *Moscow Construction* reported, Kalinin, describing the factory, hoped that:

> gradually a taste for the attractive interior would evolve among the working class, that they would reach out to porcelain, that they would understand what happiness could be derived from using beautiful pieces of porcelain to create the ever more cozy and comfortable environment for the working class family (G.N. 1927: 2).

Throughout the 1920s and 1930s, the factory's Central Asian works changed in response to differing social conditions and political policies in the area. First, until 1924, when the region was divided into new republics, Lomonosov porcelain with 'Eastern' themes depended upon figures in costumes so generalised as to convey little more than the fact that they were residents of the East. While such works did not refer specifically to Central Asia, they did work to reinforce Soviet Russian identity as 'civilised' in comparison to the persons depicted. The factory's first works to explore this theme were a series of objects dedicated to the Congress of the Peoples of the East convened under the direction of Grigorii Zinoviev, President of the Communist International, in Baku in 1920. The Congress was to be the second half of the second meeting of the Third International and was specifically devoted to questions of political organisation in colonised Asian nations. As part of the works made in honour of this meeting, factory artist Elena Danko contributed a small statuette entitled *Turkish Girl* (1921), sometimes known as *The Awakening East* (Fig. 8.1). At first glance, it does not seem to differ greatly from the 'exotic' works that most European factories, influenced by the popularity of Chinese export porcelain, had been producing since the eighteenth century (Tabakoff 1992). It is a small figurine of a size suitable for a table or bookshelf that depicts a seated young woman reading a newspaper. She is dressed in an odd amalgam which, while clearly recognisable as Eastern clothing, cannot be identified as the costume of any particular country. Sheer black material veils the lower portion of her face, which can still be seen, while her shirt has been decorated with a cut-out that bares her breasts. To a Western viewer, it is a woman's shirt as ineffectual as the veil, indeed it only serves to call attention to her breasts. In fact, it most closely resembles postcards produced in Northern Africa around the turn of the century for

Figure 8.1 Elena Danko, *Turkish Girl* or *The Awakening East*, Lomonosov Porcelain Factory, 1921. (Museum of the Lomonosov Porcelain Factory, photograph: Sergei Petrov.)

French colonials who paid native women to be photographed bare-breasted in order to create an image of a non-existent, exotic East for friends and relatives at home in France (Alloula 1986). That she is connected with Soviet Russia is clear from the headline on her newspaper announcing the 'Congress of the Peoples of the East' and Zinoviev's profile portrait decorating the centre of the newspaper page. The figurine is a complex one, because it simultaneously invokes the coy flirtations of European porcelain statuettes with its arousing suggestion of an imaginary East in which women lounge with their faces covered but their breasts bared and, at the same time, the image of the metaphorically slumbering Eastern woman, who is 'awakened' by reports of the Congress in her newspaper. With her gaze directed away from the viewer and diverted into the pages of her newspaper, the spectator is free to simultaneously enjoy the sight of the attractive young woman's bared breasts and the satisfaction of being a member of the enlightened society that sought to 'liberate' her from political, cultural and social domination.

Two years later, Natalia Danko, head of the factory's sculptural section and Elena Danko's older sister, finished a group of three small figurines that addresses a different aspect of the orientalist myth. While Elena Danko's statuette had relied upon an eroticised notion of the East, her sister's work instead took up a Russian story that presented Eastern peoples as inordinately brutal.

The set depicts the three central characters *Maria, Zarema* and *Girei* (1923) from Alexander Pushkin's 1823 poem *The Fountain of Bakhchisarai*, which tells the story of a virginal Polish princess, Maria, and her abduction by the Crimean Tatar Khan Girei during a raid on her father's castle (Fig. 8.2). Most educated Soviet Russian viewers, raised on a steady diet of Pushkin and other Russian literary classics, would have already been familiar with the poem and known that this was a 'true' story that had taken place sometime in the sixteenth or early seventeenth century, when the khanate had its capital in the Ukrainian city of Bakhchisarai. As Pushkin wrote, Girei was so struck by Maria's beauty that he fell deeply in love with her. When she arrived at his palace, Maria, who had scorned Girei's advances, became the focus of the jealousy of the Georgian Zarema, Girei's repudiated favourite. After a conversation between the two women in which they recalled their faraway childhood homes, Zarema killed Maria in a fit of jealousy and violence which Pushkin attributed to her 'Eastern' nature. Although Zarema, as a Georgian, would have been raised in the Eastern Orthodox Church, Pushkin implies that this woman of the Caucasus easily repudiated these values in favour of the 'violence' of her Tatar captors. Literary critic Leonid Grossman's 1923 speech 'Pushkin in 1823', in which he

Figure 8.2 Natalia Danko, *Maria, Zarema* and *Girei*, Lomonosov Porcelain Factory, 1923. (Museum of the Lomonosov Porcelain Factory, photograph: Sergei Petrov.)

argued that 'the advance in the *Fountain of Bakhchisarai* over previous Oriental tales was its explicit opposition between Europe and the East, represented in the poem's two heroines' indicates that in the Soviet period the poem was still seen as an accurate description of the oppositions between West and East, civilisation and barbarism (Sandler 1989: 167). Of the many points in the poem Danko could have chosen to represent, she selected the moment at which Zarema has fatally wounded Maria. Pushkin, and Danko following him, invites us to compare a woman of the West, the passive and virginal Maria, and a woman of the East, who says 'I can use a dagger, I was born near the Caucasus.' In Danko's grouping, Girei stands, helpless to intervene, having arrived after Zarema stabbed Maria. Zarema, with her thick, black braid reaching her hips, steps away from Maria, her veil billowing open to reveal her tiny shirt and sheer pants, and clutches the large dagger with which she has fatally wounded Maria. As her strength ebbs away and Maria's death approaches, she has sunk to the earth holding her rosary beads, passively looking away from the man who had abducted her and the woman who had ended her life. For the Soviet Russian viewer, these 1923 statuettes of figures from a poem of 1823 depicting a supposedly authentic event from the sixteenth or seventeenth century recalled Russia's historical and continuing mission as a defender of European culture and civilisation from the threat of Islam.

It is perhaps no coincidence that both Danko sisters, when faced with the problem of representing the East, selected figures or stories relying upon Soviet Russian conceptions of the experience of Eastern women to convey 'knowledge' of the region. Central Asian women were, as a rule, barred from any sort of participation in public life. Because of this, they were extremely important to Soviet authorities who, when faced with a lack of an urban proletariat in Soviet Central Asia, utilised women as a 'surrogate proletariat'. In their attempt to reorganise a largely agricultural society, Soviet officials in Central Asia reasoned that women were a natural substitute since they occupied the lowest position in society (Massell 1974). For Soviet authorities, the institution of veiling embodied and promoted women's subordinate status by precluding their participation in public and political life. (In many regions of Central Asia, women wore a long black garment known as *parandzha* that covered their entire body leaving only small openings for the hands and eyes.) In the summer of 1926 the party launched a campaign known as *khudzhum* against the institution of the separation of the sexes in public life embodied in the veil. The word *khudzhum* was selected because it could be translated as 'attack' or 'assault' in Turkic, Arabic or Persian, the three primary languages of Central Asia (Massell 1974: 229). This campaign took the form of Soviet-sponsored public unveilings as well as encouraging women to exercise their new found legal right to divorce their domineering or anti-Soviet husbands and to participate in public life by joining literacy classes or Soviet women's organisations.

The *khudzhum* campaign and its military imagery were, apparently, received as a challenge and were responded to in kind. Soviet newspapers, journals and magazines reported that Central Asian men harassed and beat unveiled women who appeared alone in the streets, occasionally even raping or killing them. In

March 1927, the party attempted to shield newly unveiled women through the publication of a decree protecting those woman who had removed the garment (Astapovich 1971: 91–2). Less often, Russian Soviet officials and representatives of the *Zhenotdel* (Women's Department) were attacked and assaulted. Lurid tales of savagery were widely publicised throughout the Soviet Union and created further support for colonialist incursions into Central Asian life. What had begun as a political campaign for the transformation of Central Asian society centred on women's participation in public life quickly became a ferocious struggle for the control of visual access to women's bodies centring on the existence of the *parandzha*.

After *khudzhum* had officially been launched, works such as the statuettes of the Danko sisters gave way to an almost obsessive focus on the veil in contemporary Central Asian life as an artistic theme. The Central Asian 'question' became the question of the veil. For example, in 1925 the AKhRR (Association of Artists of Revolutionary Russia) organised its eighth exhibition, *Everyday Life of the Peoples of the USSR (Zhizn' i byt narodov SSSR)*, and managed to secure state funds to send artists throughout the Soviet Union to record the daily life of its peoples (*Vos'maia vystavka* 1926: 5). At a meeting of artists preparing to depart in May 1925, the literary critic L. S. Sosnovskii delivered a speech in which he suggested appropriate topics. When he turned his attention to how these government-supported artists might depict Central Asia, he restricted his comments to the question of the veil, saying:

> I don't remember the representation (*otrazhenie*) of the women of the East in art, but whether or not it occurred, these women were faceless, covered by the [veil]. I don't know whether [nineteenth-century Russian Orientalist painter Vasilii] Vereshchagin painted women with uncovered faces, but today women are uncovering their faces, throwing off the veil, and beginning to take part in cultural, economic, and social work. This is the moment that must be recorded.
>
> (*Vos'maia vystavka* 1926: 25)

The photo-journalist Georgii Zelma, working in Uzbekistan for the Russian news agency Rosfoto and the Tashkent-based newspaper *Pravda vostoka*, seemed to be following Sosnovskii's recommendations when he took a series of photographs that were repeatedly printed in both Central Asian and Russian-language magazines and newspapers published throughout the Soviet Union. *Away with the Chador*[2] (Fig. 8.3), in which an older woman lifts a dark, heavy veil away from her face, and *Women's Day Parade, 1926, in Tashkent*[3] (Fig. 8.4), depicting a parade of veiled and unveiled women of all ages, watched by men as they travel down a tightly packed street, helped to reinforce the sense that the veil was the central question of political change within Central Asia.[4] As photographs these works could also lay claim to the status of documentary 'proof' of the fact that a great number of women, both older and younger, supported the campaign in a way that a painting or sculpture could not. Comparing these photographs to decorative works underlines the differences in the manner in which a decorative artist producing for the home approached the

Figure 8.3 Georgii Zelma, *Away with the Chador*, 1926. (Courtesy of Howard Schickler Fine Art, New York.)

same theme. Zelma's photograph of the *Women's Day Parade*, for example, might be fraught with tension from the viewer's knowledge of the male bystander's potential to attack the demonstrators, who are protected by mounted police. In 1929, when factory sculptor Natalia Danko addressed the topic, her design relied upon older porcelain figurines' doll-like faces and gestures, thus presenting a statuette offering the viewer an idealised image that was well suited to a domestic environment (Fig. 8.5). Her figurine is that of a beautiful young woman who lifts her veil and exposes her face without any sign of timidity or fear, expecting no opposition. Rather than the dark garment almost devoid of ornament worn in Central Asia, Danko's figure is removing a veil covered with small patterns. What the veil had been hiding – a young, attractive women dressed in richly decorated clothing – was also sure to satisfy the viewer's voyeurism or fantasies of the harem in which attractive young women, never the old or the ugly, were veiled and hidden. Standing alone on its base, Danko's figure is isolated from other figures or any details that might indicate where and when the woman had chosen to remove her veil. There is no indication, for example, that her unveiling took place in her home in possible defiance of her male relatives, on a street in a demonstration or under the encouraging gazes of ethnically Russian women in the office of a

Figure 8.4 Georgii Zelma, *Women's Day Parade, 1926, in Tashkent*, 1926. (Courtesy of Howard Schickler Fine Art, New York.)

Soviet women's organisation. Unlike Zelma's photograph, this tempered image suggests that unveiling was a politically less complicated process that involved no more than discarding the garment. Sitting on a bookshelf or the centre of a table in Moscow or Leningrad, rather than accompanying a journalistic account of a Central Asian woman beaten or enslaved and then throwing off the garment, it was a cheerful, comforting, and somewhat alluring view of Soviet policy in Central Asia.

As the government launched the campaign for the collectivisation of agriculture late in 1929, the debate over the veil lost its position as the central focus of the reorganisation of Soviet Central Asia.[5] The campaign for collectivisation was extremely violent and met with resistance throughout the USSR. In Central Asia, however, this opposition reached the level of a civil war. Uzbekistan became the target of an ecologically ruthless campaign to increase cotton production to pre- First World War levels in order to free the Soviet Union from the cost of importation. Central Asia as a whole is an important cotton-producing region: the first large-scale Russian invasion of the area with the intention of subjugating the local populace had coincided with the American

Figure 8.5 Natalia Danko, *Woman Unveiling Herself*, Lomonosov Porcelain Factory, 1929. (Cooper-Hewitt, National Design Museum, Smithsonian Inst./Art Resource, NY.)

Civil War and the consequent world-wide jump in the price of cotton (Fierman 1991: 12–13). Because of the importance of Uzbek cotton to the Russian and Soviet economies, during the twentieth century Russians have referred to it as 'white gold'. Despite the increased level of violence surrounding agricultural work in Central Asia, throughout the 1930s Soviet artists responded with landscapes representing a peaceful, productive countryside populated with a contented and healthy peasantry. When Moscow's Clock Factory Number Two requested that the Lomonosov Porcelain Factory supply them with a porcelain clock body for mass production, Natalia Danko selected an Uzbek theme for the commission (Kettering 1997). Her 1937 *Uzbek Woman* clock case is decorated with an unveiled young Uzbek woman whose multiple braids are

Figure 8.6 Natalia Danko, *Uzbek Woman*, Lomonosov Porcelain Factory, 1937. (Cooper-Hewitt, National Design Museum, Smithsonian Inst./Art Resource, NY.)

fanned out across her back (Fig. 8.6). The seated woman hugs a large woven basket that makes up the clock's face and which overflows with various sorts of lush pears and heavy clusters of grapes. While it has no overt narrative content, it suggests a fruitful Uzbekistan and the success of Soviet policy. In addition to rendering the woman as unveiled, Danko sculpted a wristwatch onto the woman's arm facing the viewer. Although it is a rather small detail, once rendered in stark black and white paint it could easily catch the eye and remind the viewer that in Soviet Uzbekistan, all women now had legal access to education and could read, write, do mathematical sums, and tell the time, and implied that the Uzbek woman had successfully absorbed the supposedly Western interest in punctuality and accuracy. Moreover, it suggested that the

105

Soviets had managed to eradicate the poverty that had plagued the area and that the young woman had the financial wherewithal to purchase a watch. Similarly, Natalia Danko's 1936 inkwell, *Game*, depicts a young Uzbek girl wearing the red neck-scarf of the Young Pioneers seated across from an older man (Fig. 8.7). She looks up at the man, who rubs his chin in consternation, apparently because she has defeated him at a board game. Her ability to challenge an older man in any sort of contest is, of course, connected to a whole array of new social structures symbolised by her red Pioneer's neck scarf. The fact that this teenager has been able to win also suggests that Soviet policies unleashed the formerly restrained intellectual skills of Central Asian women. The combination of these two works implies that the campaign to upset traditional social hierarchies through the substitution of Soviet institutions and their reorganisation was a resounding success.

The final event in the period before the Second World War to have an impact on the representation of Central Asians was the adoption of a new constitution reorganising administrative relationships between the republics and replacing the last vestiges of regional power with centralised control. As the Central

Figure 8.7 Natalia Danko, *Game*, Lomonosov Porcelain Factory, 1936. (Cooper-Hewitt, National Design Museum, Smithsonian Inst./Art Resource, NY.)

Committee announcement had stated in February 1935, the new constitution would reflect 'the victories and achievements that Soviet workers had won' since the adoption of the 1924 Constitution (Wimberg 1992: 314). More specifically, this new constitution was meant to signify that capitalism had been defeated and 'alien class elements' eliminated. To mark the promulgation of the new Constitution, Natalia Danko produced a seven piece desk set entitled *Uzbeks Discussing the Stalin Constitution*. The government was vitally interested in promoting the discussion of the constitution as a method of praising the advances of Soviet power. Indeed, Danko designed the desk set in 1936 while regional and local authorities were obliged to survey the opinions of their constituents and the results were published and commented upon in *Izvestiia*, *Pravda* and *Trud* (Wimberg 1992). Although the constitution was quite democratic in terms of its civil guarantees, J. Arch Getty has pointed out that the Committee members' notes for the first draft indicate that a central and unacknowledged purpose of the Constitution was 'the centralization of administrative and judicial functions at the expense of the Republics' (Getty 1990: 20).

Of the seven pieces, the inkwell is the largest and served as the centerpiece (Fig. 8.8). It was accompanied by pieces representing Uzbek folk singers (the lamp stand), young Uzbek men resting from their labours in order to read the draft Constitution (pencil holder), unveiled Uzbek women working on a rug (ashtray) and little boys and girls dreaming of a technologically modern future embodied by a toy airplane (the vase). On the surface of the inkwell, a group of seven Uzbek men and women, one of whom holds a child, discuss the draft constitution which the central figure holds in his lap. Their distinctively patterned robes and the richly decorated carpet on which they sit suggests that the discussion takes place in an 'authentically' Uzbek interior. Several more subtle factors indicate the social changes which Soviet rule had brought. The grouping suggests an active exchange between both men and women as well as older and younger members of this group, all of whom hold notes of some sort in their hands. That this disruption of pre-Revolutionary social hierarchies and organisation might have appealed more to the younger members of the group seems to be indicated by the enthusiasm of the young men and women, while the two older men hang back and still seem unconvinced. Perhaps significantly, no older female members of this community participate in what was considered a nationwide political obligation. This complex work suggests that of all the regions in the Soviet Union, Uzbekistan had benefited most from Soviet power. The scene is complicated by the knowledge that while the younger members of the group seem to assent enthusiastically to the 'most democratic constitution in the world', they are also affirming an administrative structure that will remove whatever remained of their political self-determination as it centralised power in Moscow. That the centre was willing to assert this power violently was made clear when the ethnically Uzbek leaders of the republic, Faizulla Khodzhaev and Akmal Ikramov, as well as other members of Uzbekistan's Central Executive Committee, were arrested on trumped-up charges of plotting a nationalist secession from the USSR. Khodzhaev and Ikramov were returned to Moscow where they were minor lights in the show trial of Bukharin and

Figure 8.8 Natalia Danko, inkwell from the desk set *Uzbeks Discussing the Stalin Constitution*, Lomonosov Porcelain Factory, 1936. (Cooper-Hewitt, National Design Museum, Smithsonian Inst./Art Resource, NY.)

Rykov and eventually shot. Waves of purges cleared the Central Asian administrations of native workers and replaced them with ethnically Russian cadres.

The desk set figured significantly in the Soviet Pavilion at the 1937 Paris International Exposition. Nikolai Suetin, artistic director of the Lomonosov Porcelain Factory, created the general decorative scheme of the pavilion's interior arranged thematically around the Stalin Constitution as the ultimate symbol of the political, cultural and social developments in the Soviet Union. His design for the first hall of the pavilion, dedicated to the Constitution, was decorated with a large porphyry obelisk on which the words of the Constitution were carved under profile portraits of Lenin and Stalin. Danko's set, displayed in the pavilion, demonstrated such positive changes as women's emancipation and modernisation that the Soviets had effected among national minorities in Central Asia. As such, it was related to a newly emerging motif in Soviet art. The Stalin Constitution, which its drafters emphasised could not have been written until the transformation of society had been completed, signalled the beginning of a peculiarly Soviet artistic formula, the friendship of the peoples (*druzhba narodov*), that was to be repeated throughout the Stalin period. In visual terms the friendship of the peoples was typically expressed through a visual enumeration of the Soviet republics represented by one male and one female dressed in 'native costumes'. The fact that the members of each couple are dressed in 'native costumes', a category taken from ethnographic museums, was very significant. A Muscovite or Leningrader contemplating his or her own dress would be most likely to think of it in terms of fashion or modishness, or the lack thereof. Wearing Russian 'native costume' is reserved for the times when people are trying consciously to evoke a past culture that may, in any case, never have existed. Because the Russians in these groupings were usually dressed in the smocks and tunic shirts that were associated with rural dress of the nineteenth century, members of other nationalities, wearing what was thought to be their contemporary clothing, were subtly equated with a less advanced, rural Russia of the past, a visual formula that illustrates what Homi Bhabha has termed the 'time-lag of cultural difference' (Bhabha 1994: 236–8). The exterior decoration of the Soviet Pavilion rather neatly illustrates this principle. At the top of the highest point of the structure, Vera Mukhina's monumental sculpture of an apparently Russian *Worker and Kolkhoz Woman* visually dominates Iosif Chaikov's bas-reliefs of the *Eleven Republics of the Soviet Union* decorating either side of stairs leading to the door of the pavilion. In the reliefs each republic is represented by a man and woman of the republic's dominant ethnic group, dressed in 'native costume' and engaged in productive labour, grouped around the republic's seal. Like Danko's Uzbeks, none of Chaikov's pairs representing each republic could ever come to stand visually for the entirety of the Soviet Union – this was a role reserved for ethnic Russians. In such an equation, the ethnic Russians would always dominate and lead, while the other nationalities would follow in their footsteps.

In the final analysis, Lomonosov porcelain worked to prop up Soviet policy in Central Asia and to naturalise the hierarchy of nationalities within the Soviet Union. In the early Soviet period the state had supported the production of porcelain figurines as an effective means of subtly politicising the domestic sphere, allegedly in a thoroughly Soviet, anti-bourgeois manner. Nevertheless, by failing to break with pre-revolutionary Russian culture and ethnic stereo-types, these works functioned only to bolster Russian identity as protectors of European civilisation, an identity that stretched back to Catherine the Great's battles with the Ottoman Empire and, more importantly, that justified precisely the same sorts of imperialist actions that the Soviets condemned among capitalist countries. Artists appropriated conventions of European decorative arts representing exotics in order to neutralise groups who actively resisted the disruptive 'advancements' brought by the Russians. While the works were inherently contradictory in their attempt to display 'knowledge' of the region – how, for example, was a viewer to reconcile the brutality of Zarema with the passivity of Uzbek women fought over by Russians and Uzbek men? – such images reassured viewers and makers that the policy of attempting to subdue and radically transform the peoples of Central Asia was not only justified, but, considering the 'shortcomings' of Central Asian culture, absolutely appropriate. The Russian viewer could congratulate him or herself on supporting a policy that sought to 'rescue' Central Asian women and at the same time enjoy his or her position as a member of the ethnic group that had the privilege of defining what would constitute civilisation or barbarity. With the adoption of the Stalin Constitution and the acknowledgement of the victory over 'alien class elements', however, these visual strategies abruptly gave way to a new system in which relations between men and women and between the various nationalities were unified and uncomplicated. For Russian viewers living thousands of miles away in Moscow or Leningrad, these works could serve as a daily reminder of the fruits of their labours to transform Central Asia and Central Asians' purported satisfaction with a situation in which they had lost the last vestiges of political autonomy and were relegated to an unacknowledged colonial status.

Acknowledgements

All translations from Russian are mine unless otherwise noted. I would like to thank Randi Barnes, Nancy E. Owen and Wendy Salmond for reading earlier drafts of this paper.

Notes

1   Although artists would often depict an undifferentiated Central Asian whose clothing or surroundings could be identified as an amalgam of Uzbek, Kirghiz, Kazakh and Turkmen, Uzbeks, perceived as being among the most 'backward' of all the peoples in the Soviet Union, were often singled out. This state of perceived underdevelopment was, for the Bolsheviks, indicated by the extremely low level of literacy in the area and thus many government campaigns or programmes were centred on or began in Uzbekistan. The 1926 census indicated that the rate of literacy among Uzbeks was 3.8% as compared to 76% among the Finns and 45.9% among Russians (d'Encausse 1992: 160–1).
2   Although the majority of scholars have identified this work as *Away with the Chador!*, Daniela Mrázková and Vladimir Remeš identified this work as *Old Takhtabu Showing her Face in Public for the First Time* and reproduce a slightly different version of the work in which the veil is lifted to the right (Mrázková and Remeš 1982: 79). The other version can be found in Chudakov 1990: 279.
3   The photo has been assigned varying dates between 1924 and 1927 in different publications. Because Zelma returned to complete his military service in 1927, the image most likely records a Women's Day parade that took place sometime between 1924 and 1926.
4   Throughout the 1970s and 1980s, Zelma's work from the 1920s was included in various museum and gallery exhibitions of early Soviet photography. Although typically presented in a fine art context, it should not be forgotten that they were produced and distributed through the State controlled press.
5   On 27 May 1929 the Central Committee published a resolution ordering local party organisations in Uzbekistan not to slacken the tempo of the movement against the veil at the same time as they were organising collectivisation, suggesting that they were concerned that the issue of the veil would be left along the wayside (Shams-ud-din 1982: 131).

9

Keys to the magic kingdom

The new transcultural collections of Bradford Art Galleries and Museums

Nima Poovaya-Smith

Great pomp and ceremony attended the inaugural exhibition of Cartwright Hall Art Gallery in 1904. Launched by the then Prince and Princess of Wales (later King George V and Queen Mary), the outlying Lister Park and the Hall itself became the venue for a series of festive events that drew all of the people of Bradford. One event much written about by the press of that time was the recreation of a Somali village in the grounds of the park. The Somalis attracted a great deal of attention and, judging from newspaper accounts, the curiosity was not unmixed with goodwill. The reports also record moments of poignancy and tragedy. A child was born to one of the Somali families and she was named Hadija Yorkshire. The inclement May weather hastened the death of one Somali woman who was found to have consumption. A large number of Bradford citizens turned out to mourn this sad event. What makes the whole episode so shocking to us today was the study of living, breathing human beings as though they were museum specimens or exotic animals in a zoo. It was, at best, an anthropological approach to the study of culture and very much of its time.

Today, nearly a hundred years later, and indeed in Bradford's centenary year, the social composition of this Yorkshire city has changed beyond all recognition. A rapid process of expansion had, from the 1830s, converted it into an incipient, landlocked entrepôt. Drawn by its growing prosperity, German merchants as well as shopkeepers and workers from Ireland, Scotland and Cumbria located themselves here. But it was the aftermath of the Second World War that witnessed the largest influx of settlers. Italians, Ukrainians, Poles and Pakistanis began to arrive, part of a vital process of rebuilding an enervated post-war Britain.

The manner of recording census statistics makes it difficult to place an exact figure on the number of East European residents in Bradford. But it would be safe to assume that the largest minority group in Bradford today is the South Asian community from the Indian subcontinent. Of a total population of 484,000 they comprise approximately 81,000. Although largely from Pakistan, there are also a number of people from India and Bangladesh as well.

The transcultural collections of Bradford Art Galleries and Museums are relatively new. Systematic purchasing was begun only in 1986 with an initial emphasis on contemporary art. An interesting precedent can be found in the first donation to the Bradford Art Museum in 1879, presented by one of the sons of the local industrialist Sir Titus Salt, of a suit of Japanese armour. In 1986, an evolving acquisitions policy was committed to collecting in the broad areas of the fine and decorative arts directly or indirectly related to the Indo-Pakistan subcontinent. A methodology was developed which guided the nature of the collecting. Temporary exhibitions were organised, usually as a result of community consultation. They covered a broad church, from themes as diverse as calligraphy, jewellery, manuscript paintings, textiles and contemporary art.[1]

The audience response to these exhibitions served as valuable case-studies informing the direction of Bradford's collections policy. It was clear that there were certain categories of objects, which the initial policy had not particularly highlighted, that drew a deep emotional response from particular sections of the audience. At the same time they were also of great interest to the general public. This then was the touchstone that triggered buying within certain, hitherto unemphasised, areas. Calligraphy in the Muslim world, gold and silver, *saris*, costumes and ritual textiles are some examples. This meant that the original focus on contemporary South Asian art was widened in order to give the collection added depth and range. Bradford is fortunate in having minority communities from geographic areas or cultures rich in the material arts. But the links between the holdings and the communities have been kept deliberately fluid.

These links have allowed us to collect objects whose aesthetic value is beyond question. A small number of the objects can be termed antiques, which were all purchased in this country. However, all the objects acquired directly from India or Pakistan derive from 1900 onwards. This is in compliance with the export regulations of the two countries which forbid the export of artefacts over a hundred years old. This cut-off date has actually proved quite useful. It has demonstrated, beyond doubt, that the craftsmanship of the twentieth century, too, can be of superlative quality. At the same time, the collection is also under-pinned by the ethical imperative that it reflects, to a degree, the kaleidoscopic cultures of West Yorkshire. It is, therefore, the first non-colonial collection of its kind in the country.

There are, doubtless, other equally valid methodologies but this syncretistic approach appears to be the most appropriate one for Bradford. Commonwealth and post-colonial studies have been an area of burgeoning growth over the last twenty years, particularly in the fields of literature and cultural studies. The critical discourse around this area includes the writings of well-respected scholars such as Edward Said, Homi Bhabha and Gayatri Spivak. The decoding and deconstructing of various modes of thought such as Orientalism have been invaluable to a general understanding of structures of dominance and how these infiltrate and influence culture. Many aspects of this discourse are valid and applicable to the Bradford collection, particularly the contemporary section. But this is essentially a long-term practical project and this chapter, while reaffirming a deep respect for this discourse, momentarily sets it aside in order to let the public, the Bradford collections and the exhibitions develop their own momentum.

The gallery in which the transcultural collections will be housed is sited on the same floor as the Western permanent collections. The parity between the two arms of the collection is, therefore, stated without undue emphasis. It allows for the creation, in a manner that is not forced or contrived, of a variety of contexts that cross-refer between cultures. One approach adopted is that of juxtaposing apparently unconnected objects. Closer study will, however, reveal thematic, stylistic, historical or philosophical links. For instance, Sir William Rothenstein's oil study (the finished works are sited in the Palace of Westminster) entitled *Sir Thomas Roe at the Court of Jahangir* (1926) will be displayed with a number of miniatures from the Jahangir period (reigned 1605–1627). Laila Rahman's etchings, with their essentially humanist concerns, will hang next to a selection of William Blake's engravings from the *Book of Job*, also from the Bradford collections.

The collections, at present, fall into four loose groupings: Contemporary Fine Arts and Crafts; Calligraphy in the Muslim World; Gold and Silver; and Textiles.

Contemporary fine arts and crafts

The category of contemporary arts and crafts overarches the other three categories of calligraphy, textiles, silver and gold. Indeed contemporary art makes frequent inroads into the three areas, since they too have a modern thrust. While they give it context, it gives them relevance. Contemporary art also operates as a sharp brake on any temptation to retreat into nostalgia. The primary focus of this collection is on artists of South Asian descent living and working in this country. This immediately poses a problem about the nature of definitions which was thrown into high relief by a recent event. In October 1996 Sotheby's of London held a major auction of *A Hundred Years of Modern and Contemporary Indian Art*. Before the paintings went under the hammer, they were previewed at Cartwright Hall Art Gallery.

What was noticeable about the list of selected artists, was that apart from Balraj Khanna, F. N. Souza and S. H. Raza (the post-war generation who had moved to Europe), all other artists lived and worked in India. Indeed, even these three artists continued to have strong links with India while resident respectively in England, America and France. Sotheby's were defining, no doubt unwittingly, those artists that they perceived to be properly 'Indian' or 'Pakistani'. In so doing they had almost completely left out the forty or more practising artists of Indo-Pakistan subcontinental descent living and working in Britain. This decision would have had nothing to do with their saleability or quality. For these artists included international names such as Anish Kapoor and Dhruva Mistry.

By articulating, however unselfconsciously, what they perceived to be genuinely Indian, Sotheby's had, by exclusion, defined what they perceived to be non-Indian and therefore British. This is not without irony. Since the 1980s, artists of South Asian descent have been locked in periodic conflict with the British art establishment over issues of marginalisation and interpretation. It was sixteen years ago, in 1981, that the race riots of Bristol, Birmingham, Liverpool and London galvanised the country and radicalised the thinking of a number of artists of non-British origin. Before then, artists from the Indian subcontinent and the African and Caribbean countries had lived, struggled, modestly succeeded or failed.

But the turning point was 1981, when the work of these artists began to be treated almost as a movement, producing a body of work, with shared or over-lapping concerns unique to their state of being non-European. The fact that most of them (with notable exceptions such as Rasheed Araeen) were relatively young, being either second-generation Asians or fairly recent arrivals to Britain, must have had a bearing. Artists such as Sutapa Biswas, Nina Edge, Chila Kumari Burman and Said Adruss combined both a public and private utterance in their work. Inevitably, one result of the attempt at homogenising 'Black Art' was the highlighting of public utterance in the shape of social protest, alienation and anger, often at the expense of the private utterance. To that extent the 1980s was an uneasy decade. The 1990s saw the beginning of a subtler and more introspective approach to the treatment and analysis of artists of dual heritage.

Contemporary artists practising in India and Pakistan today are very much part of the international art scene. Their work, while maintaining a distinct identity, has undoubtedly been shaped by twentieth-century Western movements in art. Shanti Panchal and Dhruva Mistry who received their initial art training in India, but who have also lived and worked in Britain, are excellent examples of this composite training. But now the majority of the artists of South Asian descent have been trained in Britain and, therefore, almost exclusively in the Western tradition. They have had to 'discover' their Indian creative selves. Many of them illustrate what Homi Bhabha described as the state of being caught up in the space between frames:

> double-lives are led in the postcolonial world, with its journeys of migration and its dwellings of the diasporic. These subjects of study require the experience of anxiety to be incorporated into the analytic construction of the object of critical attention: narratives of the borderline conditions of cultures and disciplines. For anxiety is the affective address of 'a world [that] reveals itself as caught up in the space between frames; a doubled frame or one that is split'.
>
> (Bhabha 1994: 213–14)

For many of the artists, articulating this quest has involved the shadowy realm of speculation, dreams and the unconscious; the recollections of parents, family and childhood. These become instruments of 'knowing', once described by Sutapa Biswas (in an unwitting echo of T. S. Eliot) as a 'mixing of memory and desire'. The themes of displacement and quest, a search for identity, especially for those who no longer live in their country of origin, is firmly established in literature. The writings of V. S. Naipaul, for instance, explore this in dark and ambivalent detail. But while this has been accepted as perfectly legitimate in literature, for some reason it is still slightly suspect in the visual arts and can be devalued as nostalgia, perhaps because it employs a visual vocabulary that is frequently unfamiliar to the West.

None the less, the undertaking of this quest seems vital to the artists' creative well-being and often involves a series of journeys, both metaphoric and real, to the mother-country. For many of these artists, their academic, intellectual selves seem to be embodied by the West and their intuitive, instinctual selves by the Indian subcontinent. It is a composition that is equally male and female in its makeup. The metaphysical artist Giorgio de Chirico (himself an Italian-Greek who had lived in Germany, France and Italy) believed implicitly in the theory that authentic modern art always had 'the element of surprise'. But with these artists there is often the shock of the old; an atavistic memory or arcane knowledge that can surface in the most incredible of coincidences.

For instance, Biswas used a particular patterned fabric in *Housewive with Steakknives* (1985–6) in the garment for the Kali figure, the female principle, the destroyer and protective mother goddess (incidentally, the best-known and least understood Hindu deity) (Fig. 9.1). To Biswas's amazement she discovered later, on a visit to India, that the patterned fabric was identical to a cloth with the same eye/mouth motif used to ceremonially drape Kali images in Bengal.

Through the subtleties and nuances of such quests, artists of dual heritage feel they can find their true voice; one that has both integrity and dynamism. But this carefully worked out interior process is not often reflected in the audience response. There is frequently a reductionist reaction where the work is viewed in a way that is too rigidly culture-specific. The manner in which these artists are presented and interpreted, therefore, becomes crucial.

Bradford has, arguably, one of the most comprehensive collections of contemporary South Asian art in Britain today. It gives the collection its radical edge. It will also be of increasing historical importance, capturing as it does a society in transition. Artists such as Nina Edge, Zarina Bhimji, Chila Kumari Burman and Saleem Arif, to name but a few, depict notions of empowerment and reclaiming. They also restate their centrality within the British mainstream. In the light of this Bradford has to be especially careful that the inclusion of artists from the disenfranchised Asian community does not imply their exclusion from the British mainstream.

The collection spans a period of approximately sixty years, from the 1930s to the present day. The earliest work is by one of India's great moderns, the enigmatic Amrita Sher-Gil (1913–41), who died tragically young at the age of twenty-eight. The collection itself was launched in 1986 with the purchase of fifteen works by Jamini Roy (1887–1972) another of India's important modern artists. Balraj Khanna, Bhupen Khakhar, Anish Kapoor, Dhruva

Figure 9.1 Sutapa Biswas, *Housewife with Steakknives* (1985–6), mixed media on paper. Purchased with support from the V&A/MGC Purchase Grant Fund. (Bradford Art Galleries and Museums, photograph: Richard Littlewood.)

Mistry, Arpana Caur and Salima Hashmi are some of the other notable names also represented.

The collection was given added powerful momentum with the award of an Arts Council Lottery grant in 1995. This enabled Bradford to commission works from over thirty artists and makers such as Perminder Kaur, Zarina Bhimji and Avtarjeet Dhanjal. The collection, on the whole, embodies a variety of narratives and concerns. It also reveals an impressive breadth and range of talent.

Perhaps one of the most profound works to emerge from the commissioning process is Salima Hashmi's pictographic map of the Indo-Pakistan subcontinent entitled *Zones of Dreams* (Fig. 9.2). The map, although accurate in its representation of particular locations, has a mythic presence. Hashmi presents the subcontinent as a geographic entity, a vast landmass hemmed in by oceanic waters on three sides and bordered by the majestic Himalayan mountain range on the fourth. Flashes of history, myth, fable and dream irradiate the magical realms. Wondrous fish and an Iranian *schmurgh* or phoenix move in the seas. Sri Lanka, described as 'a gem about to surface from the ocean' in an ancient Indian text, is submerged in emerald waters. Bangladesh, too often portrayed as hapless victim to the furies of nature, is symbolised by sprays of lotus

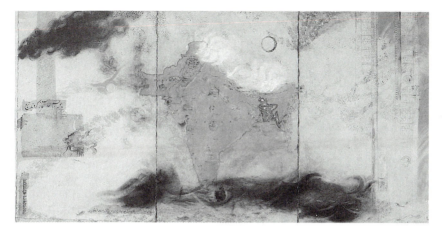

Figure 9.2 Salima Hashmi, *Zones of Dreams* (1996), mixed media on paper. Commissioned from the proceeds of the National Lottery through the Arts Council of England. (Bradford Art Galleries and Museums, photograph: Richard Littlewood.)

blossom, in memory of a land that was celebrated in poetry and song as beauteous and plentiful.

The map is like a palimpsest, simultaneously occupying different time-frames, with faint traces of history, fleeting man-made marks, echoes of past triumphs, tragedies and fragments of ancient text. A column of *kalamkari* motifs,[2] to the right, refers to the indirect, pre-colonial textile trade between India and other regions including the West. Agra, the location of the fabulous Taj Mahal is marked with a barely discernible *jali* pattern,[3] while Lucknow has a delicate paisley in celebration of the 'white on white' *chikkan kari* embroidery for which the region is famed. But although Kashmir slumbers discreetly under a blanket of snow (the artist has a sly sense of humour) the dogs of war can still be heard. Ominous clouds billow across the horizon, hinting at a social and political turbulence that threatens to overwhelm entire regions. *Zones of Dreams* is haunted by a sense of precarious balance and imminent danger.

Placed in the introductory passage to the gallery, *Zones of Dreams* heralds the entry into strange and rich magic kingdoms. Separated by a pilaster, and moving from the macrocosm to the microcosm, is *Bolton Junction: Eccleshill* (1956), a view of Bradford by David Hockney. The map and the Bradford view are visual and symbolic articulations of the journey from the Indo-Pakistan subcontinent to Bradford that so many Asians in the city undertook.

Calligraphy in the Muslim world

Although most cultures value good handwriting, it is not as central to other religious and aesthetic sensibilities as it is to Islam. The Chinese and the Japanese have a highly evolved calligraphic tradition, but in sheer ubiquity and range of materials used, they appear to be outstripped by the Muslims. The reasons for the seemingly exaggerated importance given to this art are numerous. The use of the Arabic script throughout most of the Muslim world helped forge a distinct and powerful Islamic identity. Turkey, where Arabic was officially replaced by English in 1928 by Ataturk, and Bangladesh where Bengali is used, are perhaps the only two major Islamic countries that do not use the Arabic script. Calligraphy is also revered because it is the instrument through which the Quran, the teachings of Allah as revealed to his Messenger the Prophet Mohammed (AD 571–632) was recorded.

Arabic, which is written from right to left, has twenty-eight consonantal letters to the alphabet, and long and short vowels are indicated by dots and brief strokes above and below the letters. The immense elasticity and flexibility of the script, where letters can extend into infinity or be compressed to a minute speck, lent itself to a wide variety of media outside the traditional papyrus, parchment, vellum and, after the eighth century, paper.

Calligraphy was used on stone and marble monuments, incised on gemstones like carnelian, inscribed on gold, silver and other metals, woven, printed or embroidered onto textiles, carved on wood or painted onto ceramics. The floral, entwined, arabesque and geometric patterns that characterise so much of the art in the Muslim world, were the perfect foil for Arabic calligraphy, either incorporating it into the main design or embellishing it. And, completely in keeping with the holistic nature of Islam, where the sacred and the secular sustain each other, calligraphy was firmly linked with various developments within Muslim culture, its art (both figurative and non-figurative), its sciences and its mysticism.

The small Bradford collection of calligraphy from the Muslim world was started in 1990 as a response to the enthusiasm generated by an exhibition on *Islamic Calligraphy* in 1987. Although the emphasis has been on calligraphy from the Indo-Pakistan subcontinent, the collection, as it continues to grow, is intended to be pan-Islamic and includes items from Syria, Turkey, Iran and Egypt. To reflect the versatile nature of this art-form, the collection covers a range of media – textiles, gemstones, silver, bronze, brass, wood and paper.

The calligrapher working within this seemingly circumscribed art-form, where creativity is often further fuelled by devotion, often manages to produce work of great liveliness, ingenuity and variety. The life and movement conveyed by a nineteenth-century zoomorphic horse from Iran demonstrates this perfectly. A pair of nineteenth-century walnut chairs from Syria are conceived as much as pieces of sculpture as furniture. The imagination unleashed whether in the perfect, minutely inscribed, luminous carnelians from Deccani India or in the dramatic ivory, green and gold nineteenth-century Turkish wall hanging can be both bold and conceptual.

This collection, however, is meant to be a living one. Contemporary artists from Muslim cultures use calligraphy in a far more radical or modernist manner than did their forebears. Calligraphy in the hands of a distinguished artist like

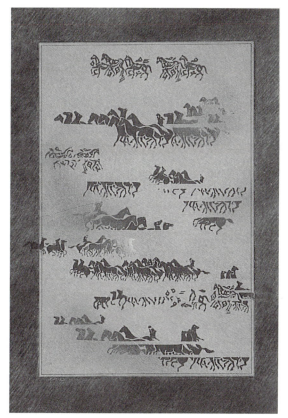

Figure 9.3 Shahzia Sikander, *Riding the Written* (1993), mixed media on paper. Purchased with support from the V&A/MGC Purchase Grant Fund. (Bradford Art Galleries and Museums, photograph: Richard Littlewood.)

Shirazeh Houshiary, becomes a tool for detachment, transcendence and the expression of alienation as revealed in *What I tell about me I tell about you*, a piece inspired by the Sufi poetry of Rumi. The endlessly repeated alphabetic characters in graphite on paper are as much gestural mark making or yantric forms as calligraphy. Shahzia Sikander uses calligraphy in fractured forms in *Riding the Written* (1993) where ornate script metamorphoses into truncated horses, symbolising historical events of disjunction and chaos (Fig. 9.3). Both artists would emphatically not see themselves as calligraphers and would perhaps fit more comfortably within the category of contemporary art in the collection. None the less, their works clearly indicate that calligraphy can still be used in unexpected ways today to plumb unsuspected depths.

Gold and silver

In 1988, in collaboration with the Victoria and Albert Museum, an exhibition of Indian jewellery was organised at Cartwright Hall. *A Golden Treasury:*

Jewellery from the Indian Subcontinent drew large audiences and it was obvious that, as with *Islamic Calligraphy*, gold and silver touched a deep chord within particular communities.

For Hindus, in particular, gold has mystical connotations. Lakshmi, the goddess of wealth, is supposed to dwell in gold. This accounts for the taboo among a large number of Hindus about wearing gold below the hip, since having one's legs or feet touch Lakshmi is disrespectful. Gold has always exercised a mysterious influence on the human mind throughout the world. A metal whose main functional use is ornamentation depends on the peculiarities of human psychology for its continuing power. The Indian subcontinent is reportedly the largest single repository of privately owned gold. But is not just the quantity of gold held that makes it so impressive. It is also the quality and range of the craftsmanship. Temple and other ritual, talismanic and marriage jewellery offer some of the best examples of the goldsmith's marvellous artistry.

Indian sculpture from Bhahrut, Sanchi and Amravati, for instance, approximately dating from the second century BC to the third century AD gives a clear idea of the extravagance and splendour of early Indian jewellery. Indeed, this is true of later Indian sculpture as well. Even today, the design vocabulary of gold and silversmiths is rich and complex. They appear to draw from a lexicon similar to that of the textile weaver and the surface decorator. Again, as with textiles, there is an immense number of regional styles. Indian jewellery can be sculptural, abstract, organic or geometric in form. The deities of the Hindu pantheon, sacred birds and beasts, mystic symbols and the fruit, flowers and other vegetal forms of the natural world are just a few examples of the motifs used in gold and silver.

The gold collection of Bradford Art Galleries and Museums is still at an early stage. Two notable new additions are a gold spiral pendant attributed to the Satavahana period (first century BC–third century AD) gifted to Bradford by the National Art Collections Fund and an early nineteenth-century plaque depicting a scene from the Ramayana from Karnataka on permanent loan from a private lender. The granulation and pierced work technique employed in these two pieces is quite superb.

Other items in the collection include a *navratna* (nine gem) pendant or a celestial talisman from Rajasthan. The nine gems when arranged in a certain order are meant to represent the nine planets. *Navratna* is popular throughout India, in the form of pendants, rings or entire suites. The collection also includes filigreed jewellery and *talis* or South Indian marriage pendants. These small gold lozenges have images and symbols of various gods from the Hindu pantheon such as Vishnu, Shiva and Parvati. The London-based contemporary jeweller Mah Rana, when commissioned to produce jewellery for Bradford, took the marriage pendants as her source of thematic inspiration. The result were two sardonically witty pieces, a pendant gold stem with sharp thorns entitled *I Never Promised You A Rose Garden* and two gold rings encased in fragile, pretty gold cages made of second-hand melted down wedding rings called *His 'n' Hers*.

The collection also includes gold on glass work from Partabgarh. In the nineteenth century, the towns of Partabgarh in Southern Rajasthan and Indore and Rutlam in Madhya Pradesh were well known for their method of producing jewellery of chased gold on coloured glass. The goldsmiths made ornaments of plaques of glass, gold and silver, the glass being poured into gold or silver frames with a delicate tracery of fine gold pressed onto the glass before it hardened. The motifs were taken equally from Hindu mythology or from Mughal courtly hunting scenes.[4] The skill required, for instance, to produce the extremely fine detailing of the peacock on the lid of one of the artefacts gives an indication of the talent of these goldsmiths.

Silver or *chandi* is a popular semi-precious metal. Because it is less expensive than gold, the craftsmen have felt free to be more experimental. Pieces can be massive and boldly executed and can cover a much wider range of domestic artefacts. The works in the Bradford collection, almost exclusively from twentieth-century Gujarat and Rajasthan, fall into two categories: ritual and secular silver. The silver is characterised by the use of minimal technology, coupled with an extraordinarily skilled craftsmanship.

The nature and function of the secular pieces provide interesting insights into the manners and customs of a more traditional and leisurely way of life for the prosperous classes in the past. The very names of the objects have a musical cadence: *attardan, dhoopdan, surmadan, sindhurdan, paandan, surahis, gulabpash* and *pichkari*. The more prosaic English translation reads as perfume, incense, kohl, vermilion and betel leaf containers, water or wine flagons and rose and coloured water sprinklers.

The *Kama Sutra* of Vatsyayana is usually too narrowly viewed as a manual for erotic instruction. It is also a minutely detailed documentary on social codes of dress and behaviour in order to live life at a sensuous, pleasurable and cultured level. A great deal of attention was paid to *shringar* or personal adornment and toilette by both men and women. In the chapter on 'The Life of a Citizen' the householder is enjoined to:

> wash his teeth, apply a limited quantity of ointments and perfumes to his body, put some ornaments on his person and collyrium on his eyelids and below his eyes, colour his lips and look at himself in the glass. Having then eaten betel leaves and other things to give fragrance to the mouth. . . . He should bathe daily, [and] anoint his body with oil every other day.[5]

The silver described earlier would obviously have been the perfect accoutrement for the process of *shringar*. They are not *objets de luxe*, for they all had a demonstrable practical use. *Shringar* in art is usually depicted in the form of a woman looking into a mirror. Fittingly, the collection includes a beautifully patterned silver vanity box with a mirror within.

The ritual silver includes an elaborately repoussé-work mobile silver shrine (Fig. 9.4), and other paraphernalia meant for *puja* or worship. Lamps, bell, conch shell and *panch pathar* (vessels for the sacramental five foods of yoghurt,

Figure 9.4 Mobile shrine. Early twentieth century, silver with repoussé and ringmatting work, Rajasthan. (Bradford Art Galleries and Museums, photograph: Richard Littlewood.)

honey, milk, ghee and sugar). Even the sacred objects have a personal, domestic quality to them. *Pujas* are conducted in either the temple or the home.

Textiles

For thousands of years Indian textiles, particularly muslins and cottons, were a major source of revenue for the subcontinent. The processes of spinning, dyeing and weaving had obviously been perfected to a high art. Indian myths often use weaving as a metaphor for the creation of the universe. The *sutra* or spun thread was the foundation, while the *sutradhara* or holder of the thread was the architect or creator of the universe.

The Industrial Revolution kept pace with the expansion of British power in India. The mechanised technology of spinning looms meant that textiles could be produced far more quickly and cheaply, albeit with a loss of quality. By 1911, so completely were the roles of buyer and seller reversed that India now bought ten per cent of Britain's exports, more than any other country in the world. The main import was cotton piece goods. Yet for a long time Indian textiles were still the standard against which British textiles were measured. There was a concerted attempt to equal or surpass, through the machine-made muslins of Europe, the legendary muslins of Dacca.

Gandhi launched the *swadeshi* movement during the struggle for Indian Independence. Indians were successfully exhorted to boycott foreign goods, particularly textiles. After Independence in 1947, Weavers' Service Centres were set up in key textile capitals all over India. They guarantee weavers a certain amount of commissioned work and supply them with equipment and designs. Surprisingly, such official support has not had a totally stultifying effect on the creativity of the textile craftsmen. But survival for the average weaver can still be a desperate and precarious business.

The Bradford collections demonstrate the weaving and surface decoration techniques in which the Indian textile worker excels and which keep millions of them in work. Brocades, *ikats*, tie-dyes, block prints and embroidered textiles are some of the areas represented. The embroidered dowry textiles of Gujarat and Rajasthan, the *phulkaris* produced mainly by Sikh women of Eastern Punjab and *saris* from all over India are three of the main areas within this collection.

The embroidery tradition of *phulkaris* (flowering work) and *baghs* (gardens) is a folk art practised with a high degree of sophistication by the women of Punjab. The date of its origin is unclear since early literature and records kept of brides' trousseaux make no mention of it. The Bradford collection consists of textiles made exclusively by Sikh embroiderers although Hindus and Muslims also practised this art. *Phulkari* is embroidery in which the, usually, earth-coloured, coarse, homespun background material is clearly visible through the stitches. The pattern is formed through an ingenious combination of thread and material. *Bagh*, which is a more elaborate form of *phulkari*, is completely covered in embroidery so that the background cloth is not visible. The embroidery appears to be the woven cloth itself.

The Bradford *sari* collection which, apart from five nineteenth-century brocades (Fig. 9.5), were all woven in the early 1990s, is proof that the Indian textile worker can still produce the most exquisite of textiles. A classic costume, one size, in high fashion for nearly two thousand years, sounds inconceivable. However, in the case of the 'unstitched but highly structured' *sari*, as Jyotindra Jain once described it, it is true. The continued popularity of the *sari* as an every day and fashion garment provides those superb master craftsmen of India, the textile workers, with a definite and continuing source of patronage in an otherwise fickle world.

Most of the *saris* in the collection are a marvel of technique and design. Perhaps one of the most unusual is an *ikat* with a coded love poem woven onto the groundcloth. No mean feat when the intricate, labour intensive nature of the *ikat* weaving technique is taken into consideration. Sections of the warp and weft threads are resist-dyed to a programmed pattern. When woven the patterning on the warp and weft mesh to produce complex designs.

Textile artists from Britain are an important part of this collection and inject an individual rather than collective creativity into the works. Fahmida Shah's sumptuous hand-painted silk is influenced by the sculptural architecture of

Figure 9.5 Wedding sari. Nineteenth century, brocaded silk. Purchased with support from the V&A/MGC Purchase Grant Fund. (Bradford Art Galleries and Museums, photograph: Richard Littlewood.)

Cartwright Hall, although abstracted out of all recognition. There is an element of light-heartedness with the introduction of mask-like faces inspired by an exhibition on heavy metal – *Sound and Fury* at Cartwright Hall in 1995. Natt's textile, *Mughal*, operates as a counterbalance. Formal rows of *Mughal* architectural shapes above and below a band of jade green skyline, immediately recall the pageantry of that glorious and oppressive world when art and architecture enjoyed a troubled golden age. Nina Edge's batik textile entitled *Zero*, on the other hand, is an extremely subtle, understated, philosophical piece. Shades of indigo blue are punctuated by a slightly irregular circle of dots, some of which are shot through by spermatozoa-type shapes. This circle surrounds a minute white central disc. The piece reflects on the nature and depiction of zero in acknowledgement of the Indian thinkers who had refined this concept by the sixth century AD. Zero had many names and many symbols including the dot before it arrived at the shape as we now know it. Zero embraces infinity, it is nothing and it is everything, and this is what Edge celebrates in this work.

This seemingly disparate grouping is united by a common cultural heritage, although interpreted very differently by different artists. United also by its aesthetic quality, it is intended to serve the collective needs, primarily, of the Bradford public. It will be displayed in a gallery without a name, in line with other numbered but unnamed galleries on the same floor, and is dedicated to the people of Bradford, the craftsmen of the Indo-Pakistan subcontinent and all the artists of this country.

Notes

1   *Islamic Calligraphy* (1987); *A Golden Treasury: Jewellery from the Indian subcontinent* (1988); *Earthen Shades: The Paintings of Shanti Panchal* (1989); *Manuscript Paintings from the Ramayana* (1989); *Warm and Rich and Fearless: An Exhibition of Sikh Art* (1991); *101 Saris from India* (1992); *Living Wood: South Indian Sculpture* (1992); *Worlds Beyond: Death and the Afterlife in Art* (1993); and *An Intelligent Rebellion: Women Artists of Pakistan* (1994).
2   Kalamkari literally translated from Persian means 'penwork'. It refers to painted and printed textiles. A pen or brush is used to apply mordants or liquid wax as a resist onto textiles. This technique particularly flourishes in Machlipatnam in Andhra Pradesh.
3   Jali is an architectural term where marble, stone or wood is pierced in arabesque or geometric patterns.
4   I am indebted to Susan Stronge of the Indian and South East Asian Collection of the Victoria and Albert Museum for information on gold and glass work.
5   Vatsyayana, *The Kama Sutra* (trans. R. Burton and F. F. Arbuthnot) Hertfordshire: Wordsworth Editions, 1995: 30.

Part 2
Ethnography and colonial objects

10

Perspectives on Hinemihi
A Maori meeting house
Eilean Hooper-Greenhill

Hinemihi at dawn

On 9 June 1995, at 4.45 am in the grounds of Clandon Park, a National Trust property near Guildford, Surrey, England, a remarkable ceremony took place. The ceremony was *Te whakatapua o nga taonga whakairo o Hinemihi ki Ingarangi* (*the blessing of carvings for Hinemihi meeting house in England*). As the sun rose, the New Zealand High Commissioner, Lord Onslow (whose family originally owned Clandon Park) and the National Trust Administrator were challenged by three warriors wearing flax kilts from Ngati Hinemihi.[1] *Kuia* (women elders) from Ngati Hinemihi called the participants in the ceremony on to the *marae* (the area in front of the meeting house) in front of Hinemihi, and *kuia* from the London Maori Club, Ngati Ranana, responded.

The Maori[2] ceremony, with its traditional rituals of encounter – *wero* (challenge), *karanga* (welcome calling), *tangi-nohonga* (moment of silence for the dead) and the *whaikorero* (speeches) was followed by the *karakia whakatapua* (blessing service) and the *hongi* (greetings) (Salmond 1974; Walker 1990: 73–4; Te Awekotuku 1991:108). The *koruru* (carved head) of Hinemihi o te Ao Tawhito (Hinemihi of the Old World) herself presided over the proceedings from the gable of the house.

In the speeches that formed part of this ceremony, certain cultural discontinuities became visible. It was not merely the Maori language which rendered the proceedings incomprehensible to the British participants. Profound differences in world view became apparent in the language used and in the way in which Hinemihi was named and presented. National Trust officers talked about the privilege of 'looking after these works of art in our care', but Hare Wzikingi, one of the Maori elders, spoke of the meeting house in quite other terms. First, as he strode backwards and forwards, carrying a carved walking stick (Salmond 1974:195), he referred to Hinemihi as 'she'. He addressed the house as though she were a living person, and described how all those Maori living in or visiting England should come to see her when they were sad or homesick, as though they were visiting a homely and nurturing elderly female relative. He further described Hinemihi as a 'symbol of unity', comparing her with the eye of the needle, through which white, red and black cotton might pass to achieve unity. In an explicit reference to white, black and hybrid peoples, he positioned Hinemihi, the ancestor figure, as a point of conjuncture for the past, the present and the future. The emotional and spiritual feeling in the words, and the sense that the carved *whare nui*[3] (meeting house) is the bearer of these feelings, is in stark contrast to the understanding of the meeting house as merely 'a work of art'. In Western terms, a work of art is inanimate, and does not have overtly personalised relationships back to the past or forward into the future. A work of art is to be cared for: it does not care for us.

In Western art history it is not seen as necessary to talk to paintings or sculptures in order to discover and elaborate their meanings. Maori, on the other hand, believe that their *taonga* (treasures) must be surrounded by *korero* (talk) that both clothes them and that enables the treasures to mediate the links between the living and the dead (Mead 1984a: 21–3). The histories of the *taonga* stay alive when it takes part in gatherings and ceremonies and is talked over, touched and wept over (Salmond 1984: 137). Each treasure is understood as a fixed point in a tribal network of names, histories and relationships. Individual objects 'belonged to particular ancestors, were passed down particular descent lines, held their own stories and were exchanged on memorable occasions' (Salmond 1984: 118). Meeting houses, which are particularly rich and elaborate treasures, are understood as spiritually animate mediators between the past and the present, which through genealogies and narratives locate individual subjects within tribal networks, and which give them 'a place to stand' in the present day (Salmond 1975).

The disjunctions and dislocations in the perceptions of Hinemihi are rooted in different ways of knowing. Nietzsche pointed out that 'the perspective decides the character of the "appearance"' (Nietzsche 1986: 207). Hinemihi would look different according to the epistemological perspective from which the house was being viewed, and the values that were being used to construct that view. Each perspective would in effect produce a different object.

We can see Hinemihi as an accumulation of discourses, both a stimulus and a repository of knowledge, gazes, behaviours and feelings. An analysis of some elements of the story of Hinemihi will reveal some of the connections, encounters, supports, blockages, strategies and plays of force that at any given moment have produced an interpretation of Hinemihi that has seemed, at least to those producing the interpretation, self-evident and obvious. As Nietzsche indicated, our values determine our understanding of things. There are no limits to the ways in which the world can be interpreted, but control and imposition of meaning offers control over the world: 'To impose upon becoming the character of being – that is the supreme will to power' (Nietzsche 1986: 213). Thus the different interpretations of Hinemihi expose a broader field of conflict – the struggle to impose and maintain truth and rationality, an unequal struggle that has taken place over the last two hundred years within the framework of colonialism.

The meanings of Hinemihi have been construed in a range of contexts, varying in both time and space. This chapter offers a partial reconstruction of some of those meanings. However, it must be acknowledged that no story can ever be told completely; there is always more to say. It is particularly difficult to try to construct a story distant from the writer in time, space and culture. The story as I tell it here is shaped by those aspects that I have found interesting and significant, by what I have been able to find out by reading and talking to other people who are also intrigued by or involved with Hinemihi.[4] I write from a feminist, post-colonial perspective: other people telling this story will tell a different one.

A version of the story can be told first in outline. The only complete Maori building in Britain, Hinemihi o te Ao Tawhito stands in the grounds of Clandon Park, Surrey. Built in Te Wairoa, near Rotorua, New Zealand, in the late 1870s, and opened in 1881, the *whare nui* acted as a religious and community centre, and was used for tourist entertainment, until it was all but buried in the cataclysmic eruption of Mount Tarawera on 10 June 1886. Left for derelict, in 1892 Hinemihi was bought for £50 by Lord Onslow, the retiring Governor of New Zealand, and shipped to his family home at Clandon. Here the *whare nui* was used as a boathouse, and remained largely neglected until the 1970s, when it was moved nearer to the house and given a preliminary restoration by the National Trust, which had meanwhile taken over responsibility for Clandon Park.

The meeting house at Clandon Park was verified as Hinemihi[5] by Bernie Kernot in 1976 (Kernot 1975; 1976). Kernot commented in detail on the house and its assembly. He pointed out that the house had been foreshortened, that the doorway, window and front wall, and their associated carvings were missing, and that it had been incorrectly assembled. He also pointed out that it was one of the oldest meeting houses still standing and one of the few to survive from the 1880s. He credited the Onslow family for having preserved the house, while many in New Zealand had been allowed to rot out of existence. He suggested that Hinemihi should be returned to New Zealand as a national monument, to be returned to its original owners as guardians on behalf of the nation. In the event of this not being possible, he suggested that every effort be made to have the house restored under the direction of a qualified carver (Kernot 1975).

In 1992, John Marsh, director of the New Zealand Maori Arts and Crafts Institute at Rotorua, and a direct descendant of the creators of Hinemihi, visited Clandon Park. The front wall, with door and window, had been rebuilt. A plan emerged to reproduce the lost carvings around the door and the window. New carvings were made in Rotorua, by descendants of the original carvers, to complement the old ones newly rediscovered in the attic of Clandon Park. Members of Ngati Hinemihi attached the new and old carvings, and refurbished and repositioned other parts of the house immediately prior to the Blessings Ceremony on 9 June 1995. This was exactly 110 years since the night of the cataclysmic eruption.

Building Hinemihi at Te Wairoa

Hinemihi o te Ao Tawhito stands in the garden at Clandon Park, the home of the Onslow family, now owned by the National Trust. In comparison with the grand eighteenth-century structure of Clandon, Hinemihi is tiny. With her English thatched roof, she does indeed have the air of a quaint summer house, standing quietly under a large tree (Fig. 10.1).

In Britain, most people are unfamiliar with New Zealand history, and do not know how to read or decode a Maori meeting house. In New Zealand, however, efforts have been made for a long time to try to grasp the complex meanings of these structures.

The basic design for what is now known as the Maori meeting house can be traced back to the twelfth century (Neich 1994: 92). However, the fully carved meeting house is a nineteenth-century development, emerging in response to the advent of Europeans. By the end of the nineteenth century, the meeting house and its *marae* formed an integral part of the village, surrounded by the houses of the people of the village.

Meeting houses are large rectangular buildings (perhaps 80 ft long by 30 ft wide by 20 ft high (24 × 9 × 6 m), with a gabled roof and a front porch. The size and degree of decoration of the meeting house makes a statement about

Figure 10.1 Hinemihi stands under a large oak tree on National Trust Property at Clandon Park, Surrey. (Photograph: Eilean Hooper-Greenhill.)

the *mana*[6] of its tribe or owner group. (Salmond 1975: 36). The *marae* is an ambiguous expression which refers both to the secular ceremonial ground in front of the meeting house, which is the centre of political debate and oratory, and to the complete complex within which stand both the meeting house and the ceremonial courtyard (sometimes called the *marae atea*).

Hinemihi was built in the late 1870s at Te Wairoa, near Rotorua in the North Island of New Zealand, commissioned and paid for by Chief Aporo Te Wharekaniwha of the Tuhourangi tribe and formally opened in 1881. One of the forces behind the need for a new large building was the development of the tourist trade. During the 1870s, although transport was still difficult, an early form of tourism was beginning in the area around Rotorua. Visitors came to see the Pink and White Terraces, Otukapuarangi and Te Tarata, of Lake Rotomanhana, close to Mount Tarawera. Te Wairoa emerged as the location from which the trips to the Hot Lakes began, and Ngati Tuhourangi quickly devised a controlled and carefully managed itinerary, over which they held the monopoly. That Ngati Tuhourangi was extremely successful in developing and managing the tourist industry can be seen from the story that Hinemihi became known as 'Hinemihi of the golden eyes', the *paua* (abalone shell) eyes of the carvings being replaced by golden sovereigns (Waaka 1986).

In addition to the commercial use of the meeting house, Hinemihi would have represented a strong statement of tribal prestige. Wero Taroi of Ngati Tarawhai was Hinemihi's main carver (Kernot 1976; Kernot 1984: 150). The carving of Hinemihi was one of Taroi's last commissions as he died in the early 1880s. In many ways, Taroi set the pattern for most subsequent Te Arawa carving, and for what ultimately would be seen as a national 'Maori' style, to be taught at the Rotorua School of Maori Arts in the 1930s and 1940s (Neich 1990a: 355).

Hinemihi was built in a region of the North Island that had been the home of carvers since earliest times. Ngati Tarawhai had managed to maintain their own distinctive carving style since pre-European days, although since the 1830s this had developed in a hybrid social context, an amalgam of old Maori, missionary and trader-settler culture (Neich 1983). The carvings produced in this mixed environment were seen, even in the 1880s, as 'traditionally Maori', and therefore conformed well to growing stereotypes which the carving style itself partly created.

However, Ngati Tarawhai carving did indeed reach back to old Maori culture. In choosing Wero Taroi as the main carver, Chief Aporo was employing the best and the most experienced person, a man whose personal experience linked him to the old ways. Hinemihi was built at a time when pre-contact times were still almost tangible. Wero Taroi's teachers would have used stone adzes and greenstone blades for their work, although he himself used metal tools; Taroi's earliest carvings were on war canoes, cultural artefacts that linked to early history and that symbolically expressed much of Maori mythology. In carving Hinemihi as one of his last pieces of work, in a political and economic context that fostered traditional ways of working, it is likely that Wero Taroi for both psychological and political reasons, would use ideas that looked to the past rather than to the future.

Interpreting cosmologies and histories

The meeting house as a cultural phenomenon consists of a complex assemblage of several different art forms. These include carving (*whakairo rakau*), painting (*kowhaiwhai*), woven latticework (*tukutuku*), and architecture (*te whaihanga*). Both men and women are employed in the production of the house: men produce the carvings, and women the latticework *tukutuku* panels that fill the spaces between the carvings; both men and women (at least latterly) work on the *kowhaiwhai* scroll paintings on the rafters and ridgepole. The various elements of the house are intended to work together as an assemblage, in combination with cosmologies, mythologies, genealogies and ritualised customs and modes of behaviour (Mead 1984b: 71; Jackson 1972: 41).

Maori cosmology is rich and complex and provides mythic descriptions and explanations which are still of relevance today (Mead 1984a). Embodied in the architectural structure and in the carved, painted and woven elements of the meeting house are creation and other myths, relationships of the past to the present, and behaviour codes that place the subject today in cosmological space. The cosmological models are not static, however, but have changed as other explanations, particularly those of Christianity, have been incorporated. As cosmological models have inflected, so the representation in the meeting house has changed (Kernot 1983; Neich 1994: 123; Amoano, Tupene and Neich 1984). Genealogies are represented through the carved figures, which are placed in the large verandah that acts as a porch, and inside, against the walls and as parts of the posts that hold up the ridgepole. The choice of which of the tribal ancestors to include in the representational scheme depends on the communicative function of the house and other contingent criteria (Neich 1994: 130–1). The meeting house can be seen as an exemplary 'site of interpretation'. Kernot has demonstrated how Christian elements have been built into a new meeting house, Ngatokowaru II, in such a way that speakers wishing to emphasise the Christian influence in the past of the owner-group may refer to the carvings of Bishop Hadfield and Father Delach, and the *tukutuku* panels that 'quote' those in a Christian church. However, those speakers who feel that it is the old Maori aspects of the past that are important refer to the large range of ancestor figures that are presented in a more stereotypically Maori way (Kernot 1983: 191–2). In any structure as complex as Ngatokowaru II, or Hinemihi, there are many systems of meaning operating. A multidimensional and fluid semiotic space is opened up which is constituted through the articulations of the fixed material elements with the social and psychological characteristics of the subjects, both speakers and listeners, within the space (O'Toole 1994: 229–30). Meaning becomes a dynamic process rather than a fixed value.

Interpretation is particularly significant in relation to Maori culture. Maori cosmology and genealogy is known through speech; it is oral rather than inscribed in fixed texts. It is learnt largely through listening on the *marae* (Windsor, personal communication, 1995), as books on tribal histories are still rare. Speaking on the *marae* is seen as creative: thus discourses are not static, but may be construed to suit the specific context or the specific speaker. Different aspects of the kin group history may be presented according to the occasion, or to relate to the specific participants. Emphases will vary, and some aspects of a story may be omitted according to who is listening (Te Awekotuku 1991: 110). Different versions of the myths through which the Maori world is represented may be offered. The distinctions between verifiable events, the fictive and the symbolic, become blurred (Binney 1984: 346).

An oral tradition leads to an understanding of history as a recitation of the deeds of the ancestors. The art of genealogy (*whakapapa*), a major aspect of Maori scholarship, enables the linking of people living in the present with immediate ancestors, tribal and sub-tribal founders, migrating ancestors, culture heroes, and ultimately Rangi and Papa, the sky-father and earth-mother, and with their offspring, the departmental gods. With colonisation, *whakapapa* became of political importance. Land claims, both in the nineteenth century and today, depend crucially on the ability to demonstrate continuity of ownership (Neich 1994: 123). Ngati Hinemihi are able, as are many Maori people, to cite their ancestors back through Hinemihi to Ngatoroirangi, Priest of the Te Arawa canoe.[7] Thus John Marsh identifies Hinemihi by showing her lineage back to Ngatoroirangi and forward to himself (Marsh, personal communication to Allan Gallop, 1992).

In analysing traditional meeting houses as models of the old Maori cosmos, it is important to bear in mind the extent to which both the cosmic model and the meeting house structure can be modified as contingent elements change. However, as Neich suggests, in some areas of more conservative groups, such as Te Arawa, the traditional meeting house model may be retained as an ideological commitment to a traditionalist cosmology (Neich 1994: 123). Hinemihi, even today, has many of the characteristics of older meeting houses, and it is certainly possible that Hinemihi can be seen as embodying a model of the traditional Maori cosmos.

Maori cosmology locates the past time to the front, where what is known can be seen, while the unknown future lies behind and is invisible. The past is therefore continually in view and the present changes into the past as each event occurs (Mead 1984b: 64; Kernot 1983: 192). Maori walk backwards into the future, looking forwards for support and direction from the past, which becomes more distinct the further away it is from the present. This reversal of the Western way of explaining historical times combines with an understanding of history as the experience of ancestors. Overlooking the past from the present means that the ancestors are always to be seen, and as a result they are spoken of as continually present.

The cosmic model is produced through the arrangement of internal and external forms within the meeting house, but the placing of the house in the landscape is also symbolically significant. The meeting house and the *marae* complex in the landscape can be seen as a cultural ordering of spatial relationships. Where possible, the meeting house faces elements of openness such as the sea or open landscape, and is backed by elements of enclosure, such as hills, mountains and bush. The open and closed elements in terms of Maori cosmology relate to the distinction between Aotearoa/New Zealand and Hawaiki. Hawaiki is the mythical homeland across the ocean, the source of food, fish, greenstone and mana, from whence the Maori came in the ancestral migration canoes, and to which the dead return (Neich 1994: 1230). New Zealand is the site of present existence, for many Maori a site of continuing struggle (Walker 1990). Whether by accident or design, Hinemihi today stands looking outwards over the open space of the garden of Clandon, with her rear to dense bushes. Away to the right of the house is the lake. In this sense, Hinemihi complies with the cosmic system, but of course, the ground on which she stands is alien ground in a foreign country. She also faces the large eighteenth-century Clandon against which she is dwarfed.

The front of a meeting house is the more public and important part, with the rear of the house being reserved as a more private domain. The front of the house and the *marae atea* is sometimes related to the world of life and light, while the rear of the house is related to the world of darkness and death. When visiting Hinemihi at Clandon, the back of the house is not at all in evidence from the outside. The visitor approaches the meeting house by walking along one of the side walls of Clandon, and then across a large lawn to arrive at Hinemihi immediately in front of the porch, on what is effectively the '*marae*'. The *amo*, or carved side-posts[8] standing to each side of the porch, act as frames for the experience of looking at the six ancestor figures and the other carvings in the verandah itself.

The names of the six ancestor figures are no longer known, although at the time when Hinemihi was constructed, these were recorded. A copy of a telegram is in existence in the New Zealand Archives from Roger Dansey, Postmaster at Rotorua, dated 23 January 1892, which says:

> I got the natives to write down the names of each carved figure with a short written statement connected with each individual represented, and numbered respectively to correspond with numbers in red paint at the back of each carving which I am translating into English; together with a short history of the whare [house] for his Excellency's information, accompanied by a small plan shewing [*sic*] the proper position of each numbered carving should it be intended to re-erect the 'whare' in England.

Unfortunately this vital document has not been traced, although the carvings are indeed numbered on the back.[9]

The verandah, or porch, of a meeting house acts as a threshold zone, not only between outside and inside, but as a transition from tribal, economic and social collaboration to family solidarity and group identity on the inside (Neich 1994: 127). The doorway is a threshold or boundary between the world of myth embodied in the actual space of the porch and the metaphorical space of the landscape, and the world of history represented within the house (Amoano, Tupene and Neich 1984: 34; Jackson 1972). The carved lintel (*pare*) above the door has a special meaning relating to the move both from the past to the present and from the external social world to the internal family framework. In traditional meeting houses, the carved figures were frequently female, and in the older carvings, explicit reference was made to the genitals. The *pare* is acknowledged as the most *tapu* carving in the house, through the dense symbolism of sexual womanhood, which is associated with both birth and death, with the lifting of *tapu* (Amoano, Tupene and Neich 1984: 34; Jackson 1972: 51–3), and with vitality and pleasure (Te Awekotuku 1991: 62). The function of the carved female figures is the mediation of the dangerous liminal zone between the world inside and the world outside.

Within Hinemihi there are several carvings. There are no carvings on the wall panels, as is the case with many meeting houses, but at the front and the back of the house there are carved posts, and also a carved centre post. The post at the back represents a well-known Te Arawa ancestor, Tutanekai, who is recognised because he holds a flute. The story of Tutanekai is a romance: Tutanekai, a young man of low birth and Hinemoa, a young woman of high birth, loved each other, but could not come together owing to their difference in social status. Each night Tutanekai, who lived on an island, played his flute to express his love and his sadness. Hinemoa could hear the flute, and eventually swam across the lake to claim Tutanekai as her husband (Stafford 1967: 84–7).

The identities of the figures carved on the central and front posts are not known. An unusual small relief panel, which shows an embracing couple, is currently hanging in the house (Fig. 10.2). Climbing down the central post is a carved lizard, 'Kataore', a pet 'taniwha', or monster, of Hinemihi, which has become a symbolic guardian (*kaitiaki*) of her descendants (Gallop 1995a) (Fig. 10.3).

Traditionally the internal space of meeting houses is divided in terms of groupings of associated major binary divisions: thus the side of the house with the window (the left side of the house when inside looking out) is called the important side – *tapu* – and associated with men, visitors, and death. The side with the door – called the unimportant side – is *noa* and is associated with women, hosts and the living (Neich 1994: 128). The internal spatial arrangements combine with the external orientations of front and back, left and right, to construct a space that relates the past to the present, men to women, hosts to visitors, and which regulates behaviours accordingly (Salmond 1978; Neich 1994: 121–60).

In addition to the cosmological model, meeting houses also serve as genealogical models. The whole house represents the founding ancestor of the group owning the house. The structure of the house represents the body of the ancestor. The carved *koruru* at the apex of the barge boards is her face, the bargeboards are her arms, the ridgepole (*tahu*) is her backbone, supported on the central post, the *poutokomanawa* (heart-supporting post), the rafters (*heke*) are her ribs and the interior her belly (*po*) or bosom. People entering the house are entering the body of the ancestor, or the heart of the tribe. Thus, when the kin group assemble in

Figure 10.2 Unusual small carved panel showing an embracing couple. (Photograph: Eilean Hooper-Greenhill.)

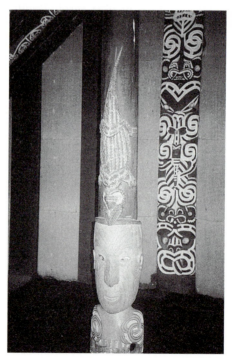

Figure 10.3 Inside Hinemihi. A carved lizard climbs down the central post, while Tutanekai plays his flute behind. The identity of the male figure below the lizard is not known. (Photograph: Eilean Hooper-Greenhill.)

the house, the living and dead are joined together in the belly of their ancestor (Salmond 1984: 120; Newton 1994: 280).

In Hinemihi meeting house, Hinemihi, the founding ancestor, is represented on the gable, at the end of the ridgepole. In the porch, *heke* carry the lines of genealogical descent from Hinemihi to what are probably succeeding ancestors. Inside the house, the *katoare* refers to Hinemihi, and Tutanekai is one of the culture heroes of Te Arawa. Thus, even after complete dismantling, and reconstruction at least twice in an alien environment, Hinemihi is still susceptible to a reading based on some aspects of the traditional Maori cosmos, and although much of the significance has been lost, is still capable of acting as a genealogical model for Ngati Hinemihi.

Disruption, displacement and new frameworks for meaning

The webs of cosmic, economic and social relations that structured the meanings of Hinemihi in New Zealand in the late nineteenth century were abruptly shattered on the night of 10 June 1886 when Mount Tarawera erupted, destroying the Pink and White Terraces and wrecking Te Wairoa (Andrews 1986; Rotorua Museum 1986).

The New Zealand Chronicle for June carried a number of reports and accounts of the event including the following from H. Dunbar Johnston in Rotorua, dated and timed at 10 June, 8.52 am:

> We are in the midst of a terrible convulsion of nature. The extinct volcanic cones of Tarawera and Rutahia burst into activity between one o'clock and two o'clock this morning. There was a constant succession of earthquakes until about five o'clock, and the thunder and lightening became almost incessant, and still continues.
>
> *(New Zealand Chronicle*, 1886: 1)

At Te Wairoa the village was effectively demolished. Approximately one hundred and fifty people died. The newspaper reports concentrate on named European families, the Haszard family (Mr Haszard was the schoolmaster) and the McRae family (Mr McRae owned the hotel). Ngati Tuhourangi are unnamed numbers – '80 Maoris have perished' (*New Zealand Chronicle*, 1886: 2). As one of the largest structures in the village, many people ran to Hinemihi when the mud and ashes began to fall. Exact numbers of people who sheltered in the meeting house are not known, but there were possibly as many as 50, including one of the carvers of Hinemihi, Tene Waitere, and his wife and daughter (Gallop 1995a; Neich 1990a: 74). The long tourist benches were used to prop up the roof to stop it falling in (Gallop 1994: 23).

For the small Maori community at Te Wairoa, the results of the eruption were catastrophic; many people were killed, and tribal lands and livelihood were devastated. Survivors from Te Wairoa moved to other locations nearby. Hinemihi was left, her walls buried up to the roof in mud, ash and debris from the eruption. Five years later Hinemihi was bought by William Hillier, 4th Earl of Onslow, who wanted a souvenir to remind him of his four years as colonial governor. A meeting house is convenient for collection and removal as it is possible to dismantle the carvings and transport them as individual pieces. Hinemihi was purchased from Mika Aporo, the son of Chief Aporo Wharek-aniwha, the original commissioner of the building. A deed of sale authorising the removal hangs in the 'Maori Room' at Clandon Park. This is signed by Mika Aporo and M. Jean Camille Malfrey, a French engineer who acted as agent for Lord Onslow:

> Received from Mr. C. Malfrey pen cheque the sum of twenty-five pounds stg (£25. 0. 0) being half the purchase money for 23 pieces of Maori carving originally part of the native meeting house at Te Wairoa and known as 'Te Hinemihi' which I have this day sold to his excellency the Governor Lord Onslow for the sum of fifty pounds sterling (£50.0.0) the balance of which is £25.0.0 together with the sum of three pounds stg (£3.0.0) for the carriage from Rotorua to Oxford to be paid to me upon my producing a receipt from the Railway Station Master at Oxford to the effect that the said 23 pieces of carving have been duly delivered to him for transmission by rail to Auckland.
>
> Signed Mika Aporo

Mika Aporo's signature is date-stamped 21/1/92 and witnessed by the interpreter:

> Witness to signature of Mika Aporo after the above had been duly interpreted to him in the Maori language and he duly appearing to understand the meaning and purpose of the same also witness to the payment pen cheque to Mika Aporo the sum of £25.0.0.
>
> (Name illegible)
> Licensed Interpreter

Written sideways next to the initial statement is a statement confirming that the balance of £25.0.0 was also received, on 29 January 1892.

Hinemihi was dismantled, loaded on to a bullock-cart and driven to a railway station at Oxford (Putaruru). From here the journey continued by rail to Auckland, and then by steamer to England, where Hinemihi was erected, without the front wall, by the lake at Clandon Park, to serve as a boat house. Later, she was moved to the present site, where an initial restoration in the late 1970s involved the installation of a damp course, cleaning and repainting of the carvings, and the re-erection of the front wall.

How can we assess the structures of meaning that enmesh Hinemihi today? Although it is clear that it would be impossible fully to explore all possible meanings, two broad perspectives from which meaning may be constructed can be identified. They are, first, the framework of ownership, second, that of the present day Maori community in Britain.

Hinemihi is owned by the National Trust. This is unequivocal. The bill of sale demonstrates that the meeting house was alienated by purchase (Kernot 1976), and it is clear the National Trust will not be relinquishing this control. Requests for repatriation in the 1980s were met with a firm refusal. The structures of ownership are fully visible in the press reports of the Blessings Ceremony: 'The National Trust handed over the property for around two hours to allow nearly 30 members of Ngari [*sic*] Hinemihi, from Rotorua, to present a gift of new wooden carvings to decorate Hinemihi' (*Surrey Advertiser*, 23 June 1995). The architectural and territorial configuration at Clandon within which Hinemihi is placed clearly reveals the legal framework of ownership. This also establishes a cultural and interpretative hegemony within which dominant meanings will be formulated and against which alternative meanings of Hinemihi must be constructed.

Hinemihi stands in the garden of Clandon, the Onslow family residence, which was built in the early 1730s for the second Lord Onslow by the Venetian architect Giacomo Leoni. A baroque eighteenth-century English stately home, the house has huge ornate formal rooms, a state bedroom, and a two-storied marble hall with elaborate plasterwork and large chimneypieces by Rysbrack. Both the hall ceiling and the marble chimneypieces are decorated with mythological scenes. The hall ceiling is covered with relief stucco-work scrolls, drapes and garlands, much of which is supported by cherubs and 'slaves', based on Michelangelo's slaves in the Sistine Chapel. The central relief represents Hercules and Omphale and the four figures in the corners are Virtues (National Trust 1994: 10).

These references place Clandon firmly within the cultural frame of European humanism, which legitimates itself by referring to ancient Greek and Roman culture. Over the west and east doors of the marble hall are busts of 'negroes', apparently alluding to the Jamaican origins of part of the Onslow fortunes (National Trust 1994: 10). The references to slavery in the ancient world, and to the African slave trade of the modern world, included as incidental motifs in a decorative scheme intended to demonstrate the cultured sophistication of the Onslow family, show all too clearly how European humanism constructed its values through exploitation and exclusion. These references are probably invisible to many who visit Clandon Park. The huge and elaborate structure of Clandon dominates and subsumes Hinemihi, reducing the complexity of a different world of myth and history to a small, somewhat exotic, garden collectable; a curiosity along with the grotto, parterre and Dutch garden.

The cultural significance of Hinemihi is invisible to visitors to Clandon, unless they bring some relevant knowledge with them. There is little information in guidebooks, interpretative panels or labels. The powerful and coherent materialisation of Western culture in the architecture of the house, the layout of the gardens and park, the furnishings and decorative schemes of the house interior form a complete and compelling narrative, with little to disturb its ideological hegemony. However, Hinemihi maintains a material existence in the garden, and as long as this remains the case, the possibilities for the activation of alternative frameworks of meaning exist.

An alternative perspective from which Hinemihi might be viewed is that of Maori people within Britain in the late twentieth century. On 2 July 1995, a performance by Ngati Ranana, the London Maori Club, was held in front of Hinemihi. As a preliminary to the programme of songs and dances, a Master of Ceremonies greeted the audience and the ancestors we brought with us. During the concert, he discussed *whakapapa* (genealogy) and pointed out its importance to the audience.

These and other references to Maori cultural pathways constitute a way of enacting Maori identity, and through enactment both creating and confirming it. Butler has shown how gender is not given, but is constructed through performative acts (Butler 1990: 139–41), and in much the same way, it is possible to see how cultural identity can be established and reinforced through the repetition of performative acts. In taking part in the posture dances, and in singing, Maori people in Britain act out their Maoriness and reaffirm their relationships to their past. Maori treasures are kept alive, and their histories reactivated by being touched, wept over and talked over and by taking part in gatherings and ceremonies (Salmond 1984: 137). Carrying out the two ceremonies with Hinemihi in the summer of 1995 reactivated her cultural significance for some of the Maori participants, and in so doing reinforced their Maori identity. The participants considered it important to bring the young Maori people in Britain to the *marae* at Hinemihi in order to pass on the cultural tradition. The use of the Maori language was crucial: although English was necessary in order to earn a living, the Maori language expressed identity, gave a cultural grounding, and was needed to describe the past (Windsor, personal communication, 1995).

Salmond suggests that it is possible that Maori people in New Zealand today are able to hold two worlds within their mental schemas – a European way of explaining the world that holds good in European situations, while in Maori situations the Maori cosmology, with its different concepts of time and space, comes into stronger focus (Salmond 1975: 211). This 'ethnography of occasions' (Salmond 1975: 212), a hybrid construction of the self, is one way of establishing personal identities within a complex post-colonial world.

John Marsh, visiting Hinemihi from New Zealand in 1992, explained how the carvings 'tell a story of our past'; he was afraid that his reactions to reading the carvings might have been too much to control. However, he found he was unable to read many of them (*Surrey Advertiser* 1992). This openness to spiritual and emotional experience, and readiness to respond to the genealogical stories is one manifestation of an 'ethnography of occasions'. Some members of the group with John Marsh did indeed feel links back to their relatives sheltering in Hinemihi during the eruption: 'We could hear their screams and feel their pain. They are still present in Hinemihi' (Gallop 1992).

During the nineteenth century in New Zealand, the meeting house was a place for oratory, for affirming genealogies and for confirming relationships and affinities. In post-contact New Zealand all of these became intimately bound up with questions of land ownership. As Maori land was taken out of their ownership, and as Europeans laid out towns which developed into the twentieth century, the *marae* and meeting house became a special place for specifically Maori activities, a special space to celebrate and confirm Maori identity, a symbolic place which visibly stated the survival of Maoritanga (Maoriness) (Salmond 1975: 81). For Maori people in Britain today, Hinemihi still has the potential to perform this function.

Notes

1 Ngati Hinemihi is the tribe of Hinemihi, who are descended from Hinemihi, an important woman from the Te Arawa tribal confederation (Stafford 1967: 66).
2 Within the traditional ritual structure, this ceremony was designed and organised according to the wishes of Ngati Hinemihi and Ngati Tuhourangi, incorporating their unique tribal history and genealogy and reflecting the nature of the importance of the occasion.
3 There are a range of names for meeting houses: *whare puni* (sleeping house), *whare whakairo* (carved house), *whare nui* (big house), *whare hui* (meeting house) and *whare runanga* (council house) (Salmond 1975: 35).
4 I am particularly grateful to Allan Gallop, and also Rachel Windsor and Peter Gathercole.
5 With reference to official correspondence in the New Zealand National Archives (Maori Affairs department Files, General Index 1891–2, MA–3–19), which also establishes that the house was alienated by purchase.
6 '*Mana*' is a complex concept that is summarised by 'power', 'prestige' and 'authority', but which also has a supernatural dimension (Lewis and Forman 1982: 47; Newton 1994: 289).
7 Maori history describes how the first people arrived in New Zealand in large canoes from Hawaiki, the mythical homeland (Walker 1990: 37–9, 45–62).
8 One of the *amo* is reproduced on each side of the old New Zealand pound note.
9 I am grateful to Alan Gallop for this information and for sending me a copy of the telegram.

11

Maori vision and the imperialist gaze

Ngapine Allen

The Treaty of Waitangi, our founding document, was signed by Queen Victoria's representatives and 'the New Zealanders', as Maori people were then identified, on 6 February 1840 (Angas 1847a). As a nation founded on colonialism, mainstream New Zealand – the Anglo-European Treaty partner – has struggled with various concepts of its own, and of Maori, identity. Recent attempts on the part of intellectuals to forge a bi-cultural identity have been largely resisted as a result of entrenched racism. This chapter re-explores the territory of identity. The establishment of Maori art history in New Zealand universities reflects an awareness, inevitable if belated, that New Zealand is a South Pacific nation. Ten years ago no one would have accepted that Maori could have an art history.

This account focuses on the travels and wanderings of a Maori house of great significance, presently displayed in one of New Zealand's major museums and at the centre of a restitution claim. The history of this Maori house, I shall argue, demonstrates a need for greater awareness of cultural difference. The intention here is a bi-cultural approach which acknowledges that museums are places where several cultures live together. Addressing this issue, and actively involving the people directly concerned with a sacred and revered cultural treasure, facilitates cultural exchange.

My visit to the Victoria and Albert Museum in 1995 marked one of those life-time, momentous personal experiences, made more poignant by the fact that a Maori house had once graced its courtyard. Ancestors immortalised in the carvings of the house were present. To follow in their *waewae tapu* – sacred footsteps – is a spiritual journey.

To introduce the ancestors, their world and worldview, is not a journey into the past, but into the future. The Maori term *i mua* describes the concept that the past is in the future. The Maori reality is that what you can see is in front of you. Hence, ancestors, viewed from a Western historical perspective as 'behind', are, from a Maori perspective, 'in front'. Conversely, the future is something you cannot see and is therefore behind you. To conceptualise this, you must reverse your notion of history. Contrary to expectations, however, the cosmological view as recorded within a Maori conceptualisation is a close corollary to the Christian Creation in Western historical accounts. In the beginning there was nothing, then there was darkness and then light. We can better understand the significance of Maori myth when we recall that George Grey (Governor of New Zealand from 1845-53 and 1861-8) attempted to record all Maori myths and superstitions – a bank of information that could potentially be used to cripple the infrastructure of Maori society (Grey 1971).

The Maori ancestral house encapsulates the spiritual world; indeed, every ancestral house is imbued with cosmological history. This was true of the house which was brought to the South Kensington Museum in the nineteenth century and the house as it survives today. Built upon the land with the sky and heavens arching above, the house metaphorically symbolises the primal parents *Ranginui* (the Sky Father), and *Papatuanuku* (the Earth Mother), their close embrace in the realm of *Te Po* (the dark and not so dark period) which followed *Te Kore* (the nothing but not the nothing) and their separation – the cause of light and enlightenment. This relationship is manifested within the physical structure of the dwelling: the supporting timbers reaching skyward evoke the male component, the insulating fibrous materials, the female element.

It is a moving experience to approach an ancestral house. Imagine a person on hands and knees with their face directly towards you, a very humble position. The house is structurally positioned with the bargeboards as arms and the two large posts on either side as legs. The front of the house is the face with an eye, the window, and mouth, the doorway, always open to welcome you inside. The gable mask is connected to the ridgepole, the backbone of the ancestor's body. From there the ribs connect to the sideposts, *poupou* and the named ancestors carry their bloodlines to these *poupou* who are named, and define the powerful allegiances (Harrison 1990).

The house which came to London in 1882, Mataatua, was named after a *waka* (canoe). As Harrison explains,

> Physically and symbolically the house can be likened to an upturned canoe and parts of it to parts of the human body. The backbone of the ancestor and its parallel is the keel of the canoe. Similarly, the *heke* (rafters) inside the house are the ribs of the ancestor which are mirrored by the thwarts of the canoe, the ends of which bear the family marks and symbols of rights to occupancy, as are the ancestral pillars in a meeting house.
>
> (Harrison 1990: 24)

Built in 1874, the house was named to evoke a powerful symbol for the people. The *mana* (prestige) of the house was measured by the named ancestors associated with it. These are all the descendants of the Awa peoples who were of the Mataatua canoe, who peopled the whole Bay of Plenty seaboard. My own great grandmother was born at the northern end and was a direct descendent of Te Rangihouhiri of the Ngaiterangi and one of the ancestors carved for the house. This house signified a powerful alliance binding the kinship ties of the Mataatua Confederation of tribes, cementing over old inter-tribal conflicts, vital in the period following the Land Wars (1860–72) and ensuing confiscations. The Mataatua Confederation sought redress and, in naming the house Mataatua, the people could establish their rights to occupancy and territory in the Land Courts that the new European regime had established.

A new house is always an important undertaking, but this house in particular reflected the urgency of the times. Mataatua was built as a meeting house to facilitate large gatherings and the occasion of the opening was organised as a show of solidarity. The government and tribes recognised the significance of this occasion as a vehicle for land negotiations; it continued for three days from 7–9 March 1875. The Minister of Native Affairs, Donald McLean, was present with the magistrate and agents (Mead 1990: 38–45). Every tribe was anxious as to where the confiscation lines would be drawn. Although the circumstances were demoralising, the descriptions recorded in the local press show the remarkable resilience of the chiefs.

My great-grandmother's grand uncle was the renowned Ngati Maniapoto, warrior chief and a key negotiator in the aftermath of the Land Wars. He was delayed in attending the opening and arrived shortly afterwards. He was invited with a government agent, whose task was to closely monitor tribal activity. The agent's own account reads:

> Monday, the 17th, (1875) the party moved on to Whakatane . . . after going through the ceremony of first entering the house, they took possession as the guests. Tukehu stood up and welcomed the guests ending with a song. Hori Kawakura (the Ngati Awa host) said, 'Welcome Maniapoto to your house Mataatua, the house that has been built for you and the Governor. You showed yourself obstinate when in the bush, never the less you are here at last. I have touched you with my greenstone (charmed him to Whakatane)' . . . A Waikato chief, Tukorehu, replied to the speeches and then Rewi spoke on his own behalf.
>
> (Mead 1990: 47)

The Under-Secretary for the Native Department was H. T. Clarke. From his remarks, it seems that the *kaupapa* (reason) for the house being built – to indicate peace – was accepted:

> Thanks for your welcome. I have nothing to talk about. I cannot help looking round the house of Ngati Awa. I was here when the house was opened. Some of the people had appealed to the hills of Whakatane to know if the house had been built for evil or good and the echo replied good.
>
> (Mead 1990: 47)

In 1990, the Ngati Awa, after two recorded requests in 1920 and 1983 for the repatriation of their *taonga* (treasure), compiled a report on the House of Representatives to present to the Waitangi Claims Tribunal. They claimed that the house was a living community house and remained so until it was rudely dismantled by Captain Preece in 1878 in an amazing exhibition of pakeha [a person of predominantly European descent] ignorance of Maori custom on the one hand and arrogance on the other to even think of asking a community to give up its premier tribal structure to be taken overseas to show off the might of the British Empire. Such a request would not be tolerated today.

(Ngati Awa 1990: 47–8)

The authors of the 1990 report asked 'Why did the chiefs agree in the face of internal opposition? What benefits did they expect would come to Ngati Awa? Were they scared of the Government?' (Ngati Awa 1990: 47-8). As the report assumes that the Crown understands the Maori background to these claims and questions, I will examine them further.

My great grandmother, Pera Te Rangihou-McMillan, was a young girl at the time. Tutored by the *tohunga* (priest), she became an authority on *whakapapa* (genealogy) and history of our Ngaiterangi tribe. The full extent of Maori deprivation began with the arrival of Europeans in our land. While the truth is often unpalatable, where it concerns colonisation it is particularly important to correct the historical record. We should recall, also, that descriptions of events by past observers are affected by their prejudices.

From a Maori viewpoint, as Herewini Ngata observes, the colonisation process began with the establishment of missions which invited further immigration. An immediate consequence was the importation of a variety of infectious diseases – from syphilis and gonorrhoea to tuberculosis and typhoid – causing the decimation of the Maori population by as much as 60 per cent by 1850 and leading, eventually, to 'dispossession, depopulation, despondency, desperation and depression' (Ngata 1994: 4–6). Suppression by the established central Parliament of Maori attempts at self-determination resulted in the Land Wars of the 1860s and the acquisition by the government of millions of acres of Maori territory (which continued well into this century). In just ten years from 1890 to 1900, three million acres of land had been purchased by the government and only three million acres remained in Maori ownership; that is, 10 per cent of the original land mass (Ngata 1994). The dispossession continued. Many people were landless. The photographs of Maoris from this period document the appalling social conditions and there is no doubt that the people did fear further repercussions of colonisation.

Mataatua had been built in 1874 through the will to survive, but the deprivation and fear of further dispossession effectively meant that Mataatua stood little chance if the government wished to bargain for it. The fear and deprivation was, I believe, the reason that it was possible for the government to seize treasures such as Mataatua. Mataatua was not the only house to be appropriated. There were others.

In the social climate of the late nineteenth century, the acquisition of a fully carved house was the supreme trophy. Maori pleas to retain such *taonga* are recorded in government records and we can identify that superiority and manipulation by government agents to extract treasures from war-defeated, impoverished people from the tenor of the reports. Such imperialistic force – the removal of treasures in an attempt to reinforce the imperial centre – is one of the key issues in the study of colonialism in relation to material culture and art. While England represented the imperial centre in relation to New Zealand, the relatively new local regime was itself a centre of imperialism.

Another Maori house, described as 'our greatest national treasure' (Mead 1984c), was built in 1842, by the master carver, Raharuhi Rukupo and, as Rongowhakaata *kaumatua* (elder) Darcy Ria, observes: 'There is still much to be learnt [as to] how the government acquired the house in 1867' (Ria 1994). According to official accounts, the carver protested against the removal of his house and sought its return by leading the petition: 'Our very valuable house had been taken away, without pretext, by the government: we did not consent to its removal . . . I did not consent, but told him [J. C. Richmond, then Minister of Native Affairs] no, it is for the people to consider' (Ria 1994). Richmond's written reply stated that he had asked to take the house at 'a large meeting of three or four hundred people and there was only one objection'. He had asked the magistrate 'to gain consent' which appears to have been achieved with a payment of one hundred pounds. But discontent continued and in 1878, after a second petition, the Native Affairs Committee voted a final payment of three hundred pounds.[1]

Mataatua, the house taken in 1878, was built by the master carver Apanui Te Hamaiwaho and his son Wepiha Apanui who both protested at its removal. Wepiha Apanui conducted major consultations between Maori and *pakeha* (Mane-Wheoki 1993). A consistent feature of both cases is the master carver's protest and the silence of the majority, which suggests that they were being manipulated. Equally telling in the official accounts is the absence of arguments actually used by the agents to procure the houses. In the case of Apanui's house, Captain George Preece, the government agent, recommended that the 'Government should give the Ngati Awas some substantial recognition in return for same' (Mane-Wheoki 1993: 63). In both cases there also appeared to be some haste on the part of the agents to arrange the removal without having settled payment.

Internal opposition arose when the house was dismantled. In uniquely Maori fashion, the women threatened to conceal the ridgepole to protect the backbone and sacredness of the ancestors. But the house was despatched and sent to the Sydney Exhibition in 1879. Later, the government, keen to tour its exhibit, would claim that the house had been given to Queen Victoria. But there is no instrument of transfer on file. When the house was removed, the government acted ruthlessly and Ngati Awa justifiably felt duped. Apanui then asked for three thousand pounds which was refused (Mead 1990: 64).

Until this point in the history of Mataatua house, we can conclude that the *tapu* (sacredness), and *mana* (sovereignty) of the house had been eroded. As the indignation of the Ngati Awa Report suggests, the separation of the house from the *whenua* (land) was a desecration. The house is obviously more than a house of ancestors of Mataatua, the foundation of the tribe; it also symbolised the tribal *waka* (social cohesion) and the cosmological connections. From this point the history of Mataatua becomes paradigmatic of the many desecrations of our houses in captivity and of *mana Maori* (the prestige of Maori people in general).

South Kensington Museum's accession number[2] for a Maori House given for a proposed Colonial and Ethnographic Museum was 422–1882, a 'desirable feature in the Colonial Annexe' according to the New Zealand Colonial Secretary (Mane-Wheoki 1993: 63). The house was shipped from the periphery to the centre of the empire and arrived, via Sydney and Melbourne, in England in 1882. Following the example set by the Sydney exhibitors the house was displayed in the quadrangle of the South Kensington Museum with the interior carvings turned outwards, maximising the exhibit's spectator appeal, but removing it from its own context. The house, as evidence of the reach of the Empire and juxtaposed with the exhibits ranging from machines to fine arts, was codified as a subordinated 'other'. A year later, the house was installed in the grounds of the museum and the carvings and weavings returned to positions in which they were originally conceived. Four years later, when new work was being carried out at the museum, the house was dismantled and stored.

New Zealanders had by this time embraced the idea of exhibitions with fervour, the first taking place in Dunedin from January to May 1865. In 1885, the first government-funded exhibition was held in Wellington, and Dunedin followed again with an exhibition which opened in November 1889 and closed in April 1890. This second exhibition heralded New Zealand's official celebration of fifty years of British rule and included a 'Maori and South Seas' exhibit.

The example of the American extravaganzas of the turn of the century provided the next New Zealand exhibition with its most ambitious plans to date, and the government, spurred towards creating a South Pacific Empire, invested in research into the latest developments in World's Fairs and International Exhibitions. In 1904 T. E. Donne, General Manager of the Government Department of Tourist and Health Resorts, was in America as New Zealand's Commissioner to the Louisiana Purchase Exposition. The New Zealand Premier who promoted the International Exhibition vigorously from 1903 requested in the Governor General's opening address to parliament, that Donne should

> visit various centres in the United States and proceed to London and Europe in order to arouse interest amongst manufacturers and others in the colony's forthcoming exhibition. Donne spent some time in London [and] other large British centres . . . the Liege International Exhibition and various European cities.
>
> (Cowan 1910: 23)

On his return to New Zealand he was appointed one of the Vice Presidents of the next exhibition.

In the International Exhibition at Christchurch in 1906 indigenous people were paraded as exhibits before the Anglo-Saxon populace – evidence of a little Pacific empire. The 1906 exhibition marked the beginning of the New Zealand search for a local and international identity. The New Zealand and South Pacific Exhibition in 1925, again in Dunedin, likewise featured an ethnographic section. The scale of the Maori section was the largest ever attempted.

At the turn of the century, Maori art was subjected to colonial disciplines: interested *pakeha* (Europeans), such as Augustus Hamilton, were instrumental in creating what has been described as a 'veiled orthodoxy' (Neich 1983) in the art of carving whereby the carvers under patronage were persuaded to carve 'classical art' contrary to their own unique traditions, thus creating a hybrid art of pseudo-carving. In the wider picture these *pakeha* had effectively set about creating a pseudo-culture on a much larger scale and with full government support.

Perhaps the most influential person in the archetypal colonial representation of the Arawa carvers and their work was the government minister, T. E. Donne. He had his own Maori House – a small standard model built for tourists, named 'Te Wharepuni a Maui', measuring 20 ft by 12 ft – which he lent for the exhibition. Similar to the 'Rauru' house now in Hamburg, Germany, this house was built by Neke Kapua to suit the *pakeha* experts as, according to the Official Record, 'a more perfect specimen' (Cowan 1910: 323).

The most remarkable feature of this *pa* (fortified settlement) was the unprecedented method by which the *pakeha* (European) experts fabricated it themselves; structures were built from borrowed carvings from museums, from various tribes and new carvings were commissioned; they even invited living exhibits – real Maori people! In this final act, the exhibition creators excelled themselves for, in Pacific empire fashion, the crowning achievement was the copy-book charade imported from the European and American imperial displays of parading Pacific Island peoples. In this show of empire, the containment of Maori culture was complete as the visiting islanders were welcomed on the place deemed appropriate, the *marae* (sacred ground in front of the meeting house). By the time the exhibition came to a close in 1907, New Zealand had gained dominion status.

In London, proposals for the Mataatua house to be exhibited at the Festival of the Empire in 1911 did not come to fruition because a whole village and Maggie Papakura's concert party from Rotorua, went to England to represent New Zealand instead. This tokenistic display of Maori culture was extremely popular and provided an exoticism central to the kind of racial ideology underpinning imperial displays.

In the first two decades of this century, a number of people from New Zealand were aware of Mataatua house in the South Kensington Museum and a wounded soldier on leave in England, Harry Devenish Skinner, pursued ways of repatriating the house to New Zealand. The Maori House remained in storage until 1924, however, when it was displayed at the British Empire Exhibition at Wembley.

It was returned to New Zealand for the New Zealand and South Seas Exhibition in Dunedin in 1925. After this exhibition, the house was removed to the Otago Museum and restoration was undertaken. Skinner, who had studied at the University of Cambridge Museum of Archaeology and Ethnology during the First World War, was appointed curator of the Otago University Museum in 1919, and under his direction the house was reconstructed according to museum orthodoxy. It was shortened and contained within its stone walls, thus losing its connection to Ranginui and Papatuanuku and thereby ceasing to represent its unique tribal origins; other tribal carvings replaced those that had suffered over the years of travel and display. Although the replacement carvings belonged to an East Coast house and established an older tribal connection, this was merely coincidental and it is doubtful whether this was a primary concern for the curator. The house Mataatua remains at the bottom of the South Island, on exhibition to this day. For one hundred and sixteen years, the Ngati Awa people have mourned the loss of their sacred treasure; yet there remains the possibility for one more, hopefully final, journey for Mataatua, to its tribal lands at Whakatane in the North Island.

The exhibition, *Te Maori: Treasures from New Zealand*, which toured cities in North America between 1984 and 1985, and the same exhibition retitled *Te Maori: Te Hokinga Mai: The return home*, which travelled the length of New Zealand for another two years, created significant attitudinal changes toward *taonga Maori*. The elevation of Maori carving from craft to fine art, through its display in museums such as the Metropolitan Museum of Art in New York and the awestruck reaction of American visitors to the exhibition, impressed the wider public at home. A contributing factor was the enthusiastic participation of Maori in opening rituals and forums which accompanied the exhibition. Although Mataatua was not included in the travelling exhibit, the Otago Museum was one host venue and the Ngati Awa people, disputing the museum's ownership, began negotiations for its restitution.

In 1990, Te Runanga o Ngati Awa published *Research Report No. 2, Nga Karoretanga o Mataatua Whare* (*The wanderings of the carved house Mataatua*) as part of a large claim to the Waitangi Tribunal seeking redress for land grievances. In November 1994, at Wairaka Marae in Whakatane, Ngati Awa presented their case before the Tribunal. The Otago Museum was invited to make a presentation to the Tribunal at Wairaka as well as the Crown. At the time of writing, the Waitangi Tribunal – a statutory body – is yet to evaluate the submissions and publish their recommendations. Although the Tribunal is the judiciary body handling Maori claims with the Crown, their decisions are not binding on the government and interested parties are still able to contest its decisions.

> From 'Mr Firth's visit to the King Party', *The Daily Southern Cross*, June 9, 1869, Auckland:
>
> PAENGAHURU: The land is like a stricken bird,
> whose wings are quivering on account of the pain.

151

Postscript (February 1997)

In contemporary New Zealand society, issues of ownership of cultural treasures are being handled with varying degrees of success. Carved burial chests and fully decorated *waka* (canoes) have been returned to tribes or local museums. At the time this chapter was presented as a paper at the AAH Conference in London, the Museum of New Zealand invited elders of the Rongowhakaata to Wellington to discuss the future of Rukupo's house, Te Hau ki Turanga (discussed above). The elders agreed for the house to be exhibited in the new museum which is scheduled to be opened in February, 1998.

In 1996, the Waitangi Tribunal recommended to the Crown that Mataatua be returned to Whakatane. By the end of the year, the carvings were sent to the Whakatane Museum and are safely there until Ngati Awa construct a new *marae* and reconstruct their premier house.

Notes

1   *Appendices to the Journal of the House of Representatives* G1 no. 12:12 (1878).
2   Personal communication with D. Anson, Otago Museum, 1995.

12

Gathering souls and objects
Missionary collections

Jeanne Cannizzo

'We turn our backs on the last traces of civilization, and our faces toward the centre of the Dark Continent . . . ' (Canadian Independent 1887: 66). With these words the young missionary who would become 'Canada's Livingstone' began his evangelical career in Central Africa. Walter T. Currie was to spend 25 years in Africa, sometimes travelling in what he described as the footsteps of his boyhood hero, David Livingstone (Figs 12.1 and 12.2). Born into a Toronto family already interested in the abolition of slavery, as a boy Currie read and re-read Livingstone's accounts of his journeys. Livingstone – a failure as a missionary and only partially successful as an 'explorer' and an obsessive personality – was a central figure in the imagination of late nineteenth-century Britain and the Dominions. This chapter compares the missionary projects of Livingstone and Currie, with particular reference to their interest in acquiring, and their subsequent use of, African objects.

There are many similarities between Livingstone and his disciple. Like his model, Currie was from a Non-conformist tradition, having completed a course at a Congregational Church training school in Montreal. He left for the then Portuguese colony of Angola in 1886. His vision, based on Livingstone's exhortations to an earlier generation, was to replace what he thought of as 'paganism' with Christianity, the slave trade with legitimate commerce and 'barbarous' customs with European forms of civilisation. This is not to suggest that either missionary found nothing to admire in the African societies he observed. Many of Livingstone's observations in *Missionary Travels* are relatively positive about African societies, while Reverend Currie in an undated report in 1896 or 1897, wrote to colleagues in Canada that 'Old Age here is regarded with a respect too often wanting at home and so provided for as to leave no room for homes of [the] aged and infirm. No orphan is without a guardian. Slaves are treated by their masters with more consideration than many hard working men in the home land' (Currie 1886–1910).

Currie had documented his experiences not only through letters, diaries and published accounts, but also in the form of a collection of over 900 African objects. This material reveals striking similarities with that collected by Livingstone decades earlier, but there are marked differences as well. This chapter will argue that such similarities stem, at least partly, from the colonial context

Figure 12.1 The Reverend Walter T. Currie as a young man. (From H. W. Barker, *The Story of Chiamba*, 1904.)

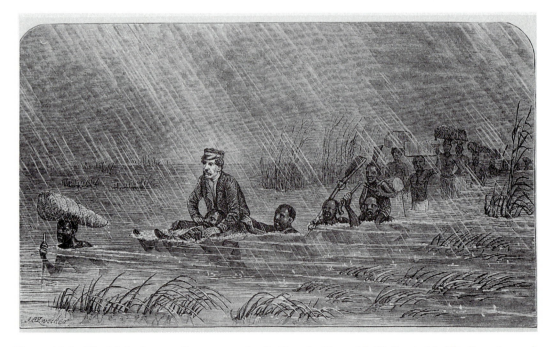

Figure 12.2 *The Main Stream Came up to Susi's Mouth.* (From H. Waller (ed.), *The Last Journals of David Livingstone*, 1874.)

in which the material was acquired. These patterns present a visible manifestation of the ideological structures and assumptions which have informed the
assemblage. The differences between the collections of Livingstone and Currie,
by contrast, are partly explained by variations in the collectors' personalities,
changing goals, conditions of travel and settlement, place and time. That is, each
collection, although grounded in an emergent or (in Currie's case, established)
colonial structure has a unique historicity and cultural specificity which will be
analysed in more detail below.

To begin with the most general similarities: if collections are forms of visual
ideology, then it comes as no surprise that Livingstone sent back physical
evidence of the horrors of slavery, the main subject of his reformist zeal. Later
missionaries, including Currie, also desperately wanted to destroy the trade in
what was sometimes called 'black ivory' and so to heal what Livingstone had
referred to as Africa's 'open sore'. In a diary entry for 10 November 1888, and
later reproduced in an evangelical magazine, Currie gives a good description of
what Livingstone called a ' slave stick' in operation.

> The young fellow's hands were tied behind his back and his neck was
> fastened in a slave-yoke – (a branch of a tree about six inches in
> diameter and seven feet long, at one end of which there is a fork formed
> by two separating boughs; one of these is placed on each of the shoul-
> ders, the neck between and fastened there by an iron pin, which passed
> in front of the throat) – in carrying which he was assisted by a man at
> the opposite end of the yoke.
>
> (Currie 1886–1910)

Just such a yoke is still in the museum at Livingstone's birthplace at Blantyre,
where it is noted that it was taken by Livingstone himself from the neck of a
slave. Currie's collection includes 'slave whips' and wooden shackles from
which he freed a child; both missionaries also sent back examples of the iron
manacles and chains with which the 'human commodities' were restrained
(illustrated in Cannizzo 1996: 140).

Livingstone had extensive contacts with Portuguese traders and administrators,
most notably during the Transversa, his journey across Africa from the Atlantic
to the Indian Ocean and later on the Zambesi expedition. He has left a description
of an early encounter:

> I was an object of curiosity to these hospitable Portuguese. They
> evidently looked upon me as an agent of the English government,
> engaged in some new movement for the suppression of slavery. They
> could not divine what a 'missionario' had to do with the latitudes and
> longitudes which I was intent on observing.
>
> (Livingstone 1857: 370)

They none the less asked him to join a feast; he went away impressed by the
'liberality with which people of colour were treated by the Portuguese' and
concluded that 'nowhere else in Africa is there so much goodwill between
Europeans and natives as here' (Livingstone 1857: 371–2).

One of Walter Currie's friends, the Portuguese traveller Silva Porto, had actually met Livingstone years earlier, although Livingstone suspected he was a slaver. It is unlikely that Currie would have agreed with Livingstone's somewhat benevolent assessment of African–Portuguese relationships. He did have Portuguese neighbours near his mission station in Angola and frequently treated them at his medical clinic. However, by July 1902 Currie's wife was writing to her mother-in-law in Canada that 'All Bihe is just ready for an uprising. They all say they are tired of rum and oppression, and the older men are ready to die rather than stand it any longer. . . . The natives say that when they have driven out the Portuguese they want us to send the King of England and America to take the country' (Currie 1886–1910). Although he denied the charges, Currie was suspected of gun running to Africans resisting Portuguese rule, as Livingstone had been by Boers in South Africa decades before.

Yet there is very little physical evidence of the relationships between either missionary and other Europeans living in Africa. Such material would undoubtedly have lacked the 'exotic' qualities which the colonial gaze projected on to items of African manufacture. As one scholar of material culture has observed, 'what was important about collecting, was not so much what could be said about or done with the specimens collected, but the way that collected material attested to the fact of having visited remote places and observed novel phenomena' (Thomas 1991: 141).

Livingstone and Currie both included natural history specimens with cultural artefacts. However, the Canadian missionary, with no particular scientific interests nor government support for investigating potential colonial enterprises, collected many fewer specimens and product samples. Such things as raw salt, spilling out of its leafy container, were saved, but often as illustrations of cultural practices – in this case salt was used as a medium of exchange by Ovimbundu traders whom Currie hoped to convert.

This is in contrast to what Livingstone and other members of the Zambesi expedition, particularly the botanist John Kirk, sent back. The latter, for example, despatched to the Royal Botanical Gardens at Kew a number of artefacts meant to demonstrate the transformation of plant material into useful objects. Baskets of various sizes, cordage, a sleeping mat and a man's cap were all included, not because of their ethnographic importance, but because they demonstrated the potential usefulness of the 'Doum palm'.

While Currie included among his items a few, partial, samples of such things as reptile skins and hippopotamus or rhinoceros hide, these cannot compare in number or scientific significance with collections from the Zambesi expedition. In reference to birds alone, Kirk obtained and preserved 193 specimens which were deposited at the Natural History Museum in London in 1860, as directed by the Foreign Office, to which he added another 39 bird skins in 1863.

Livingstone himself noted on 7 June 1859 that he had secured a set of elephant molars as requested by the biologist Richard Owen, then superintendent of natural history collections at the British Museum. Other specimens were related more directly to his visions of colonisation. Thus the Royal Museum of Scotland catalogued in 1858 'a sample of coal from Rivulet Natole above Tete, the first indication of true coal Dr Livingstone found in coming east'. He hoped that the coalfields would eventually provide fuel for the Cape and wrote extensively about their potential. However, it was not coal but the wood that Livingstone mistakenly called 'lignum vitae' (Holmes 1993: 161) that was used by the ton as fuel for most of the river travel. A sample of this most vital ingredient entered the same collection in 1863.

Beyond general similarities, there are a number of striking differences in the scale and nature of collections made by the two missionaries among their 'chosen' peoples. Currie established his base at Chisamba among the Ovimbundu, who had been active intermediaries in the slave trade in central Angola for centuries. They also controlled the rubber trade from the late-nineteenth century until its collapse in 1911, the same year the slave trade was finally ended. Livingstone may have encountered Ovimbundu among the people he called the 'Mambari' whom he referred to as 'slave dealers', mentioning their villages fortified with stockades and giving their territory as in or near 'Bihe'. Little, if any, material collected by Livingstone is identified as theirs.

The people from whom Livingstone seems to have collected most intensively are the Mang'anja, one of the most self-sufficient peoples of East Central Africa in the mid-nineteenth century (Alpers 1975: 27). It was in their highlands that Livingstone hoped to settle a few 'good Christian Scotch families' for he became convinced that it was here that his plans for the eradication of slavery and the introduction of legitimate commerce, such as the cultivation of cotton, would come to fruition.

Currie's Ovimbundu collection was the result of a long-settled residence among the same people over two and a half decades. Livingstone's Mang'anja objects were collected primarily during the Zambesi expedition when he was travelling by river with overland trips of varying lengths. Under these circumstances, it is no surprise to find that Currie's Ovimbundu objects number a few hundred while Livingstone's Mang'anja objects are only a few dozen. Given these numerical constraints, it would clearly be hard for the range of Mang'anja material culture to be as fully represented as that of the Ovimbundu. In neither case is there anything like a complete inventory of cultural materials. In any event it is impossible in a chapter of this length to discuss all the objects that either man collected.

The range and density of the Ovimbundu objects which Currie collected, now in the Royal Ontario Museum, is remarkable. For example, in reference to domestic utensils alone, he gathered together wooden ladles of various shapes and sizes, earthenware bowls and pots, gourd containers and cups, large baskets for bringing food from the fields, flat baskets for sifting ground corn and tightly-woven baskets for serving corn meal 'mush', as Currie called it.

These baskets were all made and used by women. Female converts, however, were to take up European dress, learn how to set a table with European cutlery,

157

and wash up the dishes. These changes transformed the women from producers of baskets, garden food and pottery, into consumers of pans, soaps, spoons and forks, while tying them tightly to the developing mission economy. Although describing the situation in southern Africa, the anthropologists Jean and John Comaroff suggest that 'With the colonial state ever more visible at their back, the Churchmen had a considerable impact upon African modes of production, dress and architecture' (Comaroff and Comaroff 1992: 227).

In looking at the Mang'anja materials collected by Livingstone, it is important to remember that part of the argument he had made for government support for the Zambesi expedition was that African cotton would be cheaper than the American, slave-grown, crop. The cotton plant, its cultivation and the indigenous objects associated with the production of cloth were thus an important focus of the small Mang'anja collection. Three spindles, each slightly different in design but full of cotton thread, were sent back by John Kirk. Livingstone, writing to Lord Malmesbury in 1859, suggested that 'Everyone spins and weaves cotton. Even chiefs may be seen with the spindle and bag which serves as a distaff' (Wallis 1956: 318). Thomas Baines, artist on the expedition, painted a watercolour of a spindle and bag. The division of labour, with men more active in agricultural production and manufacture than some neighbouring peoples, meant that they were less likely to be away hunting or on the trail, and thus even more amenable, in Livingstone's thinking, to providing the labour force for a European colony. A fully-rigged Mang'anja loom, with half-finished cloth, collected by Livingstone, is still to be found in the Royal Museum of Scotland. His narrative of the Zambesi trip includes an illustration of a Mang'anja man smoking a pipe with a loom behind which was considered sufficiently important to appear in two illustrations to Livingstone's *Narrative of an Expedition to the Zambesi*.

Tobacco use was widespread in Africa, and it often had medicinal and ritual, as well as recreational, functions. Some African peoples preferred taking snuff to pipesmoking and Livingstone offers a description of snuff preparation in his best-selling *Missionary Travels and Researches in South Africa*:

> The leaves are taken from the plant, and spread close to the fire, until they are quite dry and crisp; they are then put into a snuff-box, which, with a little pestle, serves the purpose of a mill to grind them into powder, it is then used as snuff.
>
> (Livingstone 1857: 318)

Like many missionaries, Livingstone and Currie disapproved of smoking and snuff-taking, but both collected examples of tobacco paraphernalia. Some of this material, in the case of Currie, may have come from converts who were encouraged to give up tobacco. In a diary entry for 10 June 1903, Mrs Currie writes of the people she called the Luchazi that

> They are the most inveterate smokers I ever met. The women and children seemed worse, if anything than the men. Some of their pipes are very curious. We have succeeded in buying a couple for curios, not for smoking.
>
> (Currie 1886–1910)

Native Mill foɪ grinding Corn.

Figure 12.3 *Native mill for grinding corn.* (From David and Charles Livingstone, *Narrative of an Expedition to the Zambesi*, 1865.)

Indeed, Currie's refusal of offers of snuff, tobacco and alcohol caused frequent comment, sometimes derision and amusement, among African observers of missionary practices. However, he did collect several Angolan pipes, some with elaborate copper or brass wire wrapping or decorated with carved figures and Ovimbundu snuffboxes made from bamboo.

The use of 'hemp' was noted with disapproval by both missionaries. Several complex Mang'anja pipes were brought back by the Livingstone expedition to the Zambesi. One, decorated with an animal figure described as a 'crocodile', was said to be for smoking cannabis. However, the collection of these pipes was unlikely to have been the result of the conversion of their owners. Rather, they were sent back, along with natural history specimens of African flora, to the Royal Botanical Gardens at Kew.

In 1903, instead of returning to North America on furlough, Currie and his wife decided to retrace some of Livingstone's journeys. He rode an ox, as Livingstone did once on his journeys, and Mrs Currie often travelled in a hammock borne by carriers who made the journey possible. As with Livingstone, Africans acted as guides and interpreters, and secured safe passage for the missionary party. The Curries were not 'eaten by cannibals' as their friends at home feared, but returned many months later, burdened with the many objects they had collected in what are now Zaire, Malawi and Zambia as well as Angola. It was on this trip that he acquired several gourd pipes and photographed a youth smoking one. He did so not in order to illustrate an ethnographic point or to document cultural practices. For him they were a very particular kind of memento, for he bought them 'from a native close to where Dr Livingstone died' (Catalogue Yearbook HAC, manuscript catalogue, Currie Collection, Royal Ontario Museum, Toronto, Canada).

Although not always appreciating each other's efforts, missionaries and the peoples they hoped to convert often shared an interest in personal grooming and hairdressing.. Livingstone indeed often exhibited his own hair, 'which is considered a curiosity in all this region. They said "Is that hair? It is the mane of a lion, and not hair at all"' (Livingstone 1857: 274).

Being properly coifed is a mark of a 'cultured' person in some African societies and it is common for hairstyles to reveal or confirm age, gender, social and marital status, and ethnicity. Livingstone's writings are full of lengthy descriptions of 'modes of wearing the hair' and sometimes illustrated with fanciful drawings.

> A circle of hair at the top of the head, eight inches or ten inches high, with an obtuse apex, bent, in some cases, a little forward, giving it somewhat the appearance of a helmet. . . . It is said that the hair of animals is added, but the sides of the cone are woven something like basket-work. The headman of this village, instead of having his brought to a point, had it prolonged into a wand, which extended a full yard from the crown of his head.
>
> (Livingstone 1857: 556)

Livingstone collected few, if any, such ornaments or hairdressing tools and devices. There is, however, a large wooden comb said to have been taken from her own hair by a chief's wife and presented to the Scottish missionary. Currie sent home to Canada scores of wooden combs and hairpins in ivory, bone, wickerwork and sometimes iron, made and worn by Ovimbundu, Lwena and Chowke. He made no distinction between ornamental and functional objects, nor did he indicate whether the hairpins were worn by men or women. A striking wooden figure of an Ovimbundu woman with an elaborate, looped hairstyle and a child on her back, was described by Currie as 'a good representation of a woman's hairdressing' (Currie 1886–1910). He may have intended such objects to suggest the basic civility of potential converts.

A comparison of objects belonging to each missionary's most important convert can also be made. The conversion of the man known as the Lion was crucial to Currie's evangelical success. Chief Kanjundu, a life-long sufferer from bronchial asthma, went to Currie's popular medical clinic after indigenous therapies provided no relief. Converted in 1898, the chief made considerable economic sacrifices. He rejected polygyny, for example, and thereby gave up a measure of prosperity based upon his wives' labour. He also freed some one hundred domestic slaves, to whom he issued documents renouncing responsibility for their welfare or any crimes they might commit. All his diviners and herbalists were driven out if they refused to convert. No beer was brewed in his capital. He was baptised in 1901, kneeling beside some of his former slaves.

All the factors on which Kanjundu based his decision to convert cannot be reconstructed at this date, but it seems fair to assume that there was a political and economic as well as a spiritual alliance between the two men. Kanjundu gained preferential credit at the mission store, the right to dispense medicine from the clinic, and access to Currie's knowledge of the European world. Kanjundu was always carefully identified by name when photographed by Currie, in what must be thought of as individual portraits (Fig. 12.4). By contrast, the unconverted were most often shown in anonymous groups. Yet there is little material in Currie's collection to represent this crucial relationship. An ensemble is described in the original catalogue entry as a 'fetish outfit belonging to an Ovimbundu chief', most probably Kanjundu, who 'embraced Christianity'. Within it is a 'charm', an animal horn wrapped in cotton cloth covered in small beads; its function was to hang from the neck of the wearer to prevent bronchitis (Fig. 12.5). Chief Kanjundu died in 1913 of bronchial pneumonia.

Livingstone retained only a few objects which belonged to his one and only convert, the Kwena chief Sechele. In a Livingstone centenary celebration in 1913, the Royal Scottish Museum, as it was then, exhibited a stool, rhinoceros horn stick, sandals, ladle and 'charms' which came from Sechele, whom the catalogue described as 'an intimate friend of Livingstone' (*A Guide to the Livingstone Centenary Exhibition* 1913). Sechele was baptised in October

Figure 12.4 Photograph of Chief Kanjundu, *c.* 1905, probably by Walter Currie. (Royal Ontario Museum.)

161

Figure 12.5 Beaded charm worn around the neck to prevent bronchitis, made of cloth, beads, horn and fibres. Part of a set offering protection against disease and misfortune which belonged to an Ovimbundu chief. Collected by Walter Currie, *c.*1901. (Royal Ontario Museum, photograph: Santiago Ku.)

1848. As part of his conversion he was required to renounce, like Kanjundu, his polygamous marriages. However, when Livingstone discovered that one of the chief's former wives was pregnant, he forbade Sechele to take communion for two years. Many Europeans seemed to view polygyny as primarily a sexual arrangement; Livingstone recognized, at least partly, the use of marriage in establishing alliances in the world of Tswana politics. Many Tswana actively opposed the imposition of monogamy; that opposition is quite understandable, for 'not only did the polygamous household form the base of the polity; it also underpinned the symbolic construction of the social world' (Comaroff and Comaroff 1991: 132).

It is also unlikely that Currie understood how profoundly disruptive some of his 'simple changes' would be. The people of Chisamba were to live, for example, in square houses of mud bricks, strung out in clearly delineated rows with carefully cultivated gardens, rather than in clusters of round, wattle-and-daub, thatched houses. These homes were to be occupied by a nuclear family, composed of a man, his wife and their children. By encouraging such living arrangements, Currie weakened alliances between lineages, discouraged the intergenerational and polygynous family, emphasised the loyalty of the couple to each other at the expense of kindred and created a different concept of privacy.

A great believer in industrial education, Currie put his faith in a carpentry shop and flour mill. He hoped these enterprises would foster not only Christianity but also legitimate commerce and what he regarded as civilised behaviour. Many new products were to result as the Ovimbundu turned out flour for bread, beds for couples to sleep in and doors to keep out their neighbours. Currie recorded this transformation by sending back to Canada a large number of shaped and sanded examples of African woods used in the carpentry shop, and cups and spoons fashioned by the carpenters who also made a small violin. There is also a hat, which Currie thought worth saving, described in the original catalogue entry as 'a grass hat made by a native in imitation of a white man's straw hat' (Catalogue Yearbook HAC).

Conversion was, of course, not only to be manifested by outer signs, but by inner transformation as well. Like many missionaries, Currie returned from the field with trophies of his victories on spiritual battlefields. Most conspicuous were the so-called 'fetishes' which his converts usually surrendered. In the African context these were objects generally used for manipulating supernatural powers or attempting to mitigate their negative effects, such as the outbreak of disease or the eruption of natural disasters. But for most missionaries these artefacts were just the harmful products of 'heathen' practices. For example, Currie's collection contains numerous animal horns still filled with beeswax and various herbal preparations, a small skin pouch labelled in Currie's hand as being 'full of poison powder to kill an enemy', and a tortoise shell used in the treatment of goitre. Others acted to prevent miscarriage and infant death and as protection against gunshot wounds. Many of these objects are marked as being 'from a native converted by Reverend Currie'.

Writing to congregations at home about the peoples of Angola, whom he was hoping to convert, Currie reminded Canadian Christians 'It is scarcely necessary to say that they are superstitious, for all ignorant people are more or less so'. Missionaries themselves sometimes remained more or less ignorant of African religious beliefs. Some did try to understand, a few quite successfully, the world-views that underpinned cultural practices like divination. Many, however, saw diviners – whom they often called 'witch doctors' – as competitors and denounced them. Livingstone was certainly irked when, in 1853, just such a diviner warned some potential carriers and companions that 'This white man is throwing you away. Your garments already smell of blood' (Livingstone 1857: 228).

A large Ovimbundu whisk of zebra or horse hair, with a handle made of a horn covered with reptile skin and studded with brass tacks, was described by Currie as the property of a 'fetish priest'. It was probably used to attract the spirit of a divination basket which then entered the body of the diviner, causing him to go into a trance. In the same collection is a diviner's headdress, consisting of a wickerwork base suffused with black feathers.

Livingstone collected few, if any, such 'fetishes'; this is at least partly explained by the fact that he was not a settled missionary like Currie and made few converts. There is also considerable variation, of course, in cultural practices and indigenous belief systems. Thus Livingstone, upon witnessing an African funeral, wrote that the mourners were 'constantly deprecating the wrath of departed souls, believing that, if they are appeased, there is no other cause of death but witchcraft, which may be averted by charms. The whole of the coloured population of Angola are sunk in these gross superstitions' (Livingstone 1857: 23).

Such a response is somewhat different from that which seems to underlie Livingstone's conversation with a Kwena (Tswana group) healer whom he called a 'rainmaker'. The annual coming of the rains for the Tswana, among whom Livingstone worked when he first arrived in southern Africa, was, in general, related to the ritual potency of their leaders but the particular skills of a ritual specialist were necessary as well (Comaroff and Comaroff 1991). Livingstone reconstructs a conversation between himself as the 'medical doctor' and the 'raindoctor'. It begins 'So you really believe that you can command the clouds? I think that can be done by God alone.' To which the 'raindoctor' replies, 'We both believe the very same thing. It is God that makes the rain, but I pray to him by means of these medicines, and the rain coming, of course it is then mine' (Livingstone 1857: 23).

Throughout this conversation Livingstone permits 'his opponent to confront him with the logical impasse of the mission. The parallel use of the title "doctor" as much as the symmetry of the actual debate, implies an ironic conviction that the contest is being waged on equal ontological grounds' (Comaroff and Comaroff 1991: 211). But it is in Currie's collection, not Livingstone's, that we find a powerfully carved sculpture in human form which Currie acquired near Lake Bangweulu, probably in 1903 (Fig. 12.6). He described it variously as being for 'rainmaking' and 'used by native doctors in divining'. There are no signs of wear on the figure, but one arm has been broken and repaired, which may explain why the carving was sold or given away rather than kept for indigenous use, as such damage may have been thought to lessen its ritual efficacy.

Besides pipes, combs and 'fetishes', Currie also seems to have been attracted to, or perhaps was given, many examples of Angolan staffs. Some are of inferior carving and were probably part of the formal attire of most males. The great skill and imagination with which others in the collection are executed suggest that they may have been displayed as emblems of rank or wealth or functioned as insignia of office. At least one of these staffs was part of an exchange between Currie and Paramount Chief Lewanika, ruler of the Lozi people. In return for the chief's gift of an ivory headed staff and several head of cattle, the Canadian missionary offered European-style doors, tables and beds.

The only artefacts sent back to Britain by Livingstone which exhibit such density of collecting activity are the many weapons – swords, spears and knives – from the people he called the 'Manyema' or 'Manyuema' who had a reputation among Swahili traders for cannibalism. Livingstone encountered them in 1869–71, during his futile search for the source of the Nile, when their lives were being dislocated by incorporation into Swahili culture and a commercial economy (Oliver and Sanderson 1985: 553). Livingstone was clearly aware that

Figure 12.6 Human figure, Zambia, wood and metal. Collected by Walter Currie, *c.* 1903. (Royal Ontario Museum, photograph: Santiago Ku.)

the 'Manyema' were made up of quite distinct peoples. Recent estimates are of some twenty-five groups in the present day part of Zaire known as Maniema (Felix 1989) although he made no attempt to differentiate the originating peoples for his weapons collection.

Why such a limited range of objects exists may be at least partly related to the actual nature of Livingstone's experiences among them. He witnessed a massacre of several hundred Manyema, mostly women and children, at a large market in Nyangwe, an event which profoundly disturbed him. In the aftermath of that massacre, Livingstone's party was attacked; he believed that the Manyema had mistaken him for one of the market murderers as he had on a red shirt or waistcoat like those worn by the slavers (Holmes 1993: 311).

He kept several Manyema weapons, including the head of a large spear which nearly killed him during the ambush; it is now on display at the museum in his Scottish birthplace. H. M. Stanley, the journalist who had been sent by an American newspaper to 'find' the 'lost' Livingstone in 1871, shipped home several of these spears for the missionary. He also illustrated some spearheads and swords in his account of how he found Livingstone and enthused that 'The Manyema are the cleverest manufacturers of weapons' (Stanley 1872: 556). The partiality of this collection promoted or reinforced stereotypical views of the peoples of Manyema.

In examining the differences and similarities between these two collections, the colonial context in which the objects were gathered together has been considered, if only briefly, as have the personalities and circumstances of the collectors, and the diversity of African cultural practices. There remains the extra-African context in which these two collections were 'consumed'. Certainly both men regularly presented family members and friends with curios, such as the Mang'anja lip ring which Livingstone sent to his daughter, with a letter jokingly explaining how to wear it.

There is ample documentary evidence that at least some of Currie's artefacts, such as the combs, pipes and musical instruments, regularly travelled on the missionary fund-raising and Sunday School circuit within Canada. Here the durability, portability, and in many cases artistry of the objects made them ideal for engaging the attention of those whose donations would support evangelical efforts to add Angolans to world-wide Christianity. The display of surrendered 'fetish' material and objects for divination spoke to the success of such efforts and offered proof that the congregation's donations were well spent. As late as 1950 divination baskets from Angola were being requested from missionaries in the field for display in Canadian Sunday Schools.

In considering Livingstone's material, while much is certainly durable, portable and some demonstrate considerable skill, his objects (or those collected by members of the Zambesi expedition), were in some cases presented directly to institutions such as the Royal Museum of Scotland, the Royal Botanical Gardens at Kew and the British Museum's Department of Natural History through the agency of the Foreign Office. Although Livingstone's goals had a certain indivisibility in his mind, these artefacts and specimens more directly embody his scientific and geographical interests and his desire to promote legitimate commerce rather than his explicitly evangelical aims.

The differences in scale, nature and focus between these two missionary collections illuminate the personal element in any collection interacting with the wider ideological demands of the historical circumstances under which it was made. The life histories of the artefacts collected by the Reverend Currie and Dr Livingstone, moving from ritual object, domestic utensil or functional weapon to missionary souvenir or government property and finally to museum specimen, illustrate the transformational power of context and suggest that the meaning and significance of objects change according to the circumstances in which they appear and are understood. The meaning of these collections, as forms of visual ideology, is inseparable from the colonial context within which they were formed.

13

Photography at the heart of darkness

Herbert Lang's Congo photographs (1909–15)

Nicholas Mirzoeff

The perfect body in Western culture has been sustained and made imaginable by the imperfect body of the racial Other. For two hundred years, Western scientists, writers and artists have attempted to create a visual taxonomy of race without long-term success. The locus of investigation has changed from the skull and skin to the gene but the mission remains the same. In fact, the recent publication of the scurrilous book, *The Bell Curve* by Charles Murray and Richard J. Herrnstein, even resurrected the old canard of a genetic connection between race and intelligence. Yet, as Henry Louis Gates forcefully reminds us,

> [r]ace as a meaningful criterion within the biological sciences has long been recognized to be a fiction. When we speak of 'the white race' or 'the black race,' or 'the Jewish race' or the 'Aryan race,' we speak in biological misnomers and, more generally, in metaphors.
>
> (Gates 1985: 4)[1]

Although the experience and heritage of ethnicity are certainly of considerable importance, Gates refers here to the search for biological signifiers of essential physical difference, categorised as 'race'. Even prior to the theory of evolution, Europeans who wished to promote theories of absolute racial difference were aware that skin colour alone was insufficient proof. In his vitriolic defence of slavery, the English colonial official Edward Long advanced the belief that Africans closely resembled the physiognomy of the European but were less advanced:

> The supposition then is well-founded, that the brain and intellectual organs so far as they are dependent upon meer [sic] matter, though similar in texture and modification to those of other men, may in some of the Negroe race be so constituted, as *not to result to the same effects*; for we cannot but allow, that the Deity might, if it was his pleasure, diversify his works in this manner, and either withhold the *superior principle* entirely, or in part only, or infuse it into the different classes and races of human creatures, in such portions, as to form the same

gradual climax towards perfection in this human system, which is so evidently designed in every other.

(Long 1774: 371)

For Long and generations of racists after him, the divine drive towards perfection was as much marked by the inferiority of the African body as by the perfection of the white. This profound interior difference was necessary to mark the superiority of the white and to convince Europeans that the Other played no part in the Self, that the coloniser was radically different from, and superior to, the colonised.

This taxonomic impulse was above all a search for convincing visual signs of difference. The anthropologist Johannes Fabian describes this impulse as 'visualism', in which 'the ability to visualise a culture or society almost becomes synonymous for understanding it' (Fabian 1983: 106). Race thus could not exist without a visual taxonomy of racial difference. In order to provide and classify such difference, entire archives of visual material came to exist in nineteenth and twentieth-century museums, private collections and laboratories. One such archive is that constituted by the mass of photography produced by colonial travellers, scientists and governments in the former colonies of Africa and Asia. These anthropological studies, postcards, views and 'scenes of native life' were quickly designated an embarrassment in the era of decolonization, their previous popularity at once forgotten. Works were consigned to a back drawer, an attic or the far corners of a museum basement and left to gather dust. As these photographs are rediscovered, a new series of questions about them must be asked. What do the colonial photographs represent, both for viewers in the period and today? What can be learnt from them about 'the creation of colonial reality', a process which implicated both colonisers and colonised (Taussig 1986: 5)? Can we observe the process by which 'race' is written onto the body, transforming the body from an individual into a specimen?

The travelling exhibition *African Reflections: Art of North-Eastern Zaire 1909–1915* (catalogue: Schildkrout and Keim, 1990) attempts to answer these questions. The show presented the collections of two travellers from the American Museum of Natural History, Herbert Lang and James Chapin, to the north-east of what was then the Congo in 1909–15. Their task was to report on the way of life of the local inhabitants, and to record, collect and identify the local flora and fauna. In the course of a five-year expedition, with over two years being spent in the Mangbetu region,[2] Lang and Chapin also collected a prodigious number of cultural products made by Mangbetu and Azande peoples, which formed the centerpiece of the exhibition. Lang was a dedicated photographer, who took no less than 10,000 plates on his travels, many of which were used to illustrate the show and its catalogue. Enid Schildkrout, one of the curators of *African Reflections*, undertook important and pioneering research into Lang's work as a photographer. From an examination of published works, the forty-volume photographic archive established by Lang at the Museum of Natural History and the contact prints from which he worked, Schildkrout concluded that Lang's work had overcome the barriers of colonial difference.

His photographs thus presented a unique view of Mangbetu peoples which 'depict a people who consciously constructed an image of themselves for outsiders that relied on their perception of outsiders' perception of them' (Schildkrout 1991: 71). Schildkrout held that the colonial photograph was not simply a reflection of the coloniser's preconceptions but a place of dialogue between the coloniser and the indigenous people. Rather than pursue the intriguing possibilities of this argument, her essay concludes:

> In some respects, [Lang] always subscribed to ideas of Western superiority and never gave up some stereotypes he brought with him . . . However, in the six years they lived together in northeastern Zaire, he and Chapin developed a deep appreciation for those African cultures and peoples they came to know. This intimacy is projected in some of Lang's photographs and it transforms them from simple contextual documents for a museum collection into works of art.
>
> (Schildkrout 1991: 85)

In a move all too familiar to art historians, the colonial photograph is transformed by intimacy from a document into art. This transcendent move is designed to shield the work from criticism that colonial photographs merely reflect the coloniser's prejudices and tell us nothing about the photograph's subject, and yet ironically has much in common with it. Both positions offer a disinterested view of art as transcending the conditions of artistic production. In these photographs, the subject is overwhelmingly the black body, sometimes named, sometimes anonymous, but always preventing a reductive analysis of the photograph. Any reading of photography is dogged by the cultural construction of the photograph as either observed truth or transcendent art. However, any engagement with the colonial photograph which is capable of giving a place to the subjects of those photographs will have to bypass such comforting certainties. Instead, it is necessary to attend to the 'ambivalence and undecidability' that Kobena Mercer has identified in Robert Mapplethorpe's contemporary photographs of black men, for both black and white spectators (Mercer 1993: 320).

In the first section of this chapter, I want to use Mercer's insight to examine the possibility of reading colonial photographs as a visual document, conforming to a certain grammar of colonial vision and yet very specific in their individual instances. Without claiming any universal verities, I shall discuss those photographs of the Congo published by Lang as a record of his journey. Lang's work will be treated in the context of the meanings given to the Congo by travel writers, politicians and novelists in the period, in order to perceive both its originality and its conformity to prevalent modes of colonial discourse. Many recent literary readings of colonial literature and travel writing have emphasised the visual dimension to such writing (Pratt 1992). In this view, travel narratives sought to describe the places visited and colonised by Europeans in terms derived from painting and photography, rather than in conventional literary metaphors. It is then simply assumed that the visual imagery of the African colonies has been derived from these literary studies, with notable exceptions

(Alloula 1986; Geary 1988). Perhaps the consistent domination of Orientalist studies over 'Africanist' work, noted by Christopher Miller, has contributed to the current situation in which Orientalist painting has been widely commented upon, but European representations of sub-Saharan Africa continue to be ignored (Miller 1985: 14–23). Photography has a unique and important role to play in the construction of such discourse, but it needs to be considered as it was presented, together with its text. Neither stands independently, for just as the photograph visualises the narrative of the text and makes it explicable, so does the text explain the details of the photograph and render them knowable.[3]

Rather than seek a transcendent interpretation of 'the' colonial photograph, I want to consider how Lang's Congo photographs constructed a cultural geography of colonialism in a specific time and place. Imperialism was never an undifferentiated phenomenon, repeating its manoeuvres regardless of time and place, but was always constructed in regard to local specificities, the domestic agenda of the colonising nation and with an eye to the other colonial powers (Wilson 1993). For the cultural geography of a place is not quite the same as its physical geography. Here landmarks are not used simply to record a terrain but to designate cultural meaning. It is an imagined geography, which identifies France by the Eiffel Tower and New York by the Statue of Liberty. These metonyms are not simply indexical signs, pointing out the locale represented, but connote the Western sense of place, regardless of the actual travel experience of the spectator. Thus in film and photography, the Eiffel Tower indicates not just Paris, but France as a place of romance and elegance. In the cultural geography of imperialism created by this process, the Congo occupied a specific and important place as the degree zero of the 'primitive' world envisaged by imperialism. Long after its interior had been explored and opened up to colonial exploitation of rubber and ivory, the Congo was considered the very 'heart of darkness', and was immortalised as such by Joseph Conrad in his eponymous novella of 1899.[4]

Envisaging the Congo

Conrad's construction of the Congo as 'a prehistoric earth' (Conrad 1969: 539) was a well-defined discourse, which was all but impervious to change. The cultural geography of imperialism and the imperial imaginary depended, and depends, on the Congo as its origin. From Schweinfurth's first published narrative of 1874, entitled *In the Heart of Africa*, subsequent travellers set out to the Congo with the specific aim of encountering the heart of darkness. Lang's first account of his expedition in 1910 was similarly entitled 'In the Heart of Africa', and the title was used yet again for the account of a rival German expedition in the same year. Such conceits have lasted until the present day. The popular novelist Michael Crichton opens his 1980 novel *Congo* in a fashion recognizable to any nineteenth-century travel writer:

> Dawn came to the Congo rain forest. The pale sun burned away the morning mist revealing a gigantic, silent world . . . [t]he basic impression

was of a vast oversized gray-green world – an alien place, inhospitable to man.

(Crichton 1980: 1)

Crichton echoes Marlow's words in *Heart of Darkness*: 'Going up that river was like travelling back to the earliest beginnings of the world, when vegetation rioted on the earth and the big trees were kings. An empty steam, a great silence, an impenetrable forest' (Conrad 1969: 536). The colonial anthropologist, traveller and writer reiterate each other's words in a vain attempt to end the silence of the Other, in defiance of actual conditions in the Congo. For by the time that Lang arrived in the region, Western travellers were far from a novelty. A series of campsites was established for the use of Western itinerants, even in the north-eastern region, enabling the British writer Marguerite Roby to cross the Congo from south to north on a bicycle in 1910. The official almanac for the Congo, published by the Belgian government, ran to over 700 pages in 1913, detailing businesses, traders and addresses of Europeans in the Congo. Even when faced with the evidence of such activity, Lang continued to perceive the Congo as the heart of darkness: 'Avakubi is a great rubber station, about twenty tons a month being received from the natives as taxes. . . . Such an isolated spot can hardly exist anywhere in the world' (Dickerson 1910: 161).[5]

Appropriately, Crichton's novel has an epigram from Henry Morton Stanley, the journalist and explorer, who gave shape to the Congo in the late nineteenth and early twentieth century in both cultural and political terms. After his famous feat in finding the missionary David Livingstone, Stanley returned to the Congo as the agent of King Leopold II of Belgium. He secured the colonial rights of the Belgian monarch to the entirety of the Congo basin as a personal fief, rights which were upheld at the Berlin conference of 1885. By the early twentieth century, thanks to the publicity generated by British consul Roger Casement and the journalist E. D. Morel, the Congo had become notorious as the site of the most extreme colonial brutality and oppression. Undoubtedly, the political impact of the reform campaign was reinforced by the European perception that the Congo was a uniquely primitive and dangerous place. Travellers expected to find what Stanley had described, and followed his tracks in order to do so. Both Lang and Adolphus Frederick of Mecklenburg, who led the German expedition of 1908, could find no other way to describe the Congo forest than to quote Stanley:

> Imagine the whole of France and the Iberian peninsula densely covered with trees 6 to 60 metres in height, with smooth trunks, whose leafy tops are so close to one another that they intermingle and obscure the sun and the heavens, each tree over a metre in thickness. The ropes stretching across from one tree to another in the shape of creepers and festoons, or curling round the trunks in thick, heavy coils, like endless anacondas, till they reach the highest point. Imagine them in full bloom, their luxuriant foliage combining with that of the trees to obscure the sunlight, and their hundreds of long festoons covered with slender tendrils hanging down from the highest

171

branches till they touch the ground, interlacing with one another in a complete tangle.

(Mecklenburg 1910: 249; Dickerson 1910: 166)

Both writers charged Stanley with exaggeration, but could not replace his words with their own. Stanley describes the Congo as a place that cannot be described in the traditional fashion, but had to be imagined. The Western heart of darkness had already been written and has yet to be rewritten.

Stanley's passage emphasised the darkness and all but unimaginable magnitude of the forest. Encountering the heart of darkness was thus a visual problem from the outset. It was, in Conrad's phrase, 'the threshold of the invisible' (Conrad 1969: 593). In order to make the darkness visible, three ways of seeing – and not seeing – were possible in the Congo of the period. The first was that of the Emperor Leopold who claimed to own the Congo. Leopold supplied some of the funds for Lang's expedition and gave numerous objects to the American Museum of Natural History, a debt repaid by Lang in a published defence of the Belgian regime in the Museum's *Journal*. Leopold's gaze may be equated with that so well described by Michel Foucault in the Emperor Napoleon I:

> At the moment of its full blossoming, the disciplinary society still assumes with the Emperor the old aspect of the power of spectacle. As a monarch who is at one and the same time a usurper of the ancient throne and the organiser of a new state, he combined into a single, symbolic, ultimate figure the whole of the long process by which the pomp of sovereignty, the necessarily spectacular manifestations of power, were extinguished one by one in the daily exercise of surveillance.
>
> (Foucault 1982: 217)

Leopold's disciplinary gaze was all-seeing in his possession and exerted its dominion through taxation, legal sanctions and property rights. It was an indifferent gaze, concerned only with the production of rubber and ivory and the maintenance of colonial order. Other events were literally invisible to this colonial gaze.

In opposition to this disciplinary gaze was the modern vision of the Congo reformers. They envisaged a Congo of free producers, whose participation in the market would be all the more effective because of their increased liberty. Casement and Morel, although undoubtedly outraged by the excesses committed in the Congo, sought to bring the colonial administration of the region into twentieth-century terms, rightly perceiving Leopold's system as an embarrasing anachronism. Their vision of the Congo was expressed by Morel:

> Seated in an imaginary airship, which we will fancy perfected and invisible, let us take a bird's eye view of the Congo as it was twenty-five years ago [i.e. before Leopold], not in the spirit of the anthropologist, naturally and rightly on the lookout for strange and repulsive rites; nor in the spirit of the moralist, lamenting the aberrations of primitive man with a zeal inducing unmindfulness of civilization's sores: but in the

spirit of the statesman, which presupposes both the student and the man of broad practical sympathies, contemplating this vast new country for the first time . . . The mightiest forest region in the world now unrolls before us its illimitable horizon, the primeval forest whither races of black, brown and copper coloured men have been attracted or driven for untold ages . . . In these fertile villages, man has settled and multiplied. He is well represented almost everywhere on the banks of the rivers except where they are very low lying and habitually flooded. But he has made many thousands of clearings in the forest too, and has cultivated the soil to such good purposes where need was, that we shall be astonished at the number and variety of his plantations. Throughout this enormous forest region . . . we shall note an intelligent, vigorous population, attaining considerable density in certain parts, digging and smelting iron, manufacturing weapons for war and the chase, often of singularly beautiful shape, weaving fibres of sundry plants into tasteful mats and cloths, fabricating a rough pottery, fishing nets, twine baskets.

(Morel 1968: 17, 21)

Power has now attained its modern form in the shape of an invisible airship, which glides above the forest, discovering a society closer to William Morris's *News from Nowhere* than the colonial travel accounts. For Morel, the technology of the all-seeing eye must replace the autocratic body of the King. For Leopold and his supporters, the primitivism of the Congo justified and necessitated traditional forms of colonial power. Neither account represents Truth, but both speak a certain truth of colonial discourse. However, what was truly invisible to Western eyes was not the primeval culture of the region but the obvious changes and upheaval taking place. Seeing the heart of darkness involved and depended upon not seeing both the local cultures and the change they were experiencing due to colonisation. Although the colonial gaze fantasised that it was the 'monarch of all I survey' (Pratt 1992: 201), it was in practice impossible for it to achieve this plenitude of vision.

Of course, the indigenous culture was not absolutely invisible, but it could only be seen in certain controlled circumstances and by the use of specific technologies. As Morel suggested, this third way of envisaging the Congo was that of anthropologist. The anthropologist did not seek to view the region as a whole, nor to judge it. He was there to record it in detail and with precision, for the scientific benefit of Western civilisation. Anthropology claimed a remarkably wide scope in the late nineteenth century, which was still in force at the time of Lang's expedition. In the words of Paul Broca, one of the founders of the discipline:

The history of the arts, that of languages, religions, literature, or political societies, that of biology, zoology, palaeontology and geology forms part of the program of anthropology. . . . [A]nthropology can exclude no branch of human knowledge which can furnish any data on the history of man and human society.

(Broca 1868: 27–8)

However, the anthropologist's obsessive recording of detail was above all applied to those countries colonised by the West, and shared much with colonial methods of dealing with tropical conditions. In *Heart of Darkness*, Marlow attributes his survival to this method: 'I had to keep a lookout for the signs of dead wood we could cut up in the night for the next day's steaming. When you have to attend to things of that sort, to the mere incidents of the surface, the reality – the reality, I tell you – fades. The inner truth is hidden – luckily, luckily' (Conrad 1969: 537). Marlow concentrated on his job of piloting the steamer up river, rather than trying to understand the Congo. By focusing on the everyday details, the colonialist could thus avoid seeing the truth that was all around him. Herbert Lang opted for this third, anthropological, way of seeing as befitted an expeditionary of the American Museum of Natural History. Even his partner Chapin was astonished by the hysterical energy Lang put into his work, collecting specimens and taking photographs by day, and developing plates by night.

Anthropology, eugenics and photography

Photography was no newcomer to the Congo. By 1913, one of the five sections of the Tervuren Musée du Congo Belge was entirely devoted to photography and the Belgian Congo was home to three photography businesses, two cinemas and one self-styled cinematographer (*Annuaire du Congo* 1913: 23, 186–8). Indeed, it was the rule for travel literature from the region to be illustrated with photographs taken by the author. The 1909 German Congo expedition returned with no less than 5,000 photographs (Mecklenburg 1910: x). As such, the photographs served as a guarantee of the authenticity of the writer's account and were extensively captioned in order to explain their subject-matter. These works, often poorly produced and weak in content, were intended to serve as documents, rather than works of art, as Molly Nesbit has argued (Nesbit 1992: 15–17). At the Fifth International Congress of Photography, held in Brussels in 1910 – capital of the Belgian empire – these works were specifically defined:

> A documentary image should be able to be used for studies of diverse kinds, ergo the necessity of including the maximum possible detail. Any image can at any time serve scientific investigation. Nothing is to be disdained: the beauty of the photograph is secondary here, it is enough that the image be very clear, full of detail and carefully treated.

Just as Lang collected animal remains, Mangbetu artefacts and plant specimens, he collected photographs as documents for the use of the American Museum of Natural History.

Lang's photography stemmed from the particular nexus of cultural concerns which caused him to be in the Congo in the first place. In this period, the Museum was increasingly turning its attention to the promotion of the new 'science' of eugenics. Eugenics, in historian George Stocking's view, 'was an attempt to compensate for the failure of natural selection under the conditions of advanced civilisation' (Stocking 1987: 145). These gloomy prophets sought to control the reproduction of the human race under conditions dictated by the laws of statistics, believing that the statistically unusual 'defective' types could be eliminated. Such theories of human breeding control were based on the model of agricultural manipulation of livestock with careful provisos taking account of social factors. Eugenicists sought to eliminate not only disabilities and retardations of all kinds, but social evils, such as alcoholism, pauperism, orphans and the catch-all category of ne'er-do-wells. Far from being confined to a lunatic fringe, these ideas achieved great currency in the early twentieth century and, by the First World War, the majority of States in the Union permitted sterilisations of the 'unfit' to take place in prisons, hospitals and asylums. These actions were ruled legal by the Supreme Court of Oliver Wendell Holmes and by 1941 41,000 Americans had been sterilised under these laws. Henry Osborn, who became director of the Museum of Natural History in 1908 and organised the Congo expedition, was excited to stand 'on the threshold of the application of science or knowledge of the laws of Nature as they bear on human morals, welfare and happiness' (Osborn 1910: 63). At the museum, a new Hall of Public Health was opened and its rationale was described by Osborn as follows: 'It is cruel to bring a child into the world predestined to disease and suffering, hence eugenics. It is cruel to bring into our country the kind of people who will produce children like this, cruel I mean to those already here, hence the survey of immigration' (Osborn 1913: 195). Osborn was further responsible for bringing the second International Congress on Eugenics to New York in 1921. This museum was an activist institution devoted, in the words of its *Journal*'s masthead, 'to natural history, exploration and the development of public education through the museum'. These goals were linked theoretically to, and motivated by, eugenics.

The Congo expedition was driven by a sense of the imminent disappearance of the indigenous cultures in the face of more 'advanced' Western civilisation. The first report from the expedition explained that its goal was

> [t]he Upper Congo region, that great, steaming land of equatorial Africa shrouded in jungle. . . . They have seen strange places and stranger primitive peoples, of whom it is time that the world obtain complete scientific record in view of the rapid advance that civilisation must make in the Congo in the immediate future.
>
> (Dickerson 1910: 147)

The disappearance of what the colonisers presumed to have been the formerly widespread practice of cannibalism was proof to the eugenically minded that such transformations were already taking place. Lang claimed that eleven million people had formerly been devoted to anthropophagy from which they had been delivered by the Belgians with mixed results: '[T]his horrible practice produced some fairly good results in eugenics, as in many tribes weakened people or crippled children helped to nourish their more sturdy brothers' (Lang 1915: 382) (Fig. 13.1). Lang therefore opposed the efforts to reform the administration of the Congo and indeed praised the 'wise decisions of a responsible government' which contrasted unfavourably with the 'impetuosity of the unfortunate campaign of the reformers' (Lang 1915: 380). Lang advocated instead a eugenic solution to the climatic, cultural and political problems of the region: 'White man's impetus must be the motive to progress, whereas the Negro will supply the activity to bring final order from chaos' (Lang 1919: 698). In other words, eugenics was to replicate in advanced society that which the cannibal variation of the survival of the fittest had achieved in the heart of darkness.

No reader of Lang's reports from the Congo in the *Journal* of the museum, now titled *Natural History*, could be unaware of the eugenic ideas which motivated Osborn's museum. In the edition of December 1919, for example, Lang published an account of his encounter with the so-called pygmies in the rainforest, the Mbuti people. In order to reach Lang's essay, it was necessary to pass through two lengthy accounts of the intelligence testing performed in the American Army during the First World War. This now notorious exercise in applied eugenics

Figure 13.1 Herbert Lang, *Chief of the Cannibals* (1909–15). (American Museum of Natural History.)

was not officially published until 1921, making the accounts in *Natural History* something of a scoop. The examiners believed that the intelligence tests had revealed important results: '[E]specially startling is the unusually large difference shown here between the distributions for Negroes and the distribution for white men' (Trabue 1919: 681). Plotted on a graph, these results formed a regular curve, with the left side indicating the high percentage of failure by 'Negroes' and the right hand side showing the corresponding degree of success achieved by the whites. According to one psychologist, 'the relationship between color and achievement was quite distinct, those with lighter skins making higher scores' (Trabue 1919: 680). It need hardly be remarked that these 'tests' were administered and conducted precisely in order to achieve such findings and have long been discredited. However, President George B. Cutten of Colgate University used them in the period to cast doubt upon the possibility of sustaining democracy in a country so widely populated with the 'feeble-minded' (Kevles 1985: 84). The diligent reader would thus not have been surprised to read that, in calling for the development of a 'national art' in the United States, Herbert J. Spinden, Assistant Curator in Anthropology at the museum, did not include Africa in the seven 'type civilisations, upon the products of which must be based any statement of what a national art can and should be' (Spinden 1919: 623). The highest realm of civilisation was inevitably the Christian. Spinden ranked other 'culture areas' in descending order with African being last, coming below even Neolithic European cultures.

Only after all of these eugenically inspired pieces does one find Lang's report, entitled 'Nomad Dwarfs and Civilisation'. This context makes it clear that the title was supposed to indicate a contrast rather than a connection. By way of example, Lang described how the Mbuti-Pygmy chief was afraid of the camera, and even when the instrument was disassembled, 'he clung to his belief in the presence of a power for evil, adding that it was evidently harbored in the dark cloth of the bellows and could be destroyed only by fire' (Lang 1919: 708). This incident accorded well with prevailing notions of the primitive, as well as the West's sense that its superiority was manifested in its technology. Indeed, it is so convenient that it seems somewhat suspicious. Twenty years previously, the British missionary Albert Lloyd published a popular account of his experiences in the Congo under the dramatic title *In Dwarf Land and Cannibal Country*.[6] As one might expect, Lloyd had little sympathy for the indigenous culture, believing that Africa sheltered 'millions of her dusky sons in as gross a state of darkness as they were a thousand years ago' (Lloyd 1899: 12). Lloyd met a group of Mbuti-Pygmies in the Congo and was able to converse with them in Swahili through an interpreter. He at once set up his camera:

> In the morning I tried to photograph my little friends, but it was quite hopeless. It was too dark in the forest itself, and I could not persuade them to come out into a clearing where I might get light enough. I tried time after time, but always failed. I exposed nearly a dozen plates, but with no good results; snapshots were useless, and I could not get them still enough for a time exposure.
>
> (Lloyd 1899: 271)

177

None the less, Lloyd did later manage to photograph a 'Pygmy lady' and reproduced the image in his book. His account mentions none of the 'primitive' fear of the camera highlighted by Lang, which would have served admirably to bolster his imperial view of the Congo, and indeed the Mbuti seem to have shown considerable patience in sitting through his repeated photographic efforts. It seems highly unlikely, therefore, that the fear of the camera encountered by Lang was a simple reaction of backward primitives to advanced Western technology. If his account is to be believed, it might rather suggest that in the intervening twenty years, Congo peoples had learnt to distrust those bearing cameras. Nor were they wrong to do so, for Lang's eugenic theory held that the 'backward' Pygmies would have to be eliminated in the interests of progress.

Lang's account of his meeting with the Mbuti provides evidence of this resistance to, and accommodation with, colonial authority in the form of mimicry. At one point, he noticed a man doing imitations:

> [T]he little fellow admirably imitated an official, taking especial advantage of the latter's habit of accentuating his instructions with peculiar abrupt gestures. When I asked him to mimic me he grinned happily. During the forenoon I had taken a number of photographs and my tripod camera was still standing in the shade. Without injury to the instrument he mimicked my every movement with just enough exaggeration to make everyone laugh. Finally he indicated that the 'evil eye had seen well' – and now came the climax to the performance. The Pygmy he had pretended to photograph, instead of unconcernedly walking away, dropped to the ground, illustrating the native superstition that the 'big evil eye' of the camera causes death. A block of salt laid on the 'dead' man's stomach instantly resuscitated him and the two entertainers walked off joyously, but only after the clown had received a reward.
>
> (Lang 1919: 712n)

The Mbuti mimicker thus connected colonial power, photography and the European belief in African fear of the camera into a satirical narrative of colonial life. Cultural critic Homi Bhabha has identified mimicry 'as one of the most elusive and effective strategies of colonial power and knowledge'. In this view, mimicry 'is the desire for a reformed, recognizable Other as a *subject of difference that is almost the same but not quite*'. This ambivalent process creates an uneasy tension between mimicry and mockery, which may turn into menace. Mimicry was not a simple exercise in colonial authority, creating masks behind which the essence of the colonial subject was concealed, but rather: 'the *menace* of mimicry is its *double* vision which in disclosing the ambivalence of colonial discourse also disrupts its authority' (Bhabha 1987: 321). Bhabha's focus was entirely upon the written text, but his analysis is central to an understanding of the colonial photograph. The mimicry Lang observed was of the coloniser's belief in the power of his practice, which was disrupted by this very imitation. The mimicker parodied both the colonial official and his means of recording the colonial vision. The photographs Lang took, then, are the intersection of the double vision of mimicry, presenting no 'authentic' vision of Africa, nor of colonialism, but a fragmentary glimpse of the interaction between the indigenous peoples and eugenic anthropology. In short, both Europeans and Mbuti had created the Pygmies.

Mimicry was an important constituent of colonial practice in the Congo, but it proved as hard to visualise as the heart of darkness itself. In *Heart of Darkness*, Conrad fictionalised this experience. As Marlow approaches the lost trader Kurtz, he meets first with his Russian deputy:

> I looked at him, lost in astonishment. There he was before me, in motley, as though he had absconded from a troupe of mimes, enthusiastic, fabulous. His very existence was improbable, inexplicable, and altogether bewildering. He was an insoluble problem. It was inconceivable how he had existed, how he had succeeded in getting so far, how he had managed to remain – why he did not instantly disappear.
>
> (Conrad 1969: 568)

Marlow pursues his tactic of not seeing anything beyond the essentials for his expedition and refuses to believe his eyes when confronted with colonial mimicry. He expects that at any moment, the phantom will disappear. The illusion of colonial normality, already all but impossible to sustain in the interior of the Congo, will soon be shattered by the discovery that Kurtz has 'gone native' and turned himself into a god. What Marlow tried so hard not to see was what Conrad famously called 'the horror, the horror'. By the time of Lang's expedition, the situation had changed sufficiently that the local people made great efforts to sustain colonial mimicry, motivated by their experience of the violence meted out by thwarted colonisers. When Lang arrived in Mangbetu, he was disappointed to find that the Great Hall described by Schweinfurth did not exist. Okondo, a chief of the Mangbetu installed by the Belgians, learnt of this disruption to colonial vision and at once set about building the hall desired by Lang. It was dutifully photographed and recorded as an authentic example of Mangbetu culture, but, as Crew and Sims remind us, '[a]uthenticity is not about factuality or reality. Objects have no authority; people do' (Crew and Sims 1991: 163). To be more precise, the objects held no meaning outside the discourse of colonial mimicry. Lang knew what he expected to discover and the Mangbetu hastened to oblige. It was no coincidence therefore that Lang held Mangbetu in great esteem, describing them as: 'the most highly cultured natives of these regions. . . . Their pottery in its best samples reminds one of Ancient Greek work' (Lang 1911: 48).

In describing his meeting with the Mbuti, Lang was principally concerned with the correct identification of their racial type, and specifically 'whether the Pygmies are merely degenerate types of Negroes and therefore of relatively recent origin, or the earliest type from which all taller African races have evolved, or one entirely distinct and as old as any living race' (Lang 1919: 699). The first two theories could easily be accommodated within mainstream

179

eugenics. The third implied a polygenetic view of the human species, that is to say, that several entirely separate varieties of the human race had coexisted for millennia. Lang finessed his own argument by deciding that the Pygmies were indeed the descendants of the first peoples to settle Africa from Asia, then held to be the place of origin of human life. Although the survival of the fittest had driven them out of the rest of Africa, the unique qualities of the heart of darkness allowed them to survive in the rainforest, like the recently discovered okapi. This sweeping assertion was maintained even in the admitted face of failure: 'At present no racial characters setting aside a majority of Pygmies from the tall Negroes can be stated and it is doubtful if physical traits have at any previous period been more uniformly pronounced' (Lang 1919: 703). However, there was no doubt in Lang's mind that these details could be discovered and he set about creating a visual record of these disappearing creatures with his camera.

Lang was careful to follow anthropological and eugenic procedures in his photography. He took ninety sets of head and shoulder shots of local people in his search for the truly typical. Each set consisted of views from the front, side and three-quarters. The three-quarter view is that traditionally used in Western portraiture and seems therefore more 'sympathetic' to eyes accustomed to reading such portraits. Lang's intention was to avoid all

> personal preference and prejudice. . . . Great is the temptation for a traveler to pick and choose the subjects for his picture gallery with an eye to beauty and interest. But we were anxious that our anthropological series of portraits should not be invalidated. After carefully ascertaining the tribal status of the natives, we lined them up indiscriminately and took every third, fifth, or seventh individual according to the number desired from any crowd.
>
> (Lang 1919: 707–8)

Such elimination of personal preference was a central tenet of scientific practice in the period, which sought to eliminate all trace of the subjectivity of the scientist, leaving judgement and discrimination to the reader (Daston and Galison 1992: 98–110). Despite this care, these portraits failed in their primary purpose: 'It would be too daring to describe as typical these remnants of a race which has not escaped mingling with large neighboring communities' (Lang 1919: 701). The discourse of colonial mimicry invalidated the colonial photograph as a pure scientific document. What was recorded was not the anthropological fantasy of unhindered, pure observation but the cultural product of the interactions between colonisers and colonised. The photographs do not tell us about 'native' life as Lang claimed, but about the ambivalences of colonial culture.

Eugenicists therefore argued for the correlation of word and image. The photograph could not stand on its own as it was an incomplete and atypical document. In his Introduction to a 1910 collection of eugenic studies, the British eugenicist Karl Pearson cautioned that

[i]t is not always possible to maintain a proper balance between the graphic and the verbal descriptions; but I wish most strongly to insist on the point that neither are to be interpreted *alone*; they are component parts of one whole, and the reader who draws conclusions from the engraved pedigrees without consulting the verbal accounts is certain to be led into error.

(Pearson 1909: ix [orig. emphasis])

In order to signify correctly, the eugenic sign required a correlation of visual representation and critical assessment, in which the latter was dominant over the former. Lang's first published photograph from the Congo showed some buildings at the edge of the forest and carried the following caption: 'The mightiest primeval forest known to man. A cold, gray picture is wholly inadequate to make vivid a tropical country, the splendid color, the sounds, the life – and the heat' (Dickerson 1910: 160) (Fig. 13.2). The caption directed the viewer's attention away from what was visible – local people and their dwellings – to that which was invisible and beyond the reach of the camera. Lang consistently treated the photograph as a partial notation, rather than the revealer of truth.

In his first article, Lang published a photograph of a Mangbetu woman, wearing a striking rafia headdress. This woman, whom Lang does not name, appears in a number of his photographs, making it reasonable to assume that Lang knew her status in the community (Fig. 13.3). For the headdress was not merely decorative, but a signifier of rank only to be worn by the ruling class (Schildkrout and Keim 1990: 125). Although visitors to *African Reflections* in 1993 were made aware of this point, Lang did not inform his readers of the signification of her headdress. Instead, Lang captioned her photograph: 'A "Parisienne" of the Mangbetu tribe', a notable departure from his usual anthropological objectivity (Lang 195: 383). To his American readers, the term 'Parisienne' was a necessarily ambiguous one. It mingled connotations of high fashion with the suspicion that the woman might be a courtesan or fallen woman for, as Molly Nesbit has observed: 'Fascination with her [the Parisienne's] sexuality grew obsessive in the decade just before the First World War' (Nesbit 1992: 133). Lang's readers, unaware of the social position of the woman he had photographed, would certainly have located his Parisienne in this hybrid discourse of fashion and sexuality. Lang was conscious of social distinctions in the region and in the same article, he published photographs of Manziga, an Azande chief (Fig. 13.4), and the 'head wife' of Abiembali, a Mayogo chief. Here, however, amongst Mangbetu whom he otherwise privileged, he described a elite woman as a prostitute. Like many other Europeans, Lang was both fascinated and repelled by the sexuality of the Africans he encountered. He noted privately of Mangbetu men that 'as a rule they behave very arrogant [*sic*] in the absence of white men and often profit of the charms so easily offered by the Mangbetu women' (Schildkrout and Keim 1990: 63). This remark is self-evidently a fantasy, for Lang could not by definition speak of the ways Mangbetu men acted in the absence of whites. Does Lang's ethnographic slip in identifying the noblewoman as a prostitute indicate that it was

Figure 13.2 Herbert Lang, *At the Edge of the Virgin Forest*. (American Museum of Natural History.)

Figure 13.3 Herbert Lang,
A 'Parisienne' of the Mangbetu Tribe.
(American Museum of Natural
History.)

Figure 13.4 Herbert Lang, *Manziga.
A Chief of the Azande*. (American
Museum of Natural History.)

Figure 13.5 Herbert Lang, *The Whir of a Pigmy's Arrow is the Crowning Step in the Pursuit of a Victim.* (American Museum of Natural History.)

in fact he who was tempted by the 'charms' of Mangbetu women? For an anthropologist and eugenicist such desire was unnameable, and yet this one uncharacteristic reference to sexual practice, which is otherwise passed over in silence, suggests that the full story of the American Museum expedition may not have been told.

The supremacy of caption over image is strikingly apparent in Lang's use of the same photograph for entirely different purposes in two publications. In 1915, Lang published a photograph of a group of Mbuti, posing with bows and arrows pointed at the camera. His caption was simply descriptive: 'Pygmies from Nala, in the Uele district. They live by hunting, and exchange their spoils with the agricultural tribes for vegetables. Two hundred of them visited the expedition and many allowed plaster casts to be made of their faces' (Lang 1915: 384). Four years later in his article on the Mbuti-Pygmies, Lang described how he had won the confidence of the Mbuti chief while being threatened with arrows. An almost identical photograph appeared to bolster the story (Fig. 13.5). It was obviously taken at the same time as the earlier picture, but had been differently cropped, revealing an extra figure at the left, whose arrow points away from the camera, and whose forced expression seems to indicate the posed nature of the scene. Such casual procedure stemmed from a belief that the caption formed the predominant impression in the reader's mind. It states:

> The whir of a Pygmy's arrow is the crowning step in the pursuit of a victim, be it man or beast. In the forest consummate skill does not depend upon shooting at great distances, but on the ability to steal up under the wind, unheard, unseen, and never miss the fleeting chance. Even among Pygmies there are only a few who have the patience, daring, and energy for such accomplishment.
>
> (Lang 1919: 705)

183

In four years, Lang's picture had changed from being evidence of his encounter with a co-operative native people to a testimony of his own bravery in confronting such skilled and lethal adversaries. This picture indicates the textual and photographic liberties Lang felt entitled to take despite his avowed desire to achieve an unmediated anthropological truth.

The politics of cultural difference

Indeed, the interpretation of photographic representations of the Congo was a politically contested field at this time. Lang and other apologists for the colonial regime in the Congo argued that the entire truth of the region could not be gleaned from photographs alone, whereas the reformers held that the photographs which had emerged from the region told the entire truth of the matter. One of the many intellectuals to become involved in the question of Congo reform was the writer Arthur Conan Doyle. He wrote a Preface to Morel's *Great Britain and the Congo*, which placed this issue at the centre of his argument:

> When we read of the ill-treatment of these poor people, the horrible beatings, the mutilation of limbs, the butt-endings, the starving in hostage-houses – facts which are vouched for by witnesses of several nations and professions, backed by the incorruptible evidence of the Kodak – we may ask again by what right these things are done?

The defenders of the Belgian regime had two answers to such accusations. Firstly, they were dismissed as untrue and, next in the words of Marguerite Roby, the British travel writer:

> As for the 'incorruptible evidence of the Kodak', it is obvious that such evidence is strictly limited in its scope, if honourably employed. I mean to say that from the photograph of a mutilated person you can only deduce the fact that the person in question has suffered according to the picture. *Where* the crime was committed is quite another matter, and unless a very careful record be kept as to where such photographs are taken, it is almost inevitable that mistakes and misunderstandings will arise. Exactly the same remarks apply to the question of *When* was the crime depicted committed? and even the most honourable men may be misled on this score when they have not taken the photographs themselves.

> (Roby 1911: 267)

The polemicists of the Congo reform question thus took directly opposed positions on the question of the accuracy of the photograph. Doyle claimed that the photograph spoke for itself, whereas Roby argued that photographs could only be interpreted with the supplement of careful textual notations.

Lang was able both to claim the authorship of his photographs, and to provide the careful documentation Roby required, which he used at length to defend the

Belgian administration. Like Roby, he argued that the natives were not oppressed by the colonial government, but rather benefited from it and needed it:

> None of the natives indulge any longer in cannibalism; yet those most anxious to help them, and many of the professional reformers, speak even now about their 'degraded condition', 'shameless manners', and 'behavior like animals', perhaps just because the warm climate allows them to walk about in just the state that seems, from all accounts, to have been the most satisfactory in Paradise. . . . It is true that they are born and die in the densest superstition, but this latter is their religion, their code of morals, their own very rigid set of laws, which binds them together in spite of all savage feeling in a true democratic spirit. . . . The greatest fallacy in judging natives is the common habit of travelers and many residents of basing their judgment about them upon information received from workmen, servants or half-civilized negroes. Even the most truthful individuals among these natives generally try and speak from the white man's point of view, displaying in this great shrewdness, so that any question asked is answered with the desire of pleasing the inquirer.
>
> (Lang 1915: 386)

This passage is exemplary of Lang's cultural politics of representation. He presents the natives as happy, worthy peoples, who live and die in inevitably primitive conditions. The colonial administration, far from hindering them, has put an end to cannibalism, introduced the principles of commerce and the means for its pursuit in the shape of railways and river steamers. However, Lang was aware that the development of colonial mimicry had made it difficult to ascertain the exact truth as to conditions in the region, and led to the deception of many of his contemporaries.

The apparent acceptance of cultural relativism by the defenders of the Belgian Congo was no more than that – apparent. Lang used his photographs to establish an image of Congo peoples as primitive, superstitious, but happy under the colonial regime. His picture of a group of local children informed the viewer that:

> There are no orphans in the Congo, in the sense of homeless children. Food is plentiful and bringing up children involves little labor or expense; thus an orphan child is always taken into another family. These children lead happy, carefree lives, and, by helping in village and garden, learn without special training the domestic and other arts of their parents.
>
> (Lang 1915)

Any evidence that mitigated this Edenic picture was suppressed. Enid Schildkrout has discovered that both in his published work and the archival albums at the American Museum, Lang 'omitted many of the images that show Western influence' (Schildkrout 1991: 84). These include a shot of the Mangbetu chief Okondo waving good-bye to the expedition, dressed in a Western uniform. This suppression was made not just in the interest of ethnographic 'authenticity' but to preserve the colonial case that the primitive nature of Congo peoples mandated an imperial presence in the region. Lang sought to establish not cultural relativism but an unbridgeable cultural difference between the 'civilised' and the 'primitive', which eugenicists held to be different ranks of humanity. Lang took pains to publish pictures showing the local acceptance of the regime. His picture entitled *Danga, a Prominent Mangbetu Chief* was captioned as follows: 'Beside him stand two female body servants and behind are some of his people. The large medal hanging from his neck is the official sign of his rank as recognized by the Belgian administration. Of this he is very proud.' Similarly, his portrait of *Manziga, a Chief of the Azande* was captioned: 'He is unusually intelligent and exhibits much tact and diplomacy in dealings with the colonial administration' (Lang 1915) (Fig. 13.4). Manziga was portrayed in traditional dress, with the caption also referring to the Azande belief that they would be reincarnated as lions. Manziga is indeed 'almost the same but not quite' (Bhabha 1987: 318). It is that difference, that not quite, to which Lang devoted his attention. Photography sought to discover the difference that the heart of darkness made all but invisible, which is to say, it seemed so apparent, so obvious, and yet resisted the taxonomic efforts of the anthropologist.

The primary motivation behind these colonial photographs was to produce an effect of cultural difference in the eyes of the Western audience. The photographic sign is not purely arbitrary, in the way attributed to the written word by philosophers since Locke in the seventeenth century. Nor is it wholly natural, revealing only that which is 'really there'. It is rather a *motivated* sign, a sign which is supposed to look like something. In this case, Lang's photographs were supposed to show racial difference marked upon the bodies of his African subjects. According to his training both as a mammologist and a eugenic anthropologist, the difference was, by its very nature, visible. Yet that difference stubbornly failed to reveal itself. Lang saw the Mbuti as 'nomad dwarfs', evidently inferior to the 'tall negro', especially the Mangbetu people, but was unable to produce such definitive categorisations. The discourse of colonial mimicry frustrated any effort to reach the 'truth' of Africa. Instead, as Bhabha notes: 'What emerges between mimesis and mimicry is a *writing*' (Bhabha 1987: 320). Lang could not visualise racial difference and was ultimately reduced, like so many of his eugenicist colleagues, to writing the difference of race on to the African body. His essays and captions seek to use the photographs as evidence, but they resist signification without Lang's direction. Like the fetishist, the colonial photographer cannot believe the evidence of his or her eyes and resorts to a dedicated belief in the averted gaze.

This failure to signify was explained and justified by the designation of Africa in general as the Dark Continent and the Congo in particular as the heart of darkness. In such conditions, the implication ran, how could even Western science be expected to see details clearly? The invisibility and inexplicability of Africa has survived into the present day. On a map of the world as served by major international airlines, it often appears that there is a void between the Mediterranean coast of Africa and the 'Western' cities of South Africa. Similarly, Africa does not yet appear on the global representation of the Internet, the computer network upon which so many utopian dreams have recently been based. Western media continue to report political events in Africa as inexplicable, rather than examining the legacies of colonial power and the neo-colonial enterprises of nations such as France and Britain, and the multinational corporations. Faced with the failure of its interpretive models, Western culture is forced to rely upon what it sees as the 'essential' difference, the visible distinction of race, while having to admit that there are no precise means by which to define how one race is to be distinguished from the next. For all its lack of profundity or interpretive power, race remains written upon our bodies.

Notes

1   I will henceforth not strain the patience of the reader by placing every racial or racist term in quotation marks, but will presume that it is understood that these categories are purely discursive, with no reference to actual bodily qualities.

2   The reports in the museum's journal indicate that Lang and Chapin arrived in Avakubi in October 1910 and had returned there by 1912. By 30 September 1914 they had returned to Stanleyville (modern Kisangani) and sailed for home on 18 November 1914.

3   I have therefore restricted my discussion to those photographs published and commented on by Lang. The daunting task of applying this contextual reading to the entire corpus of Lang's photographic archive is beyond the scope of this chapter. Ironically, the consequence is that I shall discuss very few of the photographs which were displayed in *African Reflections*, the majority of which were taken from the archives.

4   Although the Congo is not named in *Heart of Darkness*, Conrad detailed the geography, climate and culture of the region in precise fashion, down to the 50 lb weight carried by 'native' porters, the brass wire used by the Belgians to 'pay' for ivory, and the navigation conditions of the Congo river.

5   By contrast, another traveller wrote in 1910: 'Avakubi is a beautiful place, quite an ideal station. Fine, lofty buildings constructed of good sun-burnt bricks, and the whole place was most compactly arranged. The Europeans' houses, built four square, with an open quadrangle in the centre, and a high brick wall surrounding the back part, which contained the servants' quarters and outhouses. . . .The gardens at once took my fancy, for here not only was there every kind of European vegetable, but also the most beautiful flowerbeds, arranged with great taste' (Lloyd 1899: 288–9).

6   The posthumous account of the explorer Sir Richard F. Burton concerning the 'Pygmies' was also published in 1899: 'The Akkas: The Pygmies of Africa', *The Humanitarian* (January–February): 15–29; 89–100.

187

14

Taming the tusk
The revival of chryselephantine sculpture in Belgium during the 1890s

Tom Flynn

Les dents d'éléphants ont un grand prix, c'est la matière que l'on estime le plus pour les statues des Dieux.[1]

Pliny's words, rendered into French for the benefit of visitors to the 1897 Brussels-Tervuren Exhibition are an appropriate point of departure from which to explore one of the hitherto more neglected manifestations of late nineteenth-century 'chryselephantine', or ivory-based mixed media sculpture. Elephant tooth ivory was as esteemed a commodity during the last quarter of the nineteenth century as it had been in Pliny's day, but its appearance at European international exhibitions during the 1890s is significant for the problematic status it occupied at that time at the intersection of so many different, and at times antithetical, ideologies and practices. At once the fruit of colonial adventurism, an international trade commodity, art medium, industrial raw material and, within more rarefied but no less significant world-views, a source of symbolic power, ivory was at that time open to a wide variety of appropriations and interpretations.

This chapter aims to explore some of the strategies of exhibition and display employed by the organisers of the Belgian International Exhibitions during the 1890s and particularly at the colonial section at Tervuren, just outside Brussels, in 1897. It will be concerned with the ways in which the exhibition organisers inserted Belgian ivory-based sculpture into the context of the Congo section of the exhibition and will question the motives behind this particular initiative.

I will argue that the use of ivory functioned as both a promotional tool advertising the material riches to be gained from the imperial project, and as a naturalising mechanism employed in order to help efface the controversial nature of King Leopold II's Congo enterprise. More problematically, I suggest that the planned appropriation and transformation – the making over – of this particular indigenous resource by the exhibition organisers can be read as a kind of fetish practice, not only in terms of the particular fixity with which the material was treated throughout the exhibitions, but also in terms of how the fashioned object or group of objects functioned metonymically as part for whole to ward off the disavowed insecurities of the Congo project and to alleviate anxieties concerning Belgian colonial identity and its political and economic status in relation to other Western European powers.

Belgium, like other imperial nations, played upon the trope of Civilisation and Barbarism[2] to fashion and perpetuate a set of conceptual hierarchies, as though fixing on the lack of fetish traditions in the West would provide evidence of its rationalism in distinction to its uncivilised 'Other' (Apter and Pietz 1993). However, the ways in which ivory – the particular *idée fixe* of King Leopold – was commodified and transmuted at the Belgian international exhibitions prompts some corrective readings around the shifting poles of gender and capital.

Perhaps more than any other European nation, Belgium, as represented by Leopold II – who went so far as to have his portrait sculpted in ivory by the Belgian artist Thomas Vinçotte – saw Africa in a very real way as a field upon which to map out the differentiated boundaries of nationhood (Ascherson 1963; Gann and Duignan 1979).

On a more fundamental, but no less important, level the material characteristics of ivory, not least its whiteness, its malleability and its tactile qualities, make it peculiarly susceptible to reification as a 'magical' commodity, particularly when fashioned into forms other than those constituting its primary industrial applications.

While progress on the Congo project was articulated in the pro-colonial press in terms of a masculinised alliance between *la croix et l'épée* – between the cross and the sword[3] – and viewed by the officer classes as representing an opportunity to reinvigorate Belgian manhood, its domestic promotion during the 1890s mobilised the specifically feminised and feminising discourses of the decorative arts. A pivotal role was assigned to ivory in these Belgian exhibitions, appearing in 'chryselephantine' sculpture in both its raw state and in juxtaposition with the contemporary grammar of Art Nouveau, but predominantly fashioned into small-scale representations of the female nude. This underscores the problematically gendered and commodified status of the Congo as a whole as it was represented and articulated in the 1890s. Indeed, like the Congo itself, many of the ivory objects shown at the Belgian exhibitions were immediately appropriated into private ownership (Luwel and Bruneel-Hye De Crom 1967: 89–103).

Belgian public opinion had never been sympathetic to the idea of an African colony and the response to the king's imperial designs was therefore only ever, at best, lukewarm (Pakenham 1991: 13; Emerson 1979: 56–62). The Brussels-Tervuren Exhibition of 1897 thus became something of a public relations exercise designed to promote colonial adventure and its material benefits in a positive light. The subsequent harvesting of vast quantities of ivory from Central West Africa and its sale through the Antwerp markets during the last two decades of the nineteenth century contributed significantly in financing the sovereign's colonial incursion into the Congo and the subsequent establishment of the colony's administrative infrastructure.

Although ostensibly aimed at instilling in the Belgian people a more sympathetic attitude to their African colony by disseminating knowledge about its indigenous peoples, their morals, beliefs and way of life, it could also be argued that the exhibition was an attempt on the part of Leopold and his advisers to help legitimate and sustain access to what had already been identified as a highly lucrative source of national, and personal, wealth (Gann and Duignan 1979: 16).

Leopold was not entirely alone in the enterprise, however, for his considerable skills at persuasion and propaganda, combined with promises of royal privilege and prestige, brought him sufficient allies from the political and business worlds to bring the project to some form of fruition, even though Belgian public opinion remained sceptical. Naturally, geographers, well-placed journalists and others interested in exploration warmed to the project and helped to promote and disseminate Leopold's ideas. Eventually, the prospect of privileged access to potentially lucrative markets won Leopold the support of businessmen and entrepreneurs whilst others were convinced by the highly publicised humanitarian commitments behind the project, particularly its anti-slavery aims. All these elements were marshalled towards the common cause, a cause expounded through a richly symbolic language of national improvement and universal enlightenment. Not only would colonisation provide new markets and new revenues, enabling Belgium to strengthen its armed forces and thus defend its neutrality in Europe, but equally, if not more importantly, it would offer Belgium the opportunity to prove to the world that it too was an 'imperial people capable of dominating and civilising others' (Pakenham 1991: 13). Belgium as a whole conspicuously failed to respond to such exhortations, however, and instead cast something of a jaundiced eye over the prospect.

The army, on the other hand, viewed matters more positively, some officers seeing a 'civilising mission' in Africa as an opportunity to cure all manner of social ills and to deliver the armed forces from the 'depressing state of moral torpor' into which it had, in their eyes, recently sunk. One officer, Charles Lemaire, indignant at hearing the Belgian army referred to as 'old women, sabre-rattlers, coffee-house heroes and leathernecks', saw the Congo as a chance for soldiers to 'show their élan', in a world 'with its own customs, its own prejudices, a world not yet touched by the canker of money'. Eventually, he believed, 'this little world will become a tabernacle of honour, the last refuge of virtue' (Gann and Duignan 1979: 24).

Lemaire's 'little world',[4] in reality a vast uncharted expanse many times the size of Belgium, became, by the turn of the century, a territory in which vice and malpractice had become commonplace as the Congo was systematically pillaged and plundered of its natural resources, its indigenous peoples degraded, subordinated and subjected to widespread atrocity (Emerson 1979; Morel 1906; Ascherson 1963; Pakenham 1991). This contrasts with the elevated assurances Leopold had given the world back in 1876 when he stated that:

> To open up to civilisation the sole portion of the globe to which it has
> not yet penetrated, to pierce the darkness which still envelopes whole

populations, is, I venture to say, a crusade worthy of this century of progress.

(Martelli 1962: 18)

The metaphors of 'penetration' and 'piercing', immediately gendering the colonial impulse as aggressively male, conjoined with a suggestion of heroic religiosity – the 'crusade' – foreshadow the 'ambivalence of authority' which came to characterise the Congo venture in which widespread exploitation took place behind the humanitarian façade of the anti-slavery movement.[5]

By 1879, when Stanley, Leopold's emissary, had arrived with his party at the mouth of the Congo, Leopold was energised by what he promoted first and foremost as a humanitarian mission to 'peacefully conquer and subdue' (Martelli 1962: 31). The literature is scattered with numerous accounts of the manipulative ruses and trickery adopted by Stanley, De Brazza and others in their efforts to cow the native chiefs into trade and compliance.[6] Eventually their efforts came to fruition for a substantial ivory trade was established which largely financed the subsequent entrenchment of the colonial administration.[7] By 1893/4, Antwerp had usurped Liverpool and London as the centre of the world ivory market and the commodity was well established as offering the quickest and most substantial return on investment.

It is difficult to find objective statistical data regarding the ivory trade in the nineteenth century, as different countries, perhaps seeing it as an index of success in colonial endeavour, naturally wished to claim market primacy. Nevertheless, there is a broad consensus that by 1897 Antwerp had assumed primacy as the world centre of trade in the commodity, which is corroborated by figures issued in 1896 from the world's two leading ivory-trading companies: Meyer of Hamburg and Willaert of Antwerp, who submitted their statistics to the journal *Le Mouvement Géographique* in 1896.

Although highly lucrative in market terms, the trade in ivory was at no stage an unproblematic endeavour. Its negative consequences, both in terms of the effect on the indigenous peoples and on the local ecology, were recognised from the early months of its establishment. Essentially an extractive enterprise, the trade did nothing to stimulate the indigenous Congo industries and, if anything, exacerbated inter-tribal rivalries and disagreements. Furthermore, the manipulation by colonial traders of local knowledge – or lack of it – as to the difference in price between ivory at the coast and in the interior – disrupted regional economies and impacted upon the vacuum created by a diminishing slave trade (Harms 1981: 40). Without the ivory trade, Livingstone had been told by the slavers, the slave trade did not pay. Burton, too, recognised the absolute connection of the ivory and slave trades, while Swann, another pioneer trader, summarised the association of these businesses in stating that: 'By himself the slave did not pay transport, but plus ivory he was a paying game' (Moore 1931: 61).

Thus, the two central threads of the Congo enterprise, the two means of justification selected by Leopold to sell the project at home – trade and the abolition of slavery – were interconnected. Opposition to this ruinous exploitation, or *Raubwirtschaft* as it became known, was widespread. A contributor to *Chamber's Journal* of 1886 expressed alarm at the sheer quantities of ivory being harvested and offered what to modern ears has become a familiar warning:

> At this rate, these imports represent 296,016 pairs [of tusks] and consequently the same number of elephants have either died long ago, or have been recently slaughtered, to supply the demands of luxury in nine years alone [up to 1881]. At this rate of destruction . . . it will be seen how rapidly this noble animal must disappear, and how surely ivory will become a thing of the past.
>
> (*Chamber's Journal* 1886: 288)

The writer goes on to speculate that the temptation of increasing high prices will soon exhaust the large quantities of ivory still remaining in the African interior. A good deal of the indignation expressed about the ivory harvesting was stimulated by the knowledge that the material was only destined to satisfy the market for 'luxury' goods. William Booth, founder of the Salvation Army, writing in 1890, added his voice to the growing opposition to the trade when he claimed that:

> Upon the pygmies and all the dwellers of the forest has descended a devastating visitation in the shape of the ivory raiders of civilisation. . . . They exploit the domestic affections of the forest dwellers in order to strip them of all they possess in the world. That has been going on for years. It is going on today. It has come to be regarded as the natural and normal law of existence.
>
> (Booth 1890: 11)

By 1897, the year of the Brussels-Tervuren Exhibition, the need was greater than ever to disseminate a positive image of the colony. Furthermore, Leopold was also concerned that unless his subjects began to take a more sympathetic view of the African territory, his prospects of handing it over to them would disappear altogether. The Congo was at this time still the King's own personal possession but he continued to propagandise in the hope that Belgium would be willing to assume ownership on recognising the project as serving the commonweal.

Traditionally, international exhibitions tended to alight upon mundane domestic objects to communicate the diverse applications of raw materials but it was as though the Brussels-Tervuren Exhibition needed to articulate something other than purely utilitarian messages in its promotion of ivory. The use of the material in small-scale sculpture was first promoted at the Antwerp International Exhibition in 1894. The Belgian artist Fernand Khnopff told *The Studio* magazine that year that the first invitation to Belgian sculptors to use ivory in their work had come from Edmund van Eetvelde, secretary of the Congo Free State and had been greeted with enthusiasm (Luwel and Bruneel-Hye De Crom 1967: 49).

A number of French and Belgian artists had already embarked upon explorations into mixed media sculpture by the 1890s. Some brought to the practice the techniques and intricate decorative vocabularies of the jeweller and the goldsmith, combining their ivory carving and bronze casting with incrustations of precious stones and enamel work. Others employed more traditional, small-scale sculptural methods but explored innovative ways of joining ostensibly incompatible materials, while some simply carved the raw tusk, leaving it otherwise unadorned. However, the works displayed at the 1894 Antwerp exhibition constituted, Khnopff was careful to point out, a 'revival . . . of chryselephantine sculpture' (Khnopff 1894: 150).

A letter addressed to Edmund van Eetvelde, signed by seven of the sculptors contributing to the Antwerp show, expressed their gratitude for this state benevolence and confirmed their conviction that the encouragement would foster a revival of the chryselephantine technique (Luwel and Bruneel-Hye De Crom 1967: 49). Many of the artists contributing to these colonial exhibitions had been active members of those socialist artistic circles such as *l'Essor* and *Les Vingt* (later continued as *La Libre Esthétique*) and no doubt saw these state initiatives and the accompanying chance of widespread exposure as an opportunity to disseminate their own avant-garde artistic agenda, namely that of an 'art nouveau'. Nevertheless, notwithstanding their gratitude for the state's involvement in reviving the chryselephantine aesthetic in Belgian art (Luwel and Bruneel-Hye De Crom 1967: 49), it is difficult to read their collaboration as anything less than a compromise of the radical political principles which largely governed artistic activity in Belgium at this time (Herbert 1961).

According to some commentators, a disproportionate emphasis had been placed upon the origin of the materials at the 1894 Antwerp exhibition. It was therefore only when the Brussels Art Club staged a special show some months after the 1894 International Exhibition that the objects were, as it were, 'liberated' from the African connection. Thus Khnopff was able to report that: 'The Brussels Art Club recently conceived the excellent idea of giving adequate reception to the chryselephantine sculptures, which figured in the International Exhibition at Antwerp rather as products of the Congo than as objets d'art' (Khnopff 1894: 150).

A newel post at the foot of a staircase from the 1894 Antwerp exhibition (Fig. 14.1) makes clear the extent to which ivory became harnessed to broader agendas during this period, shoring up a gulf between ostensibly opposing artistic and political ideologies, that of a socialist-orientated Art Nouveau on the one hand, and of right royal imperialism on the other. A raw tusk ensnared by tendrils functions as a neat visual metaphor for Leopold's contemporary preoccupations. Furthermore, the location of the tusk at the end of the hand-rail clearly invites active engagement, foregrounding its tactile properties and incorporating them into the felt physical experience of the exhibition flâneur. One might even refer to the numerous tribal traditions in which the actions of stroking, rubbing and polishing are what activate the fetish's magical powers. Homi Bhabha has noted, following the exploration of the museum environment by the African-American artist Renée Green, how 'the stairwell as liminal space, in-between the designations of identity, becomes the process of symbolic interaction, the connective tissue that constructs the difference between upper

Figure 14.1 Elephant tusk newel post, Antwerp International Exhibition, 1894.

and lower, black and white' (Bhabha 1994: 4). The Antwerp stairway was a space susceptible to manipulation on a number of levels.

It is likely that King Leopold himself would have visited the show at the Brussels Art Club which followed the Antwerp exhibition, having for some time recognised the importance of supporting cultural projects which were connected to, or which arose from, the colonial effort. When Alexandre Delcommune, one of the king's commercial envoys, returned from his Congo-Kasai survey of 1888–9 with extensive photographs of his expedition, they too were displayed at the Brussels Art Club and the King and Queen made a public visit to the exhibition (Cornet 1953: 125).

It was therefore not surprising that the King and his 1897 committee of exhibition organisers should endeavour to develop at Tervuren the encouragement first lent to artists at Antwerp in 1894. Indeed, the man responsible for that Antwerp initiative, Edmund van Eetvelde, was made chairman of the committee in charge of the Congolese section of the Brussels-Tervuren Exhibition three years later. Once again, Fernand Khnopff – although hardly the most objective observer, given that he was himself a contributor – gave *The Studio* the benefit of his opinion in 1897:

> When the colonial section was established in the Antwerp International Exhibition of 1894, the committee paid far more attention to the

practical side of the matter than to any other; and thus it was that the few works of art in ivory displayed – or at any rate deposited – there made very little impression. . . . This year the Tervueren [*sic*] Colonial section of the Brussels Exhibition has been arranged with every regard for art.

(Khnopff 1897: 200–3)

As far as the organisers of the Brussels-Tervuren event were concerned, ivory was virtually a currency in itself, having already helped defray the initial costs of establishing the colonial administration. Although no statistics are available to assess the relative success of the Congo section of the Brussels-Tervuren Exhibition in terms of attendance,[8] there is little doubt about Leopold's hopes and aspirations.

The lawyer Félicien Cattier estimated that the Domain de la Couronne [the Crown estate region of the Congo furtively delivered into Leopold's personal possession in 1892] had made nearly £2,900,000 in clear profit for Leopold in the ten years between 1896 and 1906. Morel [E. D. Morel, the British journalist who monitored Leopold's activities during the early 1900s] calculated that Leopold had made a personal profit of £2,000,000 in six years.

(Ascherson 1963: 241)

With the prospect of further riches to be gained from the burgeoning rubber trade, it was, by 1897, arguably more important than ever for Leopold not only to maintain a firm grip on that 'slice of magnificent African cake' (Pakenham 1991: 22), but also to keep the Belgian public sympathetic to the colonial programme. Hence the official guide to the Brussels-Tervuren Exhibition was at pains to point out that of all the riches issuing from the African interior, ivory had been the most exploited and, thanks to its high value, had allowed its traders to defray the initial costs of establishing their businesses (Masui 1897: 326).

It is also clear from their repetition of their Antwerp strategy that the exhibition organisers perceived certain advantages in presenting the Belgian works within the context of the Congo component of the exhibition rather than as autono-mously located *objets d'art*, although despite these strategies of classification, the organisers continued to describe the works as 'chryselephantine' sculpture, a term whose etymology properly extends back to the literature surrounding the Athena Parthenos, that most ancient icon of imperialism.

Following the feeling among artists that their work had been 'deposited' rather than 'displayed' at the 1894 Antwerp Exhibition (Khnopff 1897: 200), and that excessive emphasis had been placed on their work as products of the Congo rather than as *objets d'art*, a compromise was reached at the Brussels-Tervuren Exhibition where a special Salon d'Honneur was established in which their work was arranged. Nevertheless it was still incorporated into the Congo section. In a chapter of the official Tervuren Exhibition guide dealing with the fauna of the Congo, the author, Masui, the general secretary of the Congo

195

section, suggested that the most 'noble use' to which ivory could be put was in chryselephantine sculpture 'so admirably represented in the Salon d'Honneur' (Masui 1897: 329). Hence it would seem that if people could be convinced of the material's more 'noble' applications first, then its economic advantages would be more easily justified and communicated.

These various ambiguities were extended into the geographical organisation of the Brussels-Tervuren Exhibition. The halls devoted to the fine arts, the sciences and Belgian industry, as well as the pavilions for the foreign sections, were distributed in the Parc du Cinquantenaire, overlooked by the spire of the Palais de Bruxelles and thus securely enclosed within the symbolic embrace of the Belgian state, while this main component was to be augmented by a special section which was planned to become a permanent museum devoted to the Congo colony.

The Tervuren site earmarked for the exhibition of the 'Independent State' of the Congo was a spacious stretch of parkland some fifteen kilometres from the centre of Brussels and part of the king's own royal domain. This location, chosen by Leopold himself, was the site of a château built by the Prince of Orange between 1817 and 1822 which had been destroyed by fire in 1879. It was to become the home of the new Congo Palace, today's Royal Museum of Central Africa.

The king conceived a scheme which comprised a 12-kilometre avenue through villages and forests and across bridges, along which would run an electric tramway linking the main exhibition site at the Parc du Cinquantenaire with the Congo Palace standing in its own expansive parkland.

This privileging of the Congolese component of the exhibition was the culmination of a plan which had been forming in Leopold's mind since the early 1880s and which was designed to broadcast what he saw as the commercial promise of the future colony while at the same time silencing his objectors (Luwel and Bruneel-Hye De Crom 1967: 47–8). From the outset, however, although the spatial arrangement of the 'palaces' and pavilions housing the exhibits reflected, on the one hand, Leopold's desire to promote the Congo to its best advantage, at the same time it underscored its distant and peripheral nature. Geographically severed from the administrative 'centre', separated from the displays of the 'civilised' European exhibitors, and even – surely the cruellest irony – reached only by a route 'qui traverse ponts, villages et forêts' (ibid.: 47), the Congo section of the exhibition was thus perhaps 'othered' to a greater extent at Tervuren than were other ethnographic displays of the 1890s (Hinsley 1991: 346).

Inside the Palace of the Colonies, however – the Congo section of the Brussels-Tervuren Exhibition – the governing initiative appears to have been an attempt to familiarise, or to domesticate, the unfamiliar nature of the Congolese component, to soften the impact of the African exhibits and to assist in the assimilation of the novel nature of the material on display. The central strategy was to position the African material – textually in the exhibition guide, and spatially in the exhibition hall – adjacent to the ivory-based works produced by European artists, or, more accurately to introduce the European-made sculpted

196

objects into the space preceding that designated for the colonial material. The important conjoining factor was ivory as it appeared both in the sculpted objects and in the interior designs by some of the leading Brussels architects and decorators such as Paul Hankar, Gustave Serrurier-Bovy and Henri Van de Velde. The particular mixture of elements which Serrurier-Bovy and Hankar developed at Tervuren became known among the general public at the time as *Le Style Congo*, 'The Congo Style' (Fierens-Gevaert 1903: 189). Indeed, it would not be too far wrong to suggest that the whole scheme was striving towards a kind of Africanised Art Nouveau *Gesamtkunstwerk*, the resulting intertextuality of which seems to have been a purposeful promotional mechanism. Fernand Khnopff, who contributed his own chryselephantine works at the Brussels-Tervuren Exhibition, revealed that in 1894:

> The more enterprising sculptors had their names registered, in order to secure picked sections of ivory, in which the grain is more compact and tougher than in the Indian variety, and the dimensions more suitable for statues; in fact, some of the exhibits reached unusual proportions, being the magnitude of the great African elephant's tusks.
>
> (Khnopff 1894: 150)

Philippe Wolfers' bronze and ivory *Caresse du Cygne* (Caress of the Swan) (Fig. 14.2), at around 6 ft (1.82 m) high, was one of the largest objects exhibited

Figure 14.2 Philippe Wolfers, *La Caresse du Cygne*, ivory, bronze. Exhibited in the Salon d'Honneur, Congo Palace, Brussels-Tervuren Exhibition, 1897.

in the Salon d'Honneur at Tervuren. This was another work which left the tusk in its virtually unadorned state, save for some low-relief Art Nouveau engraving. Indeed, close inspection reveals its conspicuously stamped Antwerp importation registration number which Wolfers clearly chose to leave visible. At around two metres high, it is hardly classifiable as an *objet d'art* but it typifies the visual euphemisms through which the relationship between coloniser and colonised was communicated in the Salon d'Honneur.

It seems to have been more important to the exhibition organisers to use ivory transformed into *objets d'art* – or *objets de fantaisie* to use the language of the official exhibition guide – as a promotional tool rather than to spotlight its more mundane domestic applications such as piano keys, knife handles, combs, etc. Better still if the objects preserved the original form of the tusk, such as that which appeared in Wolfers' swan vase, for in this context it was experienced as art rather than as purely utilitarian object, an essential strand of Leopold's initiative, as was suggested in the official exhibition guide where he declared that 'the artistic sense of a people is the most elevated expression of her perfectibility and the protection of the arts underlines the grandeur of a government' (Masui 1897: 3).

Civilisation et Barbarie – chryselephantine sculpture in the Salon d'Honneur

While the ostensible aim of the exhibition as a whole was to familiarise the Belgian people with the material culture, social organisation, flora and fauna, etc. of their king's still relatively new colonial acquisition, another aim was to present palpable evidence of the advantages issuing from the trade in ivory. As we have seen, the Congo Palace at the Tervuren section of the exhibition contained a Salon d'Honneur, a room devoted to the work of Belgian artists. The majority of these exhibits – embracing sculpture, furniture and textiles – incorporated ivory donated by the State for this specific purpose.

As the ground plan of the exhibition shows (Fig. 14.3), the Salon d'Honneur containing all the ivory-based works by Belgian artists preceded the Salle d'Ethnographie – the exhibition of Congolese material – in the suggested order of a 'tour' of the Palais and as the first room entered by the visitor, the Salon d'Honneur effectively opened the Congolese section, thus establishing the mood for the ensuing displays. This progression, through both physical and temporal dimensions from the displays of the familiar to those of the strange, corresponds to the projected diachronic narrative of colonial movement, the passage in both space and time from the here to the elsewhere. In the organisation of the Palais des Colonies, the aspirations of the active colonial agenda are enacted as enfilade. It could be argued, however, that the narrative charge stems not from a movement towards, or through, but rather as a procession away from the sovereign site of meaning, thus maintaining the primacy of centre over periphery.

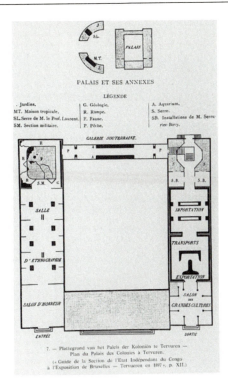

Figure 14.3   Ground plan, Congo Palace, Brussels-Tervuren Exhibition, 1897.

The section of the guide introducing the Salon d'Honneur featured an engraving representing a white European woman dressed in classical robes and wearing a laurel crown, holding a sculptor's mallet and gouge and leaning against a pedestal (Fig. 14.4). She is approached – itself a reversal of the narrative which defined the historical relationship between coloniser and colonised – by a personification of Africa, wearing a simple shift, tooth necklace and 'ethnic' bracelets who proffers a tusk to her European counterpart. It is followed by a solemn encomium informing the Exhibition visitor of the fecundity of the colonial territories which is worth quoting at length:

> The colonies, fecund sources of wealth, which so greatly extend
> our commercial and scientific horizon, besides supplying marvellous
> materials with which to work, can also bring – and this is the case for
> the new countries of central Africa – a real contribution to the domain
> of the 'beautiful', offering in the works of the primitives, naive and
> moving interpretations of nature herself. These models, of an absolute
> sincerity and purity, can help in a way altogether unforeseen in the
> development of our modern aesthetic sensibility.
>
> (Masui 1897: 3)

This conflation of political and aesthetic ideas is typical of the strategies employed throughout the exhibition and from which a number of issues arise.

Figure 14.4 Frontispiece, Salon d'Honneur, Official Guide to the Brussels-Tervuren Exhibition, 1897.

The conjunction of the European objects with the Congolese artefacts – both within the text and in the real space of the exhibition hall – seems designed to normalise the indigenous products of the colony by equating them in some vague way with European notions of 'beauty'. The suggestion that such objects possess some 'sincerity' and 'absolute purity' belongs to a set of attitudes which sees 'primitive' art as somehow childlike. As Sally Price pointed out:

> A widely accepted belief . . . is that, more than any art from the world's Great Civilisations (whether Western or Oriental), Primitive Art emerges directly and spontaneously from psychological drives. Just as children cry when they are hungry and coo when they are content, Primitive artists are imagined to express their feelings free from the intrusive overlay of learned behaviour and conscious constraints that mold the work of the Civilised artist.

(Price 1989: 34)

The gendering of both the Western artist and the personification of the colony as female serves a number of ends – to efface the patriarchal nature of imperial power, to reinforce the attributes of fertility and fecundity assigned to the colony, and to underscore the feminised and feminising nature of the decorative arts.

The various aesthetic interpretations of the Congo and its resources were largely determined by the proximity of the European objects to the Congolese artefacts – both within the text and in the real space of the exhibition hall. The tapestry created by the Belgian artist Hélène de Rudder, entitled *Le Fétichisme* (Fig. 14.5), which hung in the opening display in the Salon d'Honneur, mediated any authentic Congolese representations of their fetish traditions before the exhibition visitor had entered the ethnographic room in which such artefacts were arranged. It would seem that this severance of fetish practice from its social base, the decontextualisation, découpage and distortion of some of its constituent visual elements, effectively served to promote the Belgian decorative arts on the back of, and hence at the expense of, a coherent presentation of African material culture.

The simulated vistas of the Congo – the Congolese planted into suburban Brussels for the duration of the Exhibition, an exterior mock-up of the Ogowé river – offering a safe, mediated experience of the exotic and the unfamiliar, were presented as of the same order as an interior array of indigenous artefacts, effectively rendering the geography of the colony as available commodity.

Philippe Wolfers (1858–1929) was already an established exponent of the new decorative language of Art Nouveau with considerable experience in chryselephantine work behind him, and had explored other areas besides mixed media sculpture. It was he who constructed the bound volume of the Brussels-Tervuren Exhibition guide in ivory, bronze and precious stones mounted on a 'Heron' stand of bronze and oak. The album cover employs all the typical Wolfers devices of the period – trailing Art Nouveau foliage, flowers and bats in bronze – set against an ivory background engraved with a representation of one of his own sculptures, *La Caresse du Cygne*, which was also exhibited at the exhibition, together with a rendering in low relief of a view of the Salle d'Ethnographie. The whole scheme is pulled together by the sunrise motif. The symbolism of enlightenment, of illumination of the Dark Continent, was never far from the surface of Wolfers' work.

The bound album represents yet another example, besides the multi-functional, multi-contextual use of ivory, of how everything in the exhibition seems to refer to everything else. Objects are engraved with representations of other objects, symbolic components are common to otherwise unrelated works.

This intertextuality may have served to imbue the visual experience with a reassuring continuity so that the ensuing exposure to the Salle d'Ethnographie – another room juxtaposing ivory tusks with home-grown Art Nouveau interior decoration – would be the more easily assimilated both visually and ideologically. The assumption seems to have been that if everything could be

Figure 14.5 Hélène de Rudder, *Le Fétichisme*, silk embroidery. Exhibited at the Salon d'Honneur, Congo Palace, Brussels-Tervuren Exhibition 1897.

subordinated to an overriding 'Art Nouveauism', as it were, or, to put it another way, if the transition from display to display could be softened by the dominant domestic aesthetic, then the strange would appear familiar, the dangerous would be made safe.

The heavy-handed symbolism crops up again and again in Wolfers' mixed media work of this period, his *Civilisation et Barbarie* (Fig. 14.6) of 1896/7 plays out, with typical ambiguity, the binary equation of Civilisation and Barbarism which, as we have seen, has a more extended pedigree as part of the critical languages surrounding art and design in this period, as well as emerging as a common trope of the late nineteenth-century discourse of 'social exploration' (Booth 1890: 12).

Leopold II and his administrators also drew on these mechanisms – the tensions between light and dark and their perceived symbolic cognates of good and evil

Figure 14.6 Philippe Wolfers, *Civilisation et Barbarie*, ivory, silver, onyx. Exhibited at the Salon d'Honneur, Congo Palace, Brussels-Tervuren Exhibition 1897.

– and added them to what had become a powerful propaganda machine marshalled towards the promotion of the King's African adventures. Artists too were recruited into the front line of these exercises. Echoing its function in Periclean Athens, chryselephantine sculpture again found itself at the interstices of art and imperialism. Was Leopold casting himself as as a modern Pericles, Tervuren as his Parthenos?

Notes

1 'Elephant teeth have great value, it is the material most esteemed for the statues of the gods.' The quotation from Pliny's *Natural History* opened a section devoted to the subject of chryselephantine sculpture in the official guide to the 1897 Brussels–Tervuren Exhibition (Masui, 1897). See Pliny (1991): 113.

2 See, for example, 'Civilisation – Barbarism' in *The United States Democratic Review*, Vol. IV, 1856: 239–44. The appropriation of the trope of Civilised-Barbarian during this period is, it could be argued, an extension of the modern Western powers' identification with, and self-definition through, ancient Greek 'civilisation'. The use of ivory in this context, as a self-conscious continuation of the ancient Greek 'chryselephantine' tradition, coincides with their simultaneous quotation of the logos of Civilised/Barbarian through which the ancient Greeks identified themselves with the Persian 'Other'. As Edith Hall suggests, 'every era finds in the study of the ancient world a context in which to express its own preoccupations' (Hall, E. 1989: ix; see also Rubel 1978).

3 See, for example, the journal *Le Patriote Congolais*, May 1895.

4 I re-quote these comments here for more specific reasons than merely to outline the 'machismo' of the colonising forces. What these observations point up is the contrast between two strategies and two languages of colonial promotion, for while officers such as Lemaire drew on the 'masculinising' advantages which might be gleaned from the Congo project, its domestic promotion mobilised the specifically 'feminised' and feminising discourses of the decorative arts, nowhere more eloquently deployed than at Tervuren, in order to figure the colony as 'naturalising' and safe.

5 A number of historians have identified the impulse to disguise the true nature of the colonial project, seeing it as a defining characteristic of imperialism. See, for example, Hobson 1938: 215; Bhabha 1994.

6 Emil Torday, for example, used mechanical toy elephants as magic charms to impress and control the Bakongo people of the Congo. See Vansina, Jan, 'Photographs of the Sankuru and Kasai River Basin Expedition Undertaken by Emil Torday and M. W. Hilton Simpson' in Edwards 1992: 193–205.

7 Most secondary literature on the Belgian Congo focuses close attention on the importance of the ivory trade in funding the initial stages of the colonial project. See in particular: Morel (1906); Emerson (1979); Slade (1962); Ascherson (1963); Gann and Duignan (1979); Harms (1981); Martelli (1962); Vansina (1973).

8 'It was not unusual to have an attendance [at the Brussels Exhibition] on one or other of these days [Sunday or Monday] of 60,000 people. The entire attendance during the exposition of paying entries was stated at over six millions . . . The Exposition was a financial success' (*Report of the Commissioners of the United States to the International Exhibition held at Brussels in 1897*, Washington 1898: 34).

Bibliography

African Studies Centre (1973) *David Livingstone: Proceedings of a Seminar held on the Occasion of the Centenary of the Death of David Livingstone*, African Studies Centre, University of Edinburgh.

Agathe, J. and Strauss, K. (1985) *Waffen aus Zentral-Afrika*, Frankfurt: Museum fur Volkerkunde.

Alloula, M. (1986) *The Colonial Harem*, trans. M. and W. Godzich, Minneapolis: University of Minnesota Press.

Alpers, E. A. (1975) *Ivory and Slaves in East Central Africa*, London: Heinemann.

Altick, R. D. (1978) *The Shows of London*, Cambridge, MA: The Belknap Press of Harvard University Press.

Amoano, T., Tupene, T. and Neich, R. (1984) 'The complementarity of history and art in Tutamure meeting house, Omarumutu Marae, Opotiki', *Journal of the Polynesian Society*, 93 (1): 5–37.

Andrews, P. (1986) *Tarawera and the Terraces*, New Zealand: Wilson and Horton Publications.

Angas, G. F. (1847) *Savage Life and Scenes in Australia and New Zealand: Being an Artist's Impressions of the Countries and People at the Antipodes*, Volume 11, London: Smith, Elder and Co.

—— (1847a) *The New Zealanders Illustrated*, London: T. Maclean.

Annuaire du Congo, Belge et l'Afrique Occidentale (1913), Brussels.

Ansell, P. (1994) *The Perfect Nihilist: An Introduction to Nietzsche as Political Thinker*, Cambridge: Cambridge University Press.

Appadurai, A. and Kopytoff, I. (eds) (1986) *The Social Life of Things: Commodities in Cultural Perspective*, Cambridge: Cambridge University Press.

Apter, E. and Pietz, W. (eds) (1993) *Fetishism as Cultural Discourse*, Ithaca and London: Cornell University Press.

Arnold, E. (1868) 'Theodore the King', *Gentleman's Magazine* I: August.

Ascherson, N. (1963) *The King Incorporated*, London: Allen & Unwin.

Ashcroft, B., Griffiths, G. and Tiffin, H. (eds) (1995) *The Post-colonial Studies Reader*, London: Routledge.

Astapovich, Z. A. (ed.) (1971) *Velikii Oktiabr' i raskreposhchenie zhenshchin Srednei Azii i Kazakhstana (1917–1936 gg.), sbornik dokumentov i materialov*, Moscow: Mysl.

Baden-Powell, B. H. (1872) *Handbook of the Manufactures and Arts of the Punjab*, Lahore: Government Printing Press.

Baker, M. (1982) *The Cast Courts*, London: Victoria and Albert Museum.

Bankes, G. (1990) *Aotearoa: the Maori Collections at the Manchester Museum*, Manchester: Manchester Museum.

Banta, M. and Hinsley, C. H. (1986) *From Site to Sight: Anthropology, Photography and the Power of Imagery*, Cambridge, MA: Peabody Museum Press.

Barker, H. W. (1904) *The Story of Chisamba*, Toronto: Canada Congregational Foreign Missionary Society.

Barrett, T. H. (1989) *Singular Listlessness: A Short History of Chinese Books and British Scholars*, London: Wellsweep Press.

Barringer, T. J. (1996) 'The South Kensington Museum and the mid-Victorian moment' in H.C. Collinson (ed.), *Victorian: Style of Empire*, Toronto: Royal Ontario Museum.

Bhabha, H. K. (1987) 'Of mimicry and man: the ambivalence of colonial discourse' in Annette Michelson *et al.* (eds), *October: The First Decade*, Cambridge, MA: MIT Press.

—— (1994) *The Location of Culture*, London and New York: Routledge.

Biddick, K. *et al.* (1996) 'Aesthetics, ethnicity and the history of art: a range of critical perspectives', *Art Bulletin*, LXXVIII (4) (December): 594–621.

Binney, J. (1984) 'Myth and explanation in the Ringatu tradition', *Journal of the Polynesian Society*, 93 (4): 345–98.

Binyon, L. (1908) *The Painting of the Far East*, London: Edward Arnold.

Binyon, C. H. (1936) *The Spirit of Man in Asian Art*, Cambridge MA: Dover.

Birdwood, G. C. M. (1878) *Handbook to the Indian Section of the Paris International Exhibition, 1878*, London: Offices of the Royal Commission.

—— (1880) *The Industrial Arts of India*, London: Chapman and Hall.

—— (1881) *Portfolio of Indian Art*, London: South Kensington Museum.

Blank, S. (1994) 'Soviet reconquest of Central Asia' in H. Malik (ed.), *Central Asia: Its Strategic Importance and Future Prospects*, New York: St. Martin's Press.

Blussé, L. and Falkenburg, R. (1987) *Johan Nieuhofs Beelden van een Chinareis 1655–1657*, Middelburg: Stichting VOC Publicaties.

Booth, W. (1890) *In Darkest England and The Way Out*, London: International Headquarters.

Breckenridge, C. (1989) 'The politics of colonial collecting: India at the World's Fairs', *Comparative Studies in Society and History*, 31.

Broca, P. (1868) 'Transactions of the Anthropological Society of Paris during 1865–67', *Anthropological Review*, 22.

Broyard, A. (1950) 'Portrait of the inauthentic negro', *Commentary*, 10: 56–64.

Buckingham, J. S. (n.d.) *The Eastern and Western States of America*, 3 vols, London and Paris: Fisher, Son & Co.

Burton, A. (1985) 'The Image of the Curator', *Victoria and Albert Museum Album*, 4: 373–87.

Butler, J. (1990) *Gender Trouble: Feminism and the Subversion of Identity*, London and New York: Routledge.

Cain, P. J. and Hopkins, A. G. (1993) *British Imperialism: Innovation and Expansion 1688–1914*, London: Longman.

Cairns, H. A. C. (1965) *Prelude to Imperialism: British Reactions to Central African Society, 1840–1890*, London: Routledge and Kegan Paul.

Calcutta (1885), *Official Report of the Calcutta International Exhibition in 1883–84*, Calcutta: Bengal Secretariat Press

Campbell, L. (1996) 'The design of Leighton House: the artist's "palace of art"', *Apollo*, February: 10–16.

Cannizzo, J. (1989) *Into the Heart of Africa*, Toronto: Royal Ontario Museum.

—— (1991) 'Exhibiting cultures: "Into the Heart of Africa", *Visual Anthropology Review*, 7 (1): 150–60.

—— (1996) 'Dr Livingstone collects' in J. Mackenzie (ed.), *David Livingstone and the Victorian Encounter with Africa*, London: National Portrait Gallery.

Carpenter, F. R. (1976) *The Old China Trade: Americans in Canton, 1784–1843*, New York: Coward, McCann Geoghegan.

Catalogue of the Articles (1852) *Catalogue of the Articles of Ornamental Art selected from the Exhibition of the Works of Industry of All Nations in 1851 and Purchased by the Government*, London: Chapman and Hall.

Christie & Manson Auctioneers (1851) *Catalogue of the Celebrated Assemblage Which Formed the Chinese Exhibition, Collected by the Late Nathan Dunn, Esq.*, London, December 10–14.

Chudakov, G. (1990) *20 Sowjet Fotografen, 1917–1940*, Amsterdam: Fiolet & Draaijer Interphoto v.o.f.

Clendennen, G. (1979) David Livingstone: *A Catalogue of Documents*, Edinburgh: National Library of Scotland.

—— (1992) *David Livingstone's Shire Journal, 1861–1864*, Aberdeen: Scottish Cultural Press.

Clifford, J. (1988) *The Predicament of Culture: Twentieth-Century Ethnography, Literature and Art*, Cambridge, MA: Harvard University Press.

—— and Marcus, G. E. (1986) *Writing Culture: The Politics and Poetics of Ethnography*, Berkeley: University of California Press.

Clunas, C. (ed.) (1987) *Chinese Export Art and Design*, London: Victoria and Albert Museum.

Cohen, D. W. and Greene, J. P. (eds) (1972) *Neither Slave Nor Free, The Freedman of African Descent in the Slave Societies of the New World*, Baltimore and London: Johns Hopkins University Press.

Cole, Sir H. (1884) *Fifty Years of Public Work of Sir Henry Cole, Accounted for in his Deeds, Speeches and Writings*, 2 vols, London: George Bell.

Comaroff, J. and Comaroff, J. (1991) *Of Revelation and Revolution: Christianity, Colonialism and Consciousness in South Africa*, Chicago: University of Chicago Press.

—— (1992) *Ethnography and the Historical Imagination*, Boulder: Westview Press.

The Comic Album: A Book for Every Table (1842), London: Orr and Co.

Conrad, J. (1969) *Heart of Darkness* in *The Portable Conrad*, Harmondsworth: Penguin.

Conway, M. (1882) *Travels in South Kensington*, London: Trubner.

Coomaraswamy, A. K. (1908) *Art and Swadeshi*, Madras: Guardian.

Coombes, A. E. (1988), 'Museums and the formation of national and cultural identities', *Oxford Art Journal*, II: 57–68.

—— (1994) *Re-inventing Africa: Museums, Material Culture and the Popular Imagination*, New Haven: Yale University Press.

Cornet, R. J. (1953) [1947] *La Bataille du Rail*, Brussels: Editions L. Cuypers.

Cowan, J. (1910) *Official Record [of the Opening of the Parliament of New Zealand]*, Christchurch: Government Press.

Crew, S. R. and Sims, J. E. (1991) 'Locating authority' in I. Karp and S. Lavine (eds) *Exhibiting Cultures: The Poetics and Politics of Museum Display*, Washington DC: Smithsonian Institution Press.

Crichton, M. (1980) *Congo*, New York: Knopf.

Crook, J. M. (1981) *William Burges and the High Victorian Dream*, London: John Murray.

Cunningham, A. (1875) *Archaeological Survey of India*, 5 vols., Calcutta: Government Press.

Currie, W. T. (1886–1910) Papers and correspondence. United Church of Canada Archives, Toronto.

Daston, L. and Galison, P. (1992) 'The image of objectivity', *Representations*, 40 (Fall): 81–128.

Davidoff, L. and Hall, C. (1987) *Family Fortunes: Men and Women of the English Middle Class, 1780–1850*, London and Melbourne: Hutchinson.

Davies, P. (1985) *Splendours of the Raj: British Architecture in India 1660–1947*, London and New Delhi: Dass Media in association with John Murray.

d'Encausse, H. C. (1992) *The Great Challenge: Nationalities and the Bolshevik State, 1917–1930*, trans. Nancy Festinger, New York and London: Holmes & Meier.

Denis, R. (1995) 'The Brompton Barracks: war, peace and the rise of Victorian art and design education', *Journal of Design History*, VIII: 1.

Desmond, R. (1982) *The India Museum, 1801 – 1879*, London: India Office Library and Records.

Dickerson, M. C. (1910) 'In the Heart of Africa', *American Museum Journal*, x: 147–68.

Dictionary of New Zealand Biography (1990) *The People of Many Peaks: the Maori biographies from the Dictionary of New Zealand Biography, Volume 1: 1769–1869*, Wellington: Bridget Williams Books, Department of Internal Affairs.

Director, Public Instruction, Punjab (1873 – 88), *Reports on Popular Education in the Punjab*, Lahore: Punjab Education Department.

Dobbs-Higginson, M. (1993) *Asia Pacific: Its Role in the New World Disorder*, London: Heinemann.

Driskell, D. C. (1976) *Two Centuries of Black American Art*, New York: Alfred A. Knopf

Duncan, C. (1995) *Civilising Rituals*, London: Routledge.

Dunn, N. (1839) *Ten Thousand Chinese Things: A Descriptive Catalogue of the Chinese Collection in Philadelphia with Miscellaneous Remarks Upon the Manners, Customs, Trade, and Government of the Celestial Empire*, Philadelphia: Printed for the Proprietor.

Earle, J. (1986) 'The taxonomic obsession: British collectors and Japanese objects, 1852–1986', *Burlington Magazine*, vol. 128: 864–73.

Edwardes, M. (1961) *History of India*, London: Thames and Hudson.

Edwards, E. (ed.) (1992) *Anthropology and Photography*, New Haven and London: Yale University Press.

Emerson, B. (1979) *Leopold II of the Belgians*, London, Weidenfeld & Nicolson.

Fabian, J. (1983) *Time and the Other: How Anthropology Makes its Object*, New York: Columbia University Press

Farmakovskii, M. (1923) 'Ocherki po istorii russkogo farfora, Kruzhki v vide golovy', *Sredi kollektsionerov* 1923:11/12 (November/December): 16–21.

Felix, M. (1989) *Maniema*, Munich: Fred Jahn.

Fergusson, J. (1876) *A History of Indian and Eastern Architecture*, London: John Murray.

Fierens-Gevaert, H. (1903) *Nouveaux Essais sur l'Art Contemporain*, Paris: Alcan.

Fierman, W. (1991) 'The Soviet "transformation" of Central Asia' in W. Fierman (ed.), *Soviet Central Asia: The Failed Transformation*, Boulder: Westview Press.

First Report (1853) *First Report of the Department of Practical Art*, London.

Fortune, R. (1847) *Three Years' Wanderings in the Northern Provinces of China, Including a Visit to the Tea, Silk, and Cotton Countries: with an Account of the Agriculture and Horticulture of the Chinese, New Plants, Etc.*, London: John Murray; reprinted New York: Garland Publishing, Inc., 1979.

Foskett, R. (ed.) (1965) *The Zambesi Journal and Letters of Dr John Kirk 1853–63*, Edinburgh: Oliver and Boyd.

Foucault, M. (1970) *The Order of Things*, London: Tavistock Publications.

—— (1973) *The Birth of the Clinic*, London: Tavistock Publications.

—— (1974) *The Archaeology of Knowledge*, London: Tavistock Publications.

—— (1977a) 'Nietsche, genealogy, history' in D. F. Bouchard (ed.), *Language, Counter-Memory, Practice: Selected Essays and Interviews*, Oxford: Blackwell: 139–64.

—— (1977b) 'The political function of the intellectual', *Radical Philosophy* 17: 12–14.

—— (1980) *Power/Knowledge: Selected Interviews and other Writings*, ed. C. Gordon, Brighton: Harvester Press.

—— (1981) 'Questions of method: an interview with Michel Foucault', *Ideology and Consciousness*, 8: 3–14.

—— (1982) *Discipline and Punish: the Birth of the Prison*, Harmondsworth: Penguin.

Froude, J. A. (1898) *Oceana, or England and her Colonies*, London: Longmans, Green.

Gallop, A. (1992) 'When Maoris visited Surrey', *Surrey Advertiser*, 28 February, Surrey.

—— and Schmid, M. (1992) *The Secrets of Clandon's Maori Meeting House*, New Zealand Tourism Board Press Release.

Gallop, A. (1994) 'Surrey's secret Meeting House', *Destination New Zealand*, April, Eastbourne, East Sussex.

—— (1995a) 'Hinemihi – the house with the golden eyes: a history' in New Zealand Tourism Board and the National Trust, Southern Region, *Te Whakatapua O Nga Taonga Whakairo O Hinemihi Ki Ingarangi (The Blessings of the Carvings for Hinemihi Meeting House in England), Nga Whakaharetanga Me Nga Whakamaramatanga (Order of Proceedings and Explanations)*.

—— (1995b) 'Carving up some Maori history in Surrey', *Surrey Advertiser*, May 12, Surrey.

Gann, L. H. and Duignan, P. (1979) *The Rulers of Belgian Africa – 1884–1914*, Princeton, NJ: Princeton University Press.

Garde, H. F. (1993) 'Peter Bentzon – en vestindisk guldsmed', *Personalhistorisk Tidsskrift*, 1: 68–77.

Gates, H. L. Jr. (1985) *'Race', Writing and Difference*, Chicago: University of Chicago Press.

—— (1996) 'White like me', *The New Yorker* LXXII,16: 66–81.

Geary, C. (1988) *Images of Bamum: German colonial photography at the court of King Nyoja, Cameroon, West Africa, 1902–1915*, Washington DC: Smithsonian Institution Press.

Getty, J. A. (1991) 'State and society under Stalin: constitutions and elections in the 1930s', *Slavic Review*, 50, 1: 18–35.

Glaister, D. (1997) 'Hong Kong's nervous art collectors export works', *Guardian*, 10 February: 8.

Goings, K. W. (1994) *Mammy and Uncle Mose: Black Collectibles and American Stereotyping*, Bloomington: Indiana University Press.

Gombrich, E. (1979) *The Sense of Order*, London: Phaidon.

Gotlieb, R. (1988) '"Vitality" in British art pottery and studio pottery', *Apollo* 127: 163–7.

Greenhalgh, P. (1989) *Ephemeral Vistas: The Expositions Universelles, Great Exhibitions and World Fairs, 1851 –1939*, Manchester: Manchester University Press.

Grey, G. (1971) *Nga Mahi a Nga Tupuna*, Wellington: Read.

Grigoriev, A. V. (1926) *Chetyre goda AKhRR, 1922-1926 gg., sbornik 1*, Moscow: Izd-vo AKhRR.

Guha-Thakurta, T. (1992) *The Making of a New 'Indian' Art: Artists, Aesthetics and Nationalism in Bengal, c.1850–1920*, Cambridge: Cambridge University Press,.

Gupta, N. N. (1947) *Reflections and Reminiscences*, Bombay:

Guy, J. and Swallow, D. (eds) (1990) *Arts of India 1500–1900*, London: Victoria and Albert Museum.

Hair, P. E. H. (1973) 'Livingstone as African historian' in African Studies Centre: University of Edinburgh Press.

Hall, C. (1992) *White, Male and Middle-class*, Cambridge: Polity Press.

Hall, E. (1989) *Inventing the Barbarian – Greek Self-Definition through Tragedy*, Oxford: Clarendon Press.

Hall, N. (1989) 'Apollo Miller, freedman: his life and times', *The Journal of Caribbean History*, 23 (2): 196–213.

—— (1992) *Slave Society in the Danish West Indies, St. Thomas, St. John and St. Croix*, Mona, Jamaica: The University of the West Indies Press.

Hansford, S. H. (1956) *The Study of Chinese Antiquities*, London: School of Oriental and African Studies.

Hanson, A. (1989) 'The making of the Maori: culture invention and its logic', *American Anthropologist*, 92 (4): 890–902.

Harle, J. C. (1986) *The Art and Architecture of the Indian Subcontinent*, Harmondsworth: Penguin.

Harms, R. W. (1981) *River of Wealth, River of Sorrow – The Central Zaire Basin in the Era of the Slave and Ivory Trade 1500–1891*, New Haven: Yale University Press.

Harrison, P. (1990) 'Tanenuiarangi' in *Taonga Maori Conference*, New Zealand 18–27 November in N. McKenzie (ed.), *Cultural Conservation Advisory Council*, Wellington: Department of Internal Affairs.

Head, R. (1985) 'Bagshot Park and Indian crafts' in S. Macready and F. H. Thompson (eds), *Influences in Victorian Art and Architecture*, London: Society of Antiquaries, Occasional Paper (New Series) VII: 139–49.

Herbert, E. (1961) *The Artist and Social Reform: France and Belgium, 1885–1898*, New Haven: Yale University Press.

Herd, H. (1952) *The March of Journalism. The Story of the British Press from 1622 to the Present Day*, London: Allen & Unwin.

Hinsley, C. M. (1991) 'The world as marketplace: commodification of the exotic at the world's Columbian Exhibition, Chicago, 1893' in I. Karp and S. D. Lavine (eds), *Exhibiting Cultures: The Poetics and Politics of Museum Display*, Washington DC: Smithsonian Institution Press.

Hobson, J.A. (1938) *Imperialism – A Study*, London, Allen & Unwin.

Holmes, T. (ed.) (1990) *David Livingstone: Letters and Documents 1841–72*, Livingstone: Livingstone Museum

—— (1993) *Journey to Livingstone: Exploration of an Imperial Myth*, Edinburgh: Canongate Press

Honour, H. (1961) *Chinoiserie. The Vision of Cathay*, London: John Murray.

Illustrated London News, vol. 1, no. 12 (30 July 1842); vol. 1, no. 13 (6 August 1842); vol. 1, no. 14 (13 August 1842); vol. 2, no. 45 (11 March 1843); vol. 4, no. 90 (20 January 1844); vol. 18, no. 483 (10 May 1851); vol. 18, no. 487 (24 May 1851).

Irwin, John (1972) 'The Sanchi torso', *V&A Yearbook*, 3: 7–28.

Isaacman, A. F. (1989) 'The countries of the Zambesi basin' in J.F. Ade Ajayi (ed.), *General History of Africa*, vol. VI, Paris: UNESCO.

Jackson, M. (1972) 'Aspects of symbolism and composition in Maori art', *Bijdagen tot de Taal-, Land- en Volkenkunde*, 128: 33–80.

Jeal, T. (1993) *Livingstone*, London: Pimlico.

Jones, O. (1865) *The Grammar of Ornament*, 2 vols, London: Day and Sons.

Kaplan, F. (ed.) (1994) *Museums and the Making of 'Ourselves': The Role of Objects in National Identity*, London and New York: Leicester University Press.

Karp, I. and Lavine, S. (eds) (1991) *Exhibiting Cultures: The Poetics and Politics of Museum Display*, Washington DC: Smithsonian Institution Press.

Keith, J. B. (1886) 'Indian stone carving', *Journal of Indian Art*, I (14), August: 109–12.

Kernot, B. (1975) *Report of the Clandon Park, Surrey, Meeting House prepared for the Maori Buildings Committee*, Historic Places Trust, 7–6–75.

—— (1976) *One Year Later . . . Supplement to report of the Clandon Park, Surrey, Meeting House*, Historic Places Trust, 7–6–75.

—— (1983) 'The meeting house in contemporary New Zealand' in S. M. Mead and B. Kernot (eds), *Art and Artists of Oceania*, Palmerston North, New Zealand: The Dunmore Press 181–97.

—— (1984) 'Nga tohunga whakairo o mua (Maori artists of the time before)' in S. M. Mead (ed.), *Te Maori: Maori art from New Zealand Collections*, New York: Harry N. Abrams Inc. in association with The American Federation of Arts: 138–55.

Kettering, K. (1994) 'Idealizing collectivization: Natalia Danko's *Dancing Peasant Women*', *Hillwood Studies* 2 (1): 7–14.

—— (1997) 'Natalia Danko and the Lomonosov Porcelain Factory, 1917–1942', unpublished PhD thesis, Northwestern University.

Kevles, D. J. (1985) *In the Name of Eugenics: Genetics and the Uses of Human Heredity*, Berkeley: University of California.

Keys, D. (1993) 'House saved villagers from volcano', *Independent*, 30 November: 28.

Khnopff, F. (1894) 'The revival of ivory carving in Belgium', *The Studio*, vol. IV: 150–1.

—— (1897) 'Review of the Exposition

Internationale, Tervuren, 1897', *The Studio*, vol. VII: 200–3.

Kimambo, I. N. (1989) 'The East African coast and hinterland, 1845–80' in J.F. Ade Ajayi (ed.) *General History of Africa*, vol. VI, Paris: UNESCO.

Kipling, J. L. (1877) 'Annual Report' in *Report on the Progress of Education in the Punjab, 1876–77*, Lahore: Punjab Education Department.

—— (1884) 'Indian architecture of today', *Journal of Indian Art*, I (3), July: 1–5.

—— (1886) 'Punjab wood-carving', *Journal of Indian Art*, I (14): 101–4.

—— (n.d.) 'The Memorial of J. L. Kipling . . . to the Hon. Sir Robert Egerton, Lieut. Governor of the Punjab and its Dependencies', Kipling Papers, 3/11, University of Sussex Library.

Knell, S. J. (1994) *Bibliography of Museum Studies*, Aldershot: Scolar Press.

The Lady (1992) 'A Little Piece of New Zealand in Surrey', 51: 8–14 September.

Lang, H. (1911) 'Report from the Congo expedition', *American Museum Journal*, xi (1).

—— (1915) 'An explorer's view of the Congo', *American Museum Journal*, xv (December): 379–400.

—— (1919) 'Nomad dwarfs and civilization', *Natural History*, xix (6) December.

Langdon, W. B. (1843) *Ten Thousand Chinese Things. A Descriptive Catalogue of the Chinese Collection, Now Exhibiting At St. George's Place, Hyde Park Corner*, London: Printed for the Proprietor.

Latif, S. M. (1994) *Lahore: Its History, Architectural Remains and Antiquities*, (first published in 1872) Lahore: Snag-e-Meel Publications.

Laufer, B., Hambly, W. and Linton, R. (1930) *Tobacco and its Use in Africa*, Chicago: Field Museum of Natural History.

Lawaetz, E. (ed., trans.) (1977) *A Report from Governor General P. L. Oxholm to the Royal Westindian Chamber in Copenhagen (Det Kongelige Vestindiske Kammer) Dated May 4, 1816, St. Croix*, Christiansted, St. Croix, US Virgin Islands: Eva Lawaetz.

—— (ed., trans., comp.) (1979) *Free Coloured in St. Croix, 1744–1816, The History, Statistics and*

Selected Information Concerning the Free Coloured in the Danish West Indies, with Special Reference to St. Croix, from 1744–1816, Christiansted, St. Croix, US Virgin Islands: Eva Lawaetz.

Lee, J. G. (1984) *Philadelphians and the China Trade, 1784–1844*, Philadelphia: Philadelphia Museum of Art.

Leisure Hour (1859) 'The South Kensington Museum' in *The Leisure Hour: A Family Journal of Instruction and Recreation*, April.

Lewes, S. (1995) 'History is made', *Destination New Zealand*, July.

Lewis, D. and Forman, W. (1982) *The Maori – Heirs of Tane*, London: Orbis.

Lewis, S. (1976) *Art: African American*, New York: Harcourt Brace.

Livingstone, D. (1857) *Missionary Travels and Researches in South Africa*, London: John Murray.

—— and Livingstone, C. (1865) *Narrative of an Expedition to the Zambesi*, London: John Murray.

Lloyd, A. (1899) *In Dwarf Land and Cannibal Country*, London: Unwin.

Locke, L. (1940) *The Negro in Art*, Washington, DC: Associates in Negro Folk Education.

London, C. (ed.) (1994) *Architecture in Victorian and Edwardian India*, Bombay: Marg Publications.

Long, E. (1774) *The History of Jamaica, or General Survey of the Antient and Modern State of that Island*, 3 vols, London: T. Lowndes.

Lovelace, A. (1991) 'The African collections at the Glasgow Art Gallery and Museum', *Journal of Museum Ethnography*, 3: 15–30.

Lumley, R. (1988) *The Museum Time Machine: Putting Cultures on Display*, London: Routledge.

Luwel, M. and Bruneel-Hye De Crom, M. (1967) *Tervueren 1897*, Tervuren, Brussels: Musée Royal de l'Afrique Centrale.

Macdonald, S. (ed.) (1996) *Theorizing Museums: Representing Identity and Diversity in a Changing World*, Oxford: Blackwell.

Mackenzie, J. (1990) 'David Livingstone: the construction of the myth' in G. Walker and T. Gallagher (eds), *Sermons and Battle Hymns: Protestant Popular Culture in Modern Scotland*, Edinburgh: Edinburgh University Press.

—— (1984) *Propaganda and Empire*, Manchester: Manchester University Press.

McManus, G. M. (1988) 'Nga whare taonga me te tangata whenua o Aotearoa/Museums and the Maori people of New Zealand', unpublished MA dissertation, Department of Museum Studies, University of Leicester.

Macpherson, C. B. (1962) *The Political Theory of Possessive Individualism: Hobbes to Locke*, Oxford: Oxford University Press.

Makereti, P. (1986) *The Old-Time Maori*, Auckland: New Women's Press.

Mane-Wheoki, J. (1993) 'Mataatua: No wai tenei whare tupuna?', unpublished report for the Waitangi Tribunal.

Martelli, G. (1962) *Leopold to Lumumba – A History of the Belgian Congo 1877–1960*, London: Chapman & Hall/Martelli.

Massell, G. J. (1974) *The Surrogate Proletariat: Moslem Women and Revolutionary Strategies in Soviet Central Asia, 1919–1929*, Princeton, NJ: Princeton University Press.

Masui, T. (1897) *Guide Officiel, Exposition Internationale de Bruxelles-Tervuren*, Brussels.

Mead, S. M. (1984a) 'Nga timunga me nga paringa o te mana Maori (The ebb and flow of mana Maori and the changing context of Maori art)', in Mead (1984c): 20–36.

—— (1984b) 'Ka tupu te toi whakairo ki Aotearoa (Becoming Maori art)' in Mead (1984c): 63–75.

—— (ed.) (1984c) *Te Maori: Maori art from New Zealand Collections*, New York: Harry N. Abrams, Inc. in association with The American Federation of Arts.

—— (ed.) (1990) *Nga Karoretanga o Mataatua Whare*, Whakatane: Te Runanga o Ngati Awa: 38–45.

—— and Kernot, B. (eds) (1983) *Art and Artists of Oceania*, Palmerston North : The Dunmore Press.

Mecklenburg, A. F., Duke of (1910) *In the Heart of Africa*, trans. G.E. Maberly-Oppler, London: Cassell.

Mercer, K. (1993) 'Reading racial fetishism: the photographs of Robert Mapplethorpe', in E. Apter and W. Pietz (eds), *Fetishism as Cultural*

Discourse, Ithaca and London: Cornell University Press: 307–30.

Metcalf, T. R. (1989) *An Imperial Vision: Indian Architecture and Britain's Raj*, London: Faber & Faber.

Miller, B. S. (ed.) (1992) *Powers of Art*, Oxford: Oxford University Press.

Miller, C. (1985) *Blank Darkness: Africanist Discourse in French*, Chicago: Chicago University Press.

Miller, E. (1973) *That Noble Cabinet: A History of the British Museum*, London: Deutsch.

Miller, H. (1966) *Race Conflict in New Zealand 1814–1865*, Westport, Connecticut: Greenwood Press.

Mitter, P. (1977) *Much Maligned Monsters: History of European Reactions to Indian Art*, Oxford: Clarendon Press.

—— (1982) 'Art and nationalism in India', *History Today*, 32 (July): 28–34.

—— (1994) *Art and Nationalism in Colonial India, 1850–1922: Occidental Orientations*, Cambridge: Cambridge University Press.

Molloy, L. (1993) 'The interpretation of New Zealand's natural heritage' in C. M. Hall and S. McArthur, *Heritage Management in New Zealand and Australia: Visitor Management, Interpretation and Marketing*, Oxford: Oxford University Press: 59–69.

Moore, E. D. (1931) *Ivory – Scourge of Africa*, New York and London: Moore.

—— (1906) *Red Rubber*, London: Fisher Unwin.

—— (1968) *History of the Congo Reform Movement*, ed. R. Louis and J. Stengers, Oxford: Oxford University Press.

Morel, Edmund D. (1968) *History of the Congo Reform Movement* (ed. Roger Lewis and Jean Stengers), Oxford: Oxford University Press.

Morris, B. (1986) *The Inspiration of Design: the Influence of the Victoria and Albert Museum*, London: Victoria and Albert Museum.

Mrázková, D. and Remeš, V. (1982) *Early Soviet Photographers*, Oxford: Museum of Modern Art.

N***, G. , 'Sovetskii farfor', *Stroitelstvo Moskvy*, 1927: 2 (February), 1–4.

National Trust (1994) *Clandon Park, Surrey*, (guidebook), London: The National Trust.

Neich, R. (1983) 'The veil of orthodoxy: Rotorua Ngati Tarawhai woodcarving in a changing context' in S. M. Mead and B. Kernot (eds) *Art and Artists of Oceania*, Palmerston North: The Dunmore Press.

—— (1990a) 'The Maori carving art of Tene Waitere', *Art New Zealand*, 57: 73–9.

—— (1990b) *Wero Taroi, Dictionary of New Zealand Biography, The people of many peaks: the Maori biographies from the Dictionary of New Zealand Biography, Volume 1: 1769–1869*, Wellington: Bridget Williams Books, Department of Internal Affairs: 354–55.

—— (1994) *Painted Histories: Early Maori Figurative Painting*, Auckland: Auckland University Press.

Nesbit, M. (1992) *Atget's Seven Albums*, New Haven: Yale University Press.

New Zealand Chronicle, New Zealand, June 1886, Collectors Edition No. 1, (second printing), facsimile.

New Zealand Outlook (1993) 'Century-old Maori carvings found in English stately home', 34, December.

New Zealand Tourism Board (1992) '*Hinemihi*' – *The Maori Meeting House at Clandon Park – A Centenary Exhibition*, London: New Zealand Tourism Board.

New Zealand Tourism Board, Guidelines Public Relations, and the National Trust, Southern Region (1995) *Te Whakatapua O Nga Taonga Whakairo O Hinemihi Ki Ingarangi* (*The Blessings of the Carvings for Hinemihi Meeting House in England*), *Nga Whakaharetanga Me Nga Whakamaramatanga* (*Order of Proceedings and Explanations*).

Newton, D. (1994) 'Old wine in new bottles, and the reverse' in F. Kaplan, *Museums and the Making of 'Ourselves': The Role of Objects in National Identity*, London and New York: Leicester University Press: 269–90.

Ngata, H. (1994) 'A Glimpse into the Life of a Man', unpublished paper, *The Centenary Celebrations of the First Maori University Graduate*, Christchurch, June.

Ngati Awa (1990) 'Te Runanga o Ngati Awa' (Report to the Watangi Claims Tribunal), unpublished.

Nietzsche, F. (1986) 'The Will to Power' in M. Taylor (ed.), *Deconstruction in Context:*

Literature and Philosophy, Chicago and London: University of Chicago Press: 191–215.

Nieuhof, J. (1669) *Embassy from the East India Company . . . to the . . . Emperour [sic] of China*, trans. J. Ogilby, London: John Macock.

O'Biso, C. (1987) *First Light*, Auckland: Heinemann.

Official Catalogue of the Great Exhibition of the Works of Industry of All Nations (1851) London: Spicer and Clowes.

Oliver, R. and Sanderson, G. N. (eds) (1985) *The Cambridge History of Africa*, vol. 6: *From 1870 to 1905*, Cambridge: Cambridge University Press.

Osborn, H. (1910) *American Museum Journal*, x.

—— (1913) *American Museum Journal* xiii (4) April.

O'Toole, M. (1994) *The Language of Displayed Art*, London: Leicester University Press.

Owen, N. E. (1995) 'Ethnographic images as domestic decoration: Rookwood pottery's Native American portrait pieces', unpublished paper presented at American Culture Society of the South, Richmond, Virginia, October.

Pachai, Bridglal (1973) 'The Zambesi expedition, 1858–1864' in B. Pachai (ed.), *Livingstone: Man of Africa*, London: Longman.

Pacific Way (1994) 'Stately setting for an architectural survivor', November.

Page, M. E. (1973) 'David Livingstone, the Arabs and the slave trade' in B. Pachai (ed.), *Livingstone: Man of Africa*, London: Longman.

—— (1974) 'The Manyema hordes of Tippu Tip', *International Journal of African Historical Studies*, 7 (1): 69–84

Pakenham, T. (1991) *The Scramble for Africa*, London: Weidenfeld & Nicolson.

Pearce, Susan M. (1992) *Museums, Objects and Collections: A Cultural Study*, Leicester: Leicester University Press.

Pearson, K. (1909) 'Introduction' in *The Treasury of Human Intelligence*, London: Dulan.

Phillips, S. (1857) *Guide to the Crystal Palace*, London: Bradbury and Evans.

Physick, J. (1982a) 'From iron shed to marble halls', unpublished PhD Dissertation, London: Royal College of Art (on deposit in National Art Library, Victoria and Albert Museum).

—— (1982b) *The Victoria and Albert Museum: The History of its Building*, London: Victoria and Albert Museum.

Pliny (1991) *Natural History – A Selection*, Harmondsworth: Penguin.

Pollock, G. (1993) *Avant-Garde Gambits: Gender and the Colour of Art History*, London; Thames & Hudson.

Porter, J. A. (1992) *Modern Negro Art*, Washington DC: Howard University Press.

Pratt, M. L. (1992) *Imperial Eyes: Travel Writing and Transculturation*, London: Routledge.

Price, S. (1989) *Primitive Art in Civilised Places*, Chicago: Chicago University Press.

Purbrick, L. (1994) 'The South Kensington Museum: the building of the house of Henry Cole' in M. Pointon (ed.), *Art Apart: Art Institutions and Ideology across England and North America*, Manchester: Manchester University Press.

Report of the Commissioners of the United States to the International Exhibition held at Brussels in 1897, (1898) Washington.

Ria, D. (1994) 'Te Hau ki Turanga' in *Pipiwharauroa*, Gisborne: Te Runanganui o Turanga.

Richards, T. (1990) *The Commodity Culture of Victorian England*, Stanford, CA: Stanford University Press.

—— (1993) *The Imperial Archive: Knowledge and the Fantasy of Empire*, London: Verso.

Riegel, H. (1996) 'Into the heart of irony: ethnographic exhibitions and the politics of difference' in S. Macdonald (ed.) *Theorizing Museums: Representing Identity and Diversity in a Changing World*, Oxford: Blackwell: 83–104.

Robinson, J. C. (1858) 'Our national collections', *Athenaeum* 1587, 27/3: 403–4.

Robinson, R. and Gallagher, J. (1981) *Africa and the Victorians: The Official Mind of Imperialism*, London: Macmillan.

Roby, M. (1911) *My Adventures in the Congo*, London: Edward Arnold.

Rockel, I. (1986) 'Introduction' in Rotorua Museum *Tarawera Eruption Centennial Exhibition 1886–1986*: 8–10.

Rotberg, R. (1970) *Africa and its Explorers*, Cambridge, MA: Harvard University Press.

Rotorua Museum (1986) *Tarawera Eruption Centennial Exhibition 1886–1986*, Rotorua, New Zealand: Rotorua District Council.

Rubel, M. M. (1978) *Savage and Barbarian – Historical Attitudes in the Criticism of Homer and Ossian in Britain 1760–1800*, Amsterdam/Oxford: North-Holland.

Russell-Cotes, M. (1921) *Home and Abroad – An Autobiography of an Octogenarian*, vols 1 and 11, Bournemouth: Herbert Russell-Cotes.

Said, E. (1978) *Orientalism*, New York: Vintage Books.

—— (1993) *Culture and Imperialism*, London: Vintage Books.

Salmond, A. (1974) 'Rituals of encounter among the Maori: sociolinguistic study of a scene' in R. Bauman and J. Sherzer, *Explorations in the Ethnography of Speaking*, Cambridge: Cambridge University Press: 192–212.

—— (1975) *Hui*, Wellington, New Zealand: Reed.

—— (1978) 'Te Ao Tawhito: a semantic approach to the ancient Maori cosmos', *Journal of the Polynesian Society*, 87 (1): 5–28.

—— (1983) 'The study of traditional Maori Society: the state of the art', *Journal of the Polynesian Society*, 92 (3): 309–32.

—— (1984) 'Nga huarahi o te ao Maori (Pathways in the Maori world)' in S. M. Mead (ed.), *Te Maori: Maori art from New Zealand Collections*, New York: Harry N. Abrams, Inc. in association with The American Federation of Arts: 109–37.

Sandler, S. (1989) *Distant Pleasures: Alexander Pushkin and the Writing of Exile*, Stanford, CA: Stanford University Press.

Savage, P. (1986) 'In the shadow of the mountain' in Rotorua Museum, *Tarawera Eruption Centennial Exhibition 1886–1986*: 14–20.

Saxbee, H. (1990) 'An Orient exhibited. The exhibition of the Chinese Collection in England in the 1840s', unpublished PhD dissertation, London: Royal College of Art.

Schapera, I. (ed.) (1961) *Livingstone's Missionary Correspondence, 1841–1856*, London: Chatto & Windus.

—— (ed.) (1974) *David Livingstone: South African Papers 1849–1853*, Cape Town: Van Riebeeck Society.

Schildkrout, E. (1991) 'The spectacle of Africa through the lens of Herbert Lang: Belgian Congo photographs 1909–1915', *African Arts*, xxiv: 4.

Schildkrout, E. and Keim, C. (1990) *African Reflections: Art from North-Eastern Zaire*, New York: American Museum of Natural History.

Schoffeleers, J. M. (1973) 'Livingstone and the Mang'anja Chiefs' in B. Pachai (ed.) *Livingstone: Man of Africa*, London: Longman.

—— (1975) 'The interaction of the M'Bona cult and Christianity, 1859–1963' in T. O. Ranger and J. Weller (eds), *Themes in Christian History in Central Africa*, London: Heinemann.

Sciascia, P. (1984) 'Ka pu te ruha, ka hao te rangatahi (As the old net piles up on shore, the new net goes fishing) in S. M. Mead (ed.), *Te Maori: Maori art from New Zealand Collections*, New York: Harry N. Abrams, Inc. in association with The American Federation of Arts: 156–66.

Shams-ud-din (1982) *Secularisation in the USSR: A Study of Soviet Cultural Policy in Uzbekistan*, New Delhi: Vikas Publishing House.

Shelton, A. A. (1994) 'Cabinets of transgression: Renaissance collections and the incorporation of the New World' in J. Elsner and J. Cardinal (eds) *The Cultures of Collecting*, London: Reaktion.

Sheppard, F. W. (ed.) (1975) *Survey of London, vol. XXXVIII: The Museums Area of South Kensington and Westminster*, London: Athlone Press, University of London.

Shepperson, G. (ed.) (1980) *David Livingstone and the Rovuma*, Edinburgh: Edinburgh University Press.

Siddle, D. J. (ed.) (1973) 'David Livingstone: mid-Victorian field scientist' in African Studies Centre, University of Edinburgh Press.

Sieber, R. (1980) *African Furniture and Household Objects*, Bloomington: Indiana University Press.

—— and Walker, R. (1987) *African Art in the Cycle of Life*, Washington: Smithsonian Institution Press.

Simmons, D. R. (1969a) 'Economic change in New Zealand pre-history', *Journal of the Polynesian Society*, 78 (1).

—— (1969b) 'A New Zealand myth', *New Zealand Journal of History*, 3 (1).

—— (1984) 'Nga taonga o nga waka (Tribal art styles)', in S. M. Mead (ed.) *Te Maori: Maori art from New Zealand Collections*, New York: Harry N. Abrams, Inc. in association with The American Federation of Arts: 76–108.

Simpson, D. H. (1975) *Dark Companions: The East African Contribution to the European Exploration of East Africa*, London: Paul Elek.

Simpson, M. *et al.* (1996) 'The restitution debate', *Museums Journal*, January: 19–23.

Skelton, R. (1978) 'The Indian Collections, 1798–1978', *Burlington Magazine*, CXX (902), May: 297–304.

Slade, R. (1962) *King Leopold's Congo*, Oxford: Oxford University Press.

South Kensington Museum Guide (1857), London: South Kensington Museum, 20 June.

The Spectator, no. 730 (25 June 1842); no. 731 (2 July 1842).

Spinden, H. R. (1919) 'Creating a national art' *Natural History*, xix (6) December.

Spring, C. (1993) *African Arms and Armour*, London: British Museum Press.

Stafford, D. (1967) *Te Arawa: A History of the Arawa People*, Wellington, Auckland and Sydney: A. H. and A. W. Reed.

—— (1977) *The Romantic Past of Rotorua*, Wellington: A. H. and A. W. Reed.

Stafford, R. A. (1990) 'Annexing the landscapes of the past: British imperial geology in the nineteenth century' in J. Mackenzie, *Imperialism and the Natural World*, Manchester: Manchester University Press: 67–89.

Stanley, H. M. (1872) *How I Found Livingstone*, London: Sampson Low, Marston Low and Searle.

Stewart, S. (1993) *On Longing: Narratives of the Miniature, the Gigantic, the Souvenir, the Collection*, Durham NC: Duke University Press.

Stocking, G. W. (1987) *Victorian Anthropology*, New York: Free Press.

Sullivan, A. (1984) 'Nga paiaka o te Maoritanga (The roots of Maori culture)' in S. M. Mead, *Te Maori: Maori art from New Zealand Collections*, New York: Harry N. Abrams, Inc. in association with The American Federation of Arts: 37–62.

Surrey Advertiser (1992) 'Koha and Karanga in Meeting House centenary ceremony', 31 July.

Surrey Advertiser (1995) 'Ceremony at dawn sees traditions carved out', 23 June.

Swallow, D. A. 'The Indian Museum and the British–Indian textile trade in the late nineteenth century', forthcoming.

—— Swallow, D. A. and Guy, J. (eds) (1990) *Arts of India 1550–1900*, London: Victoria and Albert Museum.

Tabakoff, S. (1992) 'Imitation or invention: sources for eighteenth-century porcelain figurines' in C. Duval (ed.), *Figures from Life: Porcelain Sculpture from the Metropolitan Museum of Art, New York ca. 1740–1780*, St. Petersburg, FL: Museum of Fine Arts.

Tallis, J. (1851) *Tallis's History and Description of the Crystal Palace, and the Exhibition of the World's Industry in 1851*, London and New York: John Tallis and Co.

Tarapor, M. (1980) 'John Lockwood Kipling and British art education in India', *Victorian Studies*, 24 (1): 53–81.

Taussig, M. (1986) *Shamanism, Colonialism and the Wild Man: A Study in Terror and Healing*, Chicago: University of Chicago Press.

Te Awekotuku, N. (1986) 'Introduction – Makereti: Guide Maggie Papakura' in P. Makereti, *The Old-Time Maori*, Auckland: New Women's Press.

—— (1991) *Mana Wahine Maori: Selected Writings on Maori Women's Art, Culture and Politics*, Auckland: New Women's Press.

Te Rangi Hiroa (Sir Peter Buck) (1966) *The Coming of the Maori*, Wellington: Whitcombe and Tombs (first edition 1949).

—— (1991) *Mana Wahine Maori: Selected Writings on Maori Women's Art, Culture and Politics*, Auckland: New Women's Press.

Teilhet, J. (1983) 'The role of women artists in Polynesia and Melanesia', in S. M. Mead and B. Kernot (eds), *Art and Artists of Oceania*, Palmerston North: The Dunmore Press.

Temple, R. C. (1886) 'A study of modern Indian architecture', *Journal of Indian Art*, 1 (8): 57–60.

Teng S.-Y. and Fairbank, J. K. (1954) *China's Response to the West*, Cambridge, MA: Harvard University Press.

Thomas, N. (1991) *Entangled Objects: Exchange, Material Culture and Colonialism in the Pacific*, Cambridge, MA: Harvard University Press.

—— (1994) *Colonialism's Culture*, Princeton, NJ: Princeton University Press.

Thornton, R. (1983) 'Narrative ethnography in Africa, 1850–1920: the creation and capture of an appropriate domain for anthropology', *MAN* (NS) 18 (3): 502–18.

Tibbles, A. (ed.) (1994) *Transatlantic Slavery: Against Human Dignity*, London: HMSO and National Museums and Galleries on Merseyside.

Tillotson, G. H. R. (1989) *The Tradition of Indian Architecture: Continuity, Controversy and Change since 1850*, Delhi: Oxford University Press.

—— (1990) *Mughal India*, London: Viking.

Trabue, M. R. (1919) 'The intelligence of negro recruits', *Natural History*, xix (6) December.

Trevelyan, C. (1912) 'Testimony before the Select Committee of the House of Lords on the Government of the Indian Territories, 21 June 1853' reprinted in *Modern Review* (Calcutta) 11: 345–51.

Trollope, A. (1968) *Australia and New Zealand*, vol. 11, second edition (first edition 1873), London: Dawson.

Tucker, J. T. (1945) *Currie of Chisamba*, Toronto: United Church of Canada and Ryerson Press.

Vansina, J. (1973) *The Tio Kingdom of the Middle Congo 1880–1892*, Oxford: Oxford University Press.

Vellut, J. L. (1989) 'The Congo Basin and Angola' in J.F. Ade Ajayi (ed.) *General History of Africa*, vol. VI, Paris: UNESCO.

Vergo, P. (ed.) (1989) *The New Museology*, London: Reaktion.

Vogel, S. (ed.) (1988) *Art/Artifact: African Art in Anthropology Collections*, New York: Center for African Art and Prestel Verlag.

Volavka, Z. (1973) *Hidden Treasures from Central Africa*, Downsview, Ontario: Art Gallery of York University.

Volkerling, M. (1994) 'Death or transfiguration: the future for cultural policy in New Zealand', *Culture and Policy* 6, 7–27.

Vos'maia vystavka kartin i skulptura AKhRR "Zhizn' i byt narodov SSSR," spravochnik katalog s illiustratsiiami, (1926) Leningrad: Izd-vo AKhRR.

Waaka, P. (1986) 'Tarawera – 100 years before the eruption', in Rotorua Museum, *Tarawera Eruption Centennial Exhibition 1886–1986*: 11–13.

Wainwright, C. (1994) 'Principles true and false: Pugin and the foundation of the Museum of Manufactures', *Burlington Magazine*, CXXVI (1095) June: 357–64.

Walker, R. (1990) *Ka Whawhai Tonu Matou: Struggle Without End*, Auckland and London: Penguin Books.

Waller, H. (ed.) (1874) *The Last Journals of David Livingstone*, London: John Murray.

Wallis, J. P. R. (1956) *The Zambesi Expedition of David Livingstone, 1858–1863*, 2 vols, London: Chatto & Windus.

Watts, G. and Brown, P. (1979) *Arts and Crafts of India: A Descriptive Study*, (originally published in 1904) Delhi: Cosmo Publications.

White, L. (1987) *Magomero*, Cambridge: Cambridge University Press.

Wills, J. E., Jr. (1984) *Embassies and Illusions. Dutch and Portuguese Envoys to K'ang-hsi, 1666–1687*, Cambridge, MA: Harvard University Press.

Wilson, K. (1993) 'Empire of virtue: the Imperial project and Hanoverian culture' in L. Stone (ed.) *An Imperial Nation at War*, New York: Routledge.

Wimberg, E. (1992) 'Socialism, democratism, and criticism: the Soviet press and the national discussion of the 1936 draft constitution', *Soviet Studies*, 44 (2): 313–33.

Zelma, G. (1978) *Georgii Zelma. Izbrannye Fotografii*, Moscow: Planeta.

Index

217